# Publishing in a Global Village
# A Role for the Small Press

By

## William M. Brinton

Logo
Mercury House, Incorporated
San Francisco

This is not a work of fiction, except for a portion of the last chapter which is entitled *Epilogue* and is intended as satire. Names, characters, places and incidents, particularly cases cited herein, are either the product of the author's research or some use of quotations based on the research of others, most notably, the distinguished historian of the publishing and bookselling business, John Tebbel, and another historian, Leonard Shatzkin, whose book, *In Cold Type: Overcoming the Book Crisis,* was invaluable for the ideas it provided. Another historian with a sharp mind and an elegant style, Frances FitzGerald, provided some background for the textbook reforms suggested herein in her book, *America Revised,* which should be required reading for the Attorney General of the United States, whomever he may be, who should also read the First and Fourth Amendments to the Constitution, both of which were ratified in 1791.

© William M. Brinton 1988, 1989

Published in the United States by
Mercury House
San Francisco, California

© 1988 CNES, Provided by Spot Image Corporation, Reston, Virginia
Satellite photograph of San Francisco, California.

Mercury House and colophon are registered trademarks of
Mercury House Incorporated.

Manufactured in the United States of America

Library of Congress Cataloging–in–Publication Data.

Brinton, William M. 1920_____Publishing in a Global Village A Role for the Small Press.
1988   87–82608

ISBN 0–916515–41–9

# TABLE OF CONTENTS

# Prologue and Foreward

The First Amendment to the Constitution was ratified in 1791, together with the Fourth Amendment and Fifth Amendments. The Fourteenth Amendment was ratified in 1867. For over 50 years, the courts have incorporated rights guaranteed under the First, Fourth and Fifth Amendments by applying the equal protection and due process language of the Fourteenth Amendment to state action or action taken under color of state law. It has often been said that the the free speech clause of the First Amendment ("Congress shall make no law. . . abridging the freedom of speech, or of the press. . . ") is absolute in prohibiting Congress from making any law that abridges the freedom of speech. However, in Schenck v. United States, the Supreme Court held in 1919 that this right was not absolute in a case involving a conspiracy to violate the Espionage Act of 1917. Once the court found that expression could be regulated, later cases attempted to define the boundaries within which speech could be regulated. In Roth v. United States, decided in 1957, the Supreme Court held that the First Amendment did not protect obscenity and ever since then has tried to define obscenity. Miller v. California, decided in 1974, established a test which has done little more than confuse courts, juries and law enforcement officers. Stanley v. Georgia (1969), stands for the proposition that regulation of obscenity cannot reach into the privacy of a person's own home. Justice Marshall added that "if the First Amendment means anything, it means that a state has no business telling a man in his own house, what he may read or what films he may watch." The right of privacy is a protection guaranteed by, *inter alia*, the First, Fourth and Fifth Amendments.

1

A right of privacy was first acknowledged in Griswold v. Conneticut (1965), and placed certain aspects of life beyond the reach of governmental intrusion. In Griswold, the Supreme Court held that a Conneticut law criminalizing the distribution of contraceptives to married couples violated basic values "implicit in the concept of ordered liberty." In Eisenstadt v. Baird (1972), the Supreme Court struck down a state prohibiting the sale of contraceptives to unmarried persons. Paris Adult Theater I v. Slaton (1973) used the First Amendment as protection for "sexually oriented materials" for consenting adults. Over time, the Supreme Court has tended to focus on cases wherein there has been an intolerable and unjustifiable invasion of privacy in the conduct of the most intimate concerns of an individual's personal life. In early cases, the Supreme Court applied the "right of privacy" rationale to cases arising under the Fourth Amendment, and Mapp v. Ohio, together with Stone v. Powell (1976) created the so-called exclusionary rule. This is a rule that allows a defendant to move to suppress evidence secured by means of an unreaonable search and seizure. Fourth Amendment safeguards were included in the Bill of Rights as the direct result of the British imposition on the colonies of writs of assistance that allowed warrants for arbitrary searches of persons and property. Slowly, but surely ever since 1961, the Supreme Court has developed standards that have, in fact, eroded rights guaranteed under the Fourth Amendment by rationalizing a right of privacy as being subjectively reasonable on the part of a defendant. More recently, the Supreme Court has also looked to the question whether society as a whole would treat a defendant's expectation of privacy as being objectively reasonable. In Greenwood v. California and Riley v. Florida, the Supreme Court held that defendant's expectation of privacy was unreasonable. Greenwood was the *trashbag* search, and Riley was the *helicopter* search from 400 feet. Publishers and their attorneys need to read these cases in order to make the connection between the First and Fourth Amendments in view of what Congress enacted in the closing days of the Second Session of the 100th Congress.

Legislation by Congress enacted in 1988 has now placed publishers, their distributors and booksellers on a collision course with laws clearly infringing on rights guaranteed under the First, Fourth and Fifth Amendments, and the Supreme Court has given the Department of Justice, as well as many states the means with which to further encroach on these rights. A brief look at the recent past three decades or more seems worthwhile.

Ever since the Supreme Court's decision in Mapp v. Ohio in 1961,"The right of the people to be secure in their persons, houses, papers and effects against unreasonable searches and seizures shall not be violated. . . " has been subject to judicial encroachment in a manner inconsistent with what James Madison wrote in the *Annals of Congress* in 1789. "Independent tribunals of justice," he wrote, "will be naturally led to resist every encroachment upon rights expressly stipulated for in the Constitution by the declaration of rights." Those rights were "expressly stipulated" in the First and Fourth Amendments to the Constitution which were ratified in 1791. The right of the people to be secure in their homes, as quoted above from the Fourth Amendment continued by adding the Warrant Clause, which stated a proviso, "and no warrants [allowing an unreasonable search] shall issue, but upon probable cause." In Mapp v. Ohio, defendant Mapp was convicted of possession of obscene literature, and the Supreme Court reversed, holding that the rule excluding evidence unlawfully seized was "an essential part of both the Fourth and Fourteenth Amendments." In Robbins v. California, Chief Justice William Rehnquist criticized what he called the "judicially created preference for a warrant," adding that "nothing in the Fourth Amendment itself requires that searches be conducted pursuant to warrants," notwithstanding the use of the word "and" following the phrase "unreasonable search and seizures." In 1988, the Supreme Court held in Greenwood v. California that a police investigator could lawfully search trashbags left out for collection in a manner consistent with a local ordinance and do so without a warrant based on probable cause.

On January 23, 1989 the Supreme Court announced its decision in Riley v. Florida, literally eviscerating what little protection was still available under the Fourth Amendment. The plurality opinion written by Justice White with a separate concurring opinion by Justice O'Connor held that a warrantless search by a helicopter flying at 400 feet was not unreasonable, because its pilot could "observe what is visible to the naked eye, and a helicopter could lawfully fly at 400 feet pursuant to regulations of the Federal Aviation Administration (FAA). Justice O'Connor noted that FAA regulations "are intended to promote air safety and not to protect the right to be secure against unreasonable searches and seizures." Riley's reasonable expectation of privacy from aerial observation of his home was not, she wrote, "one that society is prepared to recognize as 'reasonable'. . . . because there is reason to believe that there is considerable public use of airspace at altitudes of 400 feet and above." The Federal Aviation Administration Census of U.S. Civil Aircraft, Calendar Year 1987 listed more than 10,000 helicopters registered in the United States with a population of over 232,000,000, or one helicopter for every 23,200 people.

In 1791, the First Amendment was ratified along with the Fifth Amendment as part of the Bill of Rights. Amongst other things, the First Amendment states that "Congress shall make no law respecting an establishment of religion, or prohibiting the free exercise thereof; or abridging the freedom of speech, or of the press; or the right of the people peaceably to assemble, and to petition the Government for redress of grievances." Ever since 1957, when the Supreme Court held in Roth v. United States that "obscenity" was not speech protected by the First Amendment, Congress has moved into areas affecting publishers by attempting to criminalize obscenity. Congress, as well as many states have enacted statutes to this effect concurrently with attempts of the Supreme Court to define what has been criminalized. It was not until 1974 that the Supreme Court managed to find a definition of obscenity in Miller v. California. Its four-prong test or definition has only succeeded in confusing lower courts, judges, juries and law enforcement officers. In 1987, the

Supreme Court handed down its decision in Pope v. Illinois. In this case, Justice Brennan, who wrote for the majority in Roth v. United States, dissented, noting that "The concept of obscenity cannot be defined. . . to provide fair notice to persons who create and distribute sexually oriented materials, to prevent substantial erosion of protected speech as a byproduct of the attempt to suppress unprotected speech, and to avoid very costly institutional harms."

Against this background of judicial confusion, publishers, their distributors and booksellers have to struggle just to decide what to print, publish, and sell. Not all sexually explicit material is obscene, but no one really knows where to draw the line. Congress and the states even now have decided to insulate minors from the effects of material thought to be obscene by enacting the Child Protection and Obscenity Enforcement Act of 1988 in the closing days of the 1988 Session. This enactment amended various sections of Title 18 of the United States Code. Chapter 1 of this act imposes impossible record-keeping requirements on publishers. A publisher of *any* book from 1978 to the present must be able to identify any person involved in "any visual depictions. . . of sexually explicit conduct" as to whether that person is a minor. This applies, of course, to textbooks used in sex education classes. Failure to keep such records in a place available to the Attorney General of the United States, with or without a warrant issued on probable cause, as required by the Fourth Amendment, "shall raise the rebuttable presumption that every performer in the matter was a minor." No one really knows how many foreign books, like *Ulysses,* imported in 1934 [it was finally found not to be obscene] have been published here between 1978 and 1989. Chapter 2 of the Child Protection and Obscenity Enforcement Act of 1988 appears even more ominous. A publisher selling "obscene matter" or "any person who knowingly receives or possesses any obscene book" may serve time in jail. A person convicted of an offense involving "obscene material" shall "forfeit to the United States" such person's interest in "any property, real or personal, constituting or traceable to gross profits or other proceeds obtained from such offense." What this means is *any* publisher, large or small, may be required to forfeit *all* the real property used as part of the publishing process — everything from typewriters to a 24 story office building. Moreover, with respect to property ordered forfeited, the Attorney General may "grant petitions. . . restore forfeited property to *victims* of a violation of this chapter" or "award compensation to persons providing information resulting in a forfeiture under this section." The word "victim" is not defined. Presumably, Congress meant persons suffering emotional distress after reading a book subsequently found obscene. Congress clearly meant to reward informants for providing information leading to conviction of any publisher or bookseller "knowingly" in possession of a book subsequently found obscene, thereby encouraging a flood of complaints concerning literature regarded as classic, such as *Tom Sawyer,* War and Peace, Madame Bovary or *Catcher in the Rye.*

As if this were not enough, the Attorney General may apply *ex parte,* that is, without notice or hearing, and obtain a temporary restraining order if he "demonstrates that there is probable cause to believe that the property with respect to which the order is sought [a book] would in the event of a conviction, be subject to forfeiture." What this means is that any publisher will have to think carefully whether any book or books it publishes, even with one page of sexually explicit material, should be published at all. No one wants to test the reach of this law for the first time, so many books with protected speech will not be published. It is something of an understatement to say that this law will have a chilling effect on publishers, even though their lawyers have advised them that the book or books about to be published enjoy protection under the First Amendment, as its provisions guaranteeing free speech have been currently construed by the courts. This law is only part of the Reagan-Meese legacy.

Many states, including Virginia and Minnesota, have enacted laws for the protection of minors in cases where it is thought harmful for minors to peruse material "displayed" in bookstores and falling within a definition of obscene. In American Booksellers Association v. Commonwealth of Virginia, for example, the Supreme Court has not yet decided which books may be displayed in a place accessible to juveniles without being in violation of a Virginia statute enacted in 1985.

In view of the political environment which allowed the Child Protection and Obscenity Enforcement Act to slip through Congress without deleting the record keeping requirements, the forfeiture of property provisions and the power to obtain a temporary restraining order enjoining the publication of a book or books thought to be obscene, publishers must think in terms of connecting the rights guaranteed under the First and Fourth to the Constitution. No one wants to defend the ccommercial exploitation of minors which, by itself, does not involve rights guaranteed under the First Amendment and is unconscionable to begin with. Surely, however, Congress need not create a police state by enacting a law to prevent such exploitation and enacting additional provisions unrelated to this worthwhile objective. Congress here was not dealing with drugs which do indeed represent a scourge ripe for eradication. It was legislating with respect to intellectual diversity, the world of ideas which must be allowed to compete in the marketplace for acceptance or rejection.

Justice Brennan who, together with Justice Marshall and Justice Stevens dissented in Riley v. Florida noted that "If the Constitution does not protect Riley's marijuana garden against such surveillance, it is hard to see how it will forbid the Government from aerial spying on the activities of a law-abiding citizen on her fully enclosed outdoor patio." Later, in this dissent, Justice Brennan also said that "I hope it will be a matter of concern to my colleagues that the police surveillance methods they sanction were among those described in George Orwell's dread vision of life in the 1980's" in his book, *1984*. The combination of this case and many others too numerous to cite, together with statutes enacted by both Congress and some states, unless challenged in the courts, do indeed invoke "George Orwell's dread vision of life in the 1980's," and the publishers and booksellers have to consider a judicial challenge to this patchwork of aberrant legislation before we reach the point described in Ray Bradbury's book, *Fahrenheit 451*. This is the temperature at which books burn, and this book was first published in 1953. Its most recent paperback version in 1988 was published by Ballantine Books of New York, its 74th printing.

## FOREWORD

Having said much about the election of November 8, 1988 in the Prologue, I feel that something must be said about what we may be able to publish in the future. At this time, the Supreme Court of the United States has four justices elevated or appointed by President Reagan. During his four years in office, President Bush may have an opportunity to nominate more of the same conservative orthodoxy as those nominated by his predecessor. President Bush, for example, might be pressured to nominate Vice-President Quayle or Senator Orrin Hatch of Utah. Both are lawyers, although it appears that the former may have tunnelled under law school rather than going through it. Only a Senate with a Democratic majority stands between these nominations and both men becoming justices of the Supreme Court.

*Publishing in a Global Village* looks to both the past in terms of First Amendment cases decided in the last thirty years. Only in a very limited way does this book look at the future in terms of the First Amendment with the identity of President Bush's nominations, if any, only a matter of speculation. All publishers need to be concerned, and so do the booksellers of the United States. During 1988, the 100th Congress was asked to consider and enact laws, some of which would clearly violate rights guaranteed under the First Amendment. While eternal vigilance is said to ensure freedom, mere watchfulness may not be enough. Even the small preses will not be somehow be immunized by laws criminalizing conduct thought by the extremely orthodox right to be dangerous to our young people. The display of "sexually explicit" books in a bookstore available for "perusal" by juveniles has already been challenged by the Commonwealth of Virginia, and the outcome is still in doubt. On a more economic basis, the small presses must somehow publish books worth reading and make a profit to stay in business. *Publishing in a Global Village* is really dedicated to them and the role they may play in the future.

The small presses of a global village are unlikely ever to be able to compete for market share with any of the publishing "giants" of today, even though all of them began as small presses themselves. However, in terms of quality and the sheer excitement of creating something for the pleasure of others without more than a prudent look at net income from operations, the small presses which publish quality books, including textbooks, can compete and will continue to do so. They may want to think about the text of I Daniel, Chapter 17 from the Books of the Old Testament (Authorized King James Version — 1611) later republished in 1896 by the Oxford Press.

What we all read now and in the future — books and textbooks — are likely to be determined by the Supreme Court of the United States as well as the highest courts of the 50 states. What we learn from textbooks in schools and colleges, as well as from the free exchange of ideas in the classroom is also likely to determine the content of books read later for pleasure and information — even how we think. At all age levels, the courts affect what we learn and what we can say, use or publish.

In 1924, for example, the Supreme Court of California ruled that the King James version of the Bible was not prohibited for reference and library purposes in the public schools against an argument that it was "used in Protestant churches" while the Douai version, was "used by the Roman Catholic church in English-speaking countries." The Douai version consists of a translation of the New Testament in 1582. The books of the Old Testament were translated in 1609. Both parts of the Douai version was based on the text of the Latin Vulgate, while the King James version was based on the Hebrew and Greek texts. In its opinion in Evans v. Selma Union High School District (1924) 193 Cal. 54, the Court noted it was not deciding the question whether the use of either version for instruction in the classroom amounted to the teaching of "sectarian or denominational doctrine" and could be purchased with public funds for use in a library, because it was "the book of a certain religious sect." One may wonder what might happen, if *this* book were ever used as a textbook in the public schools. It actually contains a quotation from the King James version of the Bible used by Protestants. It also contains what are thought to be constitutionally protected expressions of opinion.

Here, however, is what what was "Translated out of the original tongues: And with the former translations diligently compared and revised by his Majesty's special command." This means that a Privy Council reviewed the text to make certain that no heretical language appeared in it. Here it is.

*Elah, fighting with the Philistines.*

*(49)And there went out a champion out of the camp of the Philistines, named Goliath, of Gath, whose height was six cubits and a span.*

*(49)And David put his hand in his bag, and took thence a stone, and slang it, and smote the Philistine in his forehead, that    (1) Now the Philistines gathered together their armies to battle, and were gathered at Shochoh, which belongeth to Judah.*

*(19) Now Saul, and they, and all the men of Israel, were in the valley of Elah, fighting with the Philistines.*

*(49)And there went out a champion out of the camp of the Philistines, named Goliath, of Gath, whose height was six cubits and a span.*

*(49)And David put his hand in his bag, and took thence a stone, and slang it, and smote the Philistine in his fore stone sunk into his forehead, and he fell upon his face to the earth.*

# Chapter 1
## The Business of Publishing:
## Content, Production and Marketing

The small presses of the United States have seen a revolution in electronic publishing which they started only a very few years ago. Their publishers have become players in an exciting period of profound change. The use of computers and word processing software was only the beginning. Then, the use of telecommunications software, optical character readers, typesetting software and laser printers increased the speed of output and reduced the cost of book production. Now, small presses must not only become more technologically innovative but also more *niche* oriented. Nonfiction and fiction for the mature adult, for example, will expand over the next decade or so, as more and more of the mid-30s to mid-50s age group continues to increase as a percentage of the total population. Almost unnoticed, however, is a growing trend toward regulation of book content supported by judicial fiat, much of it occuring in the last thirty years. *Publishing in a Global Village* represents an effort to tie all these concepts together in a seamless web from the author to the person who buys his book in one of the 5,700 or more general bookstores in the United States. The small presses have a role to play in all this, and the two factors, other than quality of content, which define that role are the law and money—the competition of ideas in the marketplace.

Regulation of content works in many different ways, but the result is the same. The quality of literature, defined as writing having excellence of form and expressing ideas of permanent or universal interest, tends to decline, and mediocrity multiplies. How does an editor determine *content* of a book before recommending it for publication? Publishers, editors and authors all know that a book, whether fiction or nonfiction, represents the

1

communication of ideas which may or may not stimulate the reader to think or reason. The eloquence with which any book is written may set fire to reason. So long as a book does not incite the reader to overt antisocial conduct, however, a publisher should be free to publish and sell it to the public. Emile Zola's *J'accuse,* for example, led to penal reform, and Rachel Carson's *Silent Spring* is thought by many to have led to enactment of the National Environmental Policy Act in 1968. James Joyce's *Ulysses* represented a new and exciting literary genre. He attempted — with astonishing success — to show how a stream of consciousness with its shifting impressions affects the focus of each one of the characters as they went about a city in Ireland on a single day in June, 1904, and what many of them thought about during their day. It was because Joyce wrote honestly and sincerely to describe fully what his characters thought about that he was the subject of many attacks. Many of these attacks were prompted by his preoccupation with sex in the thoughts of his characters. One need not enjoy the technique used by Joyce, but anyone reading *Ulysses* was free at any time to put this book aside or throw it away. His preoccupation with sex was not meant to titillate the reader, but an honest attempt to show a true picture of the life of Celts in the Dublin of 1904.

In a rather gross sense, publishers and editors know that sex sells, but when does explicit sexual content cross a borderline drawn by would-be censors? May a book be suppressed merely because some jury finds that it appeals to a prurient interest or excites lustful thoughts not followed by antisocial conduct? The book which represents the communication of ideas may just as easily stimulate thoughts followed by socially acceptable conduct. Dr. Martin Luther King, Jr.'s *I Have a Dream* played a significant part in the civil rights revolution of the 1960's. Mark Twain's *Huckleberry Finn* was a childhood classic read by millions, and Edmund Wilson's *Memoirs of Hecate County* was found obscene in New York, but not in California. A bookseller indicted in California for selling the same book was acquitted. The United States has fifty separate centers for social and literary experimention, and juries in every state will have different attitudes toward the same work of literature. *God's Little Acre,* for example, was found obscene in Massachusetts, but not in New York or Pennsylvania.

There seems to be no great danger to the nation from the freedom to experiment with literature, unless and until Congress attempts to impose a blanket ban on some books throughout the United States on the ground that they fail to satisfy judicially imposed standards of what constitutes obscenity. For Congress to enact legislation like this represents an intolerable form of censorship, and Congress has no business, whether under the postal or commerce clauses, in banning the sale of books because they might lead to any kind of thoughts not manifested in overt antisocial conduct. Punishing an author, a bookseller or a publisher for publication of a book, the legality of which turns on the purity of thought it instills in the mind of the reader is an intolerable denial of rights in a free society. Such thought are and should be the concern of the individual and his or her spiritual advisors. To allow Congress to invade this sensitive area and punish mere speech or publication that a jury finds has an undesirable impact on thought or reason is a gross violation of rights guaranteed under the First Amendment, an impermissible regulation of content by Congress.

The First Amendment to our Constitution was ratified in 1791, and its various provisions were designed to protect sensitive areas of personal belief and opinion, but the courts seem to have forgotten why the Framers of the Constitution included certain rights and extended protection to freedom of speech and the press. Those colonists who left England in the 17th Century did so to escape religious persecution, but they brought with them the principles set forth in the Magna Carta presented to King John in 1215. This document stands as permanent testimony to the human belief in the importance of written law, the limits of absolute monarchy and the right of rebellion against tyranny. Some of its language was incorporated into the constitutions of the early American states and into the Constitution of 1787. The text of the Fifth Amendment—due process of law and the privilege against self-incrimination—was taken almost verbatim from Sir William Blackstone's *Commentaries on the Laws of England,* first published in the 18th Century. The First Amendment is also an extension of his discussion of freedom of the press. Thus, the Constitution under which we live today springs from almost ancient history. Principles of the Magna Carta, for example, were incorporated into the Bill of Rights, the First Ten Amendments to the Constitution. Article III of the 1787 Constitution vested the judicial power of the United States "in one supreme court, and in such inferior courts as the Congress may from time to time ordain and establish." When there was opposition to ratification of the 1787 Constitution on the ground that it did not secure to the people certain fundamental rights, the Bill of Rights was enacted in 1789 and ratified in 1791. In 1789, James Madison wrote in the Annals of Congress that "independent tribunals will be naturally led to resist every encroachment upon rights expressly stipulated for in the Constitution by the declaration of rights." Over the last sixty years, however, the Supreme Court has not resisted "every encroachment" upon certain rights, principally those guaranteed under the First and Fourth Amendments. In Greenwood v. California, decided in 1988, the Supreme Court sanctioned a warrantless search of sealed trash bags with the wholly specious argument that the search of Greenwood's garbage did not violate his subjective expectation of privacy in his own garbage, because society did not accept that expectation as "objectively reasonable." It now remains to be seen whether the Supreme Court will use a sanitized Fourth Amendment to encroach upon rights guaranteed by the First Amendment. A person who inadvertently bought a book and found upon reading it to be trash should not throw this book away. A local police investigator may now search sealed trash bags without a warrant. Thus, a book banned by Congress may now be used as evidence of a criminal act by the person who threw it away as trash. Is this person's expectation of privacy in what he or she reads an expectation which is "objectively reasonable" to society as a whole? One would think so, but the Supreme Court held otherwise in Greenwood v. California.

The First Amendment states in part that "Congress shall make no law. . . . abridging the freedom of speech, or of the press. . . " Ever since 1925, however, books and the ideas expressed in them have been subjected to a form of censorship that has become more pervasive with the passage of time, and the "independent tribunals" mentioned by James Madison have not always resisted "every encroachment upon rights" guaranteed under the First Amendment. In Gitlow v. New York (1925), the Supreme Court held that expression (criminal syndicalism) could be restricted where its expression created a "clear and present danger" of antisocial *conduct,* i.e., an injurious result. Both Justice Holmes and Justice Brandeis disented. "Every idea," said Justice Holmes, "is an incitement. It offers itself for belief, and, if believed, it is acted on unless some other belief outweighs it, or some failure of energy stifles the movement at its birth. The only difference between the expression of an opinion and an incitement in the narrower sense is the speaker's enthusiasm for the result. Eloquence may set fire to reason."

With this language, Justice Holmes established free speech in terms of ideas that compete in the marketplace for attention. Gitlow v. New York, however, was one of the first cases in which ideas, if sufficiently unpopular at the time, could be suppressed by legislatively established standards under state law. Long before this, 1873, Congress enacted legislation known as the Comstock Act. Anthony Comstock was one of the leading figures in the long dishonorable history of censorship in the United States. The Comstock Act made it a criminal offense to send "obscene literature" through the mail, but Congress did not bother to define this phrase. Comstock, however, was named a special agent of the U.S. Post Office with police power, and the Society for the Suppression of Vice, which was founded by him, was given part of the fines collected from successful prosecutions under the federal law. Tireless zealotry paid off for Comstock, and he died in 1915, unmourned.

In 1957, the Supreme Court reminded us of the legacy left by Anthony Comstock. In Roth v. United States, the court held that "obscenity" was not protected by the express language of the

First Amendment. "Obscenity," said the court, "was not speech." In another case decided on the same date as Roth, Kingsley Books, Inc. v. Brown, the Supreme Court approved other techniques to control the distribution of books thought to be obscene. In this case, the court affirmed the right of a New York state court to enjoin further distribution of booklets thought to be obscene and authorized their destruction. The New York statute authorizing this "book burning" empowered the chief executive or legal officer of a municipality to bring an action for an injunction to prevent the sale or distribution of obscene written or printed matter without a hearing. A temporary restraining order could be issued *ex parte,* enough of a threat to publishers who stood to lose money even though a hearing on the merits followed the temporary restraining order. Writing for four justices in dissent, Justice Douglas thought that "the provision for an injunction *pendente lite* [an *ex parte* order] gives the State the paralyzing power of censorship. . . it guarantees that the power to restrain publication before even a hearing is held. This is prior restraint and censorship at its worst. Second, the procedure for restraining by equity decree the distribution of all the condemmed literature does violence to the First Amendment."

In Roth v. United States, Justice Brennan, writing for the majority, stated: "We hold that obscenity is not within the area of protected speech or press." The trial court judge had instructed the jury that "The words 'obscene, lewd and lascivious' as used in the law [18 U.S.C. 1461] signify that form of immorality which has relation to sexual impurity and has a tendency to excite lustful *thoughts."* (Emphasis in original.) The majority, almost apologetically, found it unnecesary to reach the question whether obscene literature could perceptibly create a clear and present danger of antisocial conduct by its recipient. Eloquence may set fire to reason, but not if it's reduced to writing about sex, a great and mysterious motive force in human life which has indisputably been a subject of absorbing interest to mankind through the ages. Justice Brennan even observed that "[sex] is one of the vital problems of human interest and public concern." But, he added, if it's found obscene by contemporary standards, i.e., related to sexual impurity and has a tendency to excite lustful thoughts, the writing is not protected speech as "being utterly without redeeming social importance."

Justice Douglas, in a dissent joined by Justice Black, wrote that "the tests by which these convictions were obtained, require only the arousing of sexual thoughts," something that happens every day in normal life. The danger of influencing a change in the current moral standards of the community, or of shocking or offending readers, or of stimulating lustful thoughts or desires, can never justify the losses to society that result from the interference with literary freedom. The courts seem unwilling to acknowledge that people who read have the intellectual capacity to reject noxious literature and to separate the real from the unreal, the true from the false.

Now, in 1989, Congress has taken a final step toward the regulation of "content" of books. It enacted the Child Protection and Obscenity Act of 1988, and President Reagan signed it before leaving office on January 20, 1989. The decision of the Supreme Court in Fort Wayne Books v. State of Indiana on February 21, 1989__U.S.__ seems to foreshadow what it will do when an appropriate case challenging this legislative aberation reaches the Supreme Court.

As a footnote to Salman Rushdie's *The Satanic Verses,* it is worth noting that blasphemy was a criminal offense in at least six states of the United States, including Massachusetts, New York and Pennsylvania.In State v. Mockus, 113 A. 39 (1921), The Supreme Judicial Court of Maine held that Maine's statute making blasphemy a criminal offense did not deny religious freedom or the freedom of speech guaranteed under the First Amendment. Fortunately, this statute was repealed, but not until 1975. One can only guess what the National Writers Union or the Authors Guild will do to resist the legislative dictate of the Child Protection and Obscenity Enforcement Act of 1988. Will book chains, for example, remove a book from their shelves after some religious zealots say it's obscene? Will publishers take the position that there will be no further concessions to literary "terrorism," even if a conviction may mean the forfeiture of all their property to the United States? How will television use its immense power of communication to resist book burning? Will scholarly panelists discuss the definition of obscenity, a definition that seems to have eluded the Supreme Court? As recently as 1970, the U.S. Commission on Obscenity and Pornography, after a two-year study, determined that the standards developed by the Supreme Court beginning with Roth v. United States "interfere with constitutionally protected materials." This Commission went on to say that standards like "an appeal to prurient interest," "patently offensive in light of community standards," and "lacking in redeeming social value" were useless as definitional standards. They were, and still are vague and highly subjective, aesthetic, psychological and moral tests that do not provide meaningful guidance to law enforcement officials, juries or courts.

In Pope v. Illinois, decided in 1987, the Supreme Court seemed to agree in part with this conclusion. In this case, two salesmen in a Rockford, Illinois bookstore were convicted of violating an Illinois obscenity statute by selling allegedly obscene magazines. On appeal, the Illinois Court of Appeals affirmed the conviction, rejecting the argument that the work, taken as a whole, lacked serious literary value and must be determined on an objective basis and not by contemporary community standards. The Illinois Supreme Court denied review. On certiorari, the U.S. Supreme Court vacated the judgment of conviction and remanded the case to the Illinois Court of Appeals for a ruling whether, if properly instructed, a jury could find value in the magazines, and that the trial court's instruction represented harmless error, citing the "value" test in Miller v. California. In Miller v. California, the Supreme Court held that the test of obscenity, to the extent it required a finding that the work was "utterly without redeeming social value" was not constitutionally mandated, because it imposed a burden of proof on the state that "was virtually impossible to discharge under our criminal standards of proof." In Pope v. Illinois, the jury was instructed that the obscenity determination was to be made by reference to a state-wide standard rather than the standard of any single community within the state.

Justice White wrote the plurality opinion. "The proper inquiry," he wrote, "is not whether an ordinary member of any community would find serious literary, artistic, political, or scientific value in allegedly obscene material, but whether a reasonable person would find such value in the material, taken as a whole. The instruction at issue in this case was therefore unconstitutional." Justice Scalia concurred with the "reasonable person" standard, but Justice Brennan, who wrote the majority opinion in Roth v. United States, went even further. He wrote that "my view that *any* regulation of such material with respect to consenting adults suffers from the defect that 'the concept of obscenity' cannot be defined with sufficient specificity and clarity to provide clear notice to persons who create and distribute sexually oriented materials, to prevent substantial erosion of protected rights as a byproduct of the attempt to suppress unprotected speech and to avoid very costly institutional harms." Justice Stevens, with whom Justice Marshall joined, dissented, saying that the "Court's attempt to clarify the constitutional definition of obscenity is not faithful to the First Amendment; and. . . Illinois may [not] criminalize the sale of magazines to consenting adults who enjoy the constitutional right to read and possess them."

The ambiguity present in Justice White's opinion in Pope v. Illinios muddies the waters even further than the Court did in Miller v. California. The ideas a book represents need not obtain majority approval to merit protection under the First Amendment. The "reasonable person" standard does not tell the jury how to decide cases where some reasonable people would find literary, artistic or political value in a book, and other people would conclude that the book had no such value. Publishers, authors, distributors and bookstore owners will be forced to "level" the books they publish, write, distribute or sell to the majority to the lowest common denominator of the population. A reconsideration of Roth v. United States is long overdue, if only because from the multitude of competing offerings from publishers, the public will pick and choose. The expression of an idea — content — may be trash for one person and have enduring value for others. We must rely on the capacity of the free marketplace of ideas to distinguish that which is useful or beautiful from that which is ugly or worthless.

However, only one year earlier than the Court's decision in Pope v. Illinois, 1986, the Meese Commission on Obscenity and Pornography arrived at wholly new and subjective standards. This Commission seems to done the impossible by politicizing "obscenity," and the Supreme Court did not wait very long before placing its seal of approval on most of the Meese Commission's recommendations in Fort Wayne Books v. State of Indiana, a case involving a state statute virtually the same as that just enacted by Congress. Chapter 2 of this law would clearly perpetuate indiscriminate censorship in publishing, and it has ignored at least three generations of people who find judicially established standards defining obscenity to be utterly incomprehensible. In 1933, for example, a U.S. Customs official found *Ulysses* by James Joyce "obscene." Random House, much to its credit successfully resisted this officially sanctioned censorship. In the U.S. District Court (United States v. One Book Called Ulysses ), Judge Woolsey, in holding that *Ulysses* was not obscene, observed that sex in this book was emetic, not aphrodisiac," thus elevating into legal principle the proposition that nausea was not immoral.

Aside from quality of content, money is the other factor in what the small presses may decide to publish. Most small presses are not willing or able to pay the five or six figure advance to an author, so they must learn to use their money in innovative ways and continue to publish quality books in a marketplace where the pleasure and importance of reading exists to raise the level of awareness of those who appreciate good books.

Publishing at its best is a combination of business and culture. Insofar as business is concerned, all publishers have a perfectly legitimate concern with the profit motive. In order for them to stay in business, they must make money. The profit motive applies in equal measure to the small presses of the United

States. The small press community, and it numbers an estimated 12,000 to 15,000 publishers, accounts annually for an estimated 50% of *all* books published each year, about 52,000 of them. Many times a year, there are conferences, seminars and other meetings where the needs of the small press community have been subjected to scrutiny by experts in the field, and the combined experience of these people has been dedicated to helping those attending these seminars to make money, basically by cutting the costs of publishing trade books (fiction, nonfiction and poetry). With one or two major exceptions, these seminars take a hard look at the book production process — how to get an idea into print and sell the result at a profit. New magazines have recently been the beneficiaries of these seminars. A few of them, like *Small Press,* have even organized such seminars, such as that held in April, 1988, in New York City. From July 10 to July 23, 1988 the Eleventh Annual Stanford Professional Publishing Course was held in Palo Alto, California, and its next course will be offered in July, 1989. According to its brochure, one of the principal objectives of the Stanford Course was "To provide in the most time-efficient manner a total immersion in either book or magazine publishing." Cost: $1,650 for nonmembers of the Stanford Alumni Association. In May, 1988 The Folio Show was held in New York City. It was sponsored by two magazines: *Publish!* and *Folio.* Only one of the ten roundtable seminars addressed book publishing *per se,* however, but it was an excellent overview of trade book publishing on the desktop. The phrase, desktop publishing" (DTP) seems to have moved into the big time world of major publishers from its real origins in the small press community, where DTP began as a solution to the big time costs of getting a book or magazine into the market place. A look at one of these seminars seems appropriate. It certainly separates the business of publishing from its culture.

Desktop publishing (DTP) seems to have come of age, and the Seybold Seminar 1988 in San Francisco (March 7-11, 1988) made the point quite well. It stressed what its organizer, Jonathan Seybold, described as the *Fourth Wave* of technology. Focusing primarily on *Fortune* 500 users, seminar panelists discussed talked about technology beyond the reach of the small presses as being far too expensive. Tyler Peppel of Apple Computer summed up the entire subject of desktop publishing this way. "We see," he said, "strong market growth, increasing competition and rapidly increasing user and product sophistication." He also said that desktop publishing, as we know it today, has had most of its impact within the traditional publishing industry. If, by this, he meant the publishers of trade books, the major publishers were conspicuous by their absence.

The list of book publishers who are clearly end users of much of this technology, included McGraw-Hill, Commerce Clearing House Inc. Addison-Wesley Publishing Co., Bertelsmann AG (West Germany's largest publisher and owner of Doubleday Publishing Co.) and Mercury House Inc., a small press in San Francisco. These five were the only publishers of trade books listed as attending this important seminar, the theme of which was *The Fourth Wave* of new technology. A representative of Value Line, Inc., its Director of Automation, was a panelist. *Value Line* is the largest periodical with investment advisory bulletins in the U.S., and its huge financial database resides in a Tandem computer. A major problem for Value Line, Inc. was assembling the data for and compiling the complex graphs for which it is noted. It was solved by Computer Associates' Tell–A–Graph software together with Xyvision for page makeup. The graphs were placed on one page for each company with text and tables composed on PCs. The results are seen daily by analysts at Drexel, Burnham Lambert, Citicorp, Morgan Guaranty Trust Co. and many more. Value Line, Inc. itself manages mutual funds with assets of $2.2 billion. These graphs, even though a relatively small part of its total business, got the attention of Value Line, Inc.'s systems analysts, because the solution was cost-effective. They are all part of its investment advisory services which have a combined circulation of over 100,000 and about 100 security analysts. Value Line, Inc. is clearly a publisher in the traditional sense even though its publications are essentially paperbacks-close to trade books.

Representatives of Simon & Schuster, Random House, Harper & Row (now owned by Rupert Murdoch) and Harcourt Brace & Jovanovich were simply not in evidence. Nor were there any representatives of New American Library, William Morrow & Co., Inc., Macmillan Publishing Co., Little Brown & Co., Inc., Houghton Mifflin or Farrar Strauss & Giroux, Inc. However, representatives of Time, Inc. and *Newsweek* were at the Seybold Seminar on electronic publishing which ended in March, 1988. So were there representatives of PCW Communications, Inc., *PC World, PC Magazine, PC Week* and *Print Magazine.*

The missing majors might have learned a great deal. With an estimated 900 people paying over $900 to hear many industry leaders describe their products, partly, it must be said, in terms too technical for about 50% of those attending, the Seminar must be considered a great success. Scott McNealy, President of Sun Microsystems, Inc. talked about *Fourth Wave* system architectures and Sun's 1987 agreement with A.T.& T. to develop the Unix workstation. The Unix operating system, McNealy explained, used reduced instruction set (RISC) architecture. This architecture with Unix was designed essentially for computing in an engineering environment, i.e., manufacturing or structural design, where complex algorithms are used for mathematical computations. It works well there, but the business community is not too enthusiastic. It seems to prefer the disk operating system (DOS) environment for output like spreadsheets.

A.T.& T. aggressively licenses the Unix operating system, both to establish an industry standard and to compete with IBM which uses its own architecture. In January, 1988, A.T.& T. paid $300 million for a 20% interest in Sun Microsystems. IBM has announced at least one or two new versions of its PS/2 Model 80. It is supposed to include both a 20–MHz 80386 processor, with RISC architecture. If true, it can probably run Unix and MS–DOS or OS/2 concurrently, using IBM's Micro Channel bus which, in Model 50 and above, will support multiple master processors on the same bus. As someone once said: "Don't write off Big Blue."

McNealy was followed by Ronald Eich, Director of Development, Publishing Systems Business Unit, at International Business Machines, Lawrence Tesler, Vice President of Advanced Technology at Apple Computer, Inc. and Howard Woolf, Manager for Digital Equipment Corporation's Electronic Publishing Systems Group. Additionally, Adrian King, Director of Operating Systems for Microsoft Corporation, Paul Brainerd, President of Aldus Corporation and Charles Geschke, Chief Operating Officer of Adobe Systems, Inc. were some of the many panelists. Others included Harold Evans of R.R. Donnelley & Sons, Inc., William Givens, President of ECRM, Inc., John Warnock, President of Adobe Systems, Inc., and Louis Tortora, Director of Marketing and Product Planning at the Linotype Company. Since electronic imaging and graphics were very hot topics, the Linotype booth got a great deal of attention. Its flat bed scanner, for example, can scan catalog artwork and, using its proprietary system, digitize the image scanned and show a grayscale reproduction on the monitor in about 2 minutes. The image itself can then be transferred to a disk for use by a catalog publisher such as J.C. Penney or Sears Roebuck & Co. — cost, about $21,000. Datacopy Corporation is another company offering scanners and image processing software. Its Model 840-i, the 400 dpi resolution, 8 — bit flatbed scanner with built — in image processing capabilities, attracted a great deal of attention. Unfortunately, an 8½ x 11" file with 256 levels of grayscale imaging uses 15.0MB of disk space. This can be reduced by compression to a 3:1 ratio, but then, it must be decompressed for use, and this seems to require a remote user to have compatibility with the host computer.

An image computer requires a very large memory — over 100MB — and processors powerful enough to deal with this much memory — about 120 MIPS (120 million instructions per second). Its cost is staggering. The problem of placing images into a computer for this sort of use is simply explained but not easily solved. Product vendors, however, know there is a market for this technology. Its use is often referred to as Computer Aided Design and Drawing (CADD). Take an illustration for a book cover as an example, one done by an artist — illustrator combination. The most expeditious way of getting this into a computerized environment is to auto—digitize the illustration, using a desktop scanner and raster to vector conversion. This means converting bit-map (dots) images into vector (line representations). A circle, for example, becomes a dot with a radius value for recording, using and storing this sort of image. A computer must be able to "recognize" this value, and this is most often done by a scanner which recognizes common shapes. Island .Graphics, for example, will photograph an existing illustration-the equivalent of scanning-and store this image for use. Publishers of books, magazines and other print media, as well as advertising agencies represent a very large and growing market for this technology. Many of the companies working on this were founded in the 1980s. Currently, only grayscale images can be handled this way on a reasonable cost/performance basis, but color technology is on the way.

In November, 1987, at Comdex–87 in Las Vegas, Qume Inc. exhibited a color printer which had beautiful color graphics output—cost, $17,000. Many of the product vendors at The Seybold Seminar were working on this same technology, and many of those attending reached a level of interest that was unusual. They felt that later in 1988 or early in 1989, there would be a real breakthrough that was affordable. According to Alvy Ray Smith of Pixar, a disk with 1.2GB (gigabytes) can hold 25-340 full-color pages without compression. The cost of this was not specified. However, NPS, Inc. offers Image Express system which supports options such as high resolution scanners (300 dpi or better), video cameras and RGB (red, green blue bit-mapping) with a price that starts at $28,500. Impressive but expensive. Jovian Logic Corporation, which was not an exhibitor at the Seybold Seminar, offers a simpler and far less expensive image capture system. Using an ordinary VCR camera and a Video Input Adapter (VIA), its software will digitize an image "frozen" from the camera. By using a PS/2 computer which has a visual graphics adapter (VGA) built—in, the cost of the entire Jovian Logic system is $595, and the camera is about $900. With an IBM or compatible, a user will need a VGA—cost, $400. The image captured by the Jovian Logic system will show on a color monitor in up to 256 colors. It, too, is impressive and affordable.

The list of exhibitors was impressive, including companies from Abaton Technologies to ECRM, Inc., Eastman Kodak Company, Lotus Development Corporation, Xerox Corporation, Interleaf, Inc., Microtek Lab, Inc., Quark, Frame Technology, Networked Picture Systems, Inc. and Island Graphics Corporation.

Notwithstanding all this high powered talent, the average user of all the new hardware and software must have had a difficult time understanding what one listener described as "marketing techno-babble." Multitasking, networking, systems network architecture and user interface," he said, "were little more than 'buzzwords' and without much meaning to most users of all the technology marketed by the panelists." Then, he added, "Don't tell me about raster conversion and pixels. Just tell me what prepress work I have to do to get color artwork in my catalogs. Or what's a cost-effective way of putting 'grayscale' graphics in my magazine or book?" One wonders if the nontechnical users all felt the same way. One panelist noted the marketing hype by using the "What you see is what you get" phrase (WYSIWYG) used by other panelists. What you see is what you. . . " and then pausing for 5 seconds, he added, "see." His point was then made when he said: "What you see is what you'll get on paper when it's printed. What's so new and different about that? And why does it all cost so much? Then, in a quite refreshing change of pace, he added: "You're paying all that extra money to get a computer simulation of crushed wood pulp — paper." Even the product company representatives in the audience joined in the laughter.

Later in the week, Theodore Holm Nelson, the author of *Literary Machines,* offered a vision of the future and what, in his opinion, electronic publishing had to become. He called it *Project Xanadu.* "What you hear," he said, "is true. *[Project Xanadu]* is a plan for a worldwide network, intended to serve hundreds of millions of users simultaneously from the corpus of the world's stored writings, graphics and data." What he seems to be saying is that people everywhere can collect literature, news and data on disk drives, not bookshelves. Researchers could use an arsenal of knowledge by accessing the *Project Xanadu* system and seeing it all on their own computer's monitor and paying a modest fee for its use. It would seem that all the product vendors at the Seybold Seminar might see the market potential of this worldwide system which will not be fully operational for at least 20 years.

Other than representatives of product companies (Apple Computer had 19, Adobe Systems had 12, Bitstream, Inc. had 5, Compugraphic Corporation had 11, Digital Equipment Corporation had 18, Hewlett-Packard had 17, Linotype Company had 21 and Xerox Corporation had 14), most of the other people attending, many of them users, came from newspapers all over the country. Those represented included *The New York Times, The Washington Post, The San Francisco Chronicle, The San Francisco Examiner, The Santa Rosa Press–Democrat, The Chicago Tribune, Newsday, Baltimore Sun Co., Minneapolis Star Tribune, The Cleveland Plain-Dealer* and *The Philadelphia Inquirer.*

It seems clear that desktop publishing has so far been seen as a cost-effective way of printing corporate newsletters, annual reports, magazines and newspapers. These are all heavy with graphics, both color and grayscale. It's no wonder that Pixar, a corporate spinoff from the computer graphics division of Lucasfilm, was there for the *Fourth Wave.*

The publishers of trade books, i.e., fiction and nonfiction sold in America's bookstores, seem to be the stepchildren of the *Fourth Wave* and its technology. With the few exceptions mentioned, publishers of trade books — the literature of America — were conspicuous by their absence. They appear to be indifferent to technology, according to one observer who asked not to be identified. He also added: "The major publishers need this technology more than ever, even if the only result of having it reduces the cover price of a book by a dollar or so a copy."

In fact, the January 31, 1988 issue of *The Seybold Report on Publishing Systems* made a slight bow in the direction of trade book publishers in its lead article, "Publishing Joins the Computer Mainstream." However, except for mentioning Gutenberg once and early prepress technology, this article didn't even mention books. It dwelt principally on power (memory size, disk capacity and speed as millions of instructions per second— MIPS), all of which is both relevant and important. Then, the same issue had this to say about the Seminar theme:

> "We will do everything wrong if we try to base our future on the technical foundations of the past.
> . . . If we add 1990 technology to a 1970 architecture, we are being very short sighted and will only delay (and in the long run substantially increase the cost of) modernization.

This statement seems only partly true. The personal computer (PC) revolution did not even get off the ground until early 1982 when IBM offered its PC XT, followed by Apple Computer. Apple's latest products were first offered in 1987, e.g., the Macintosh SE. By 1988, the mass market for the PC had succeeded in reducing the prices of computers and peripherals, and the same thing occurred with periphals like the Hewlett-Packard LaserJet and Apple's LaserWriter. What the *Fourth Wave* seems to overlook is a simple point. Equipment never becomes obsolete if it does what the user wants it to do. Except in color technology, which still leaves much to be desired in terms of both cost and performance, 1988 hardware (computer architecture) and software used by publishers of trade books is quite satisfactory. Incompatibility of systems hardware and software has been a problem for years, and it's still a problem. IBM, with its Systems Application Architecture (SAA) has gone a long way in providing a consistent programming environment for all of *its* products, but it has not yet come up with color graphics. Some vendors are moving toward standard hardware and software for linking peripherals to each other, but there simply must be an industry standard for computers, printers and modems as well as software before real progress can become possible. The assembly of a complete system for publishing trade books takes great care now, and it's almost *caveat emptor* as things now stand.

Mercury House, which did take great care in acquiring both hardware and software — it was all compatible — considers itself a member of the small press community where "desktop publishing" probably got its name. This community has been estimated to include 12,000 publishers and annually publishes an estimated 50% of all trade books in the United States. This means new titles each year from all publishers. Publishing of *all* books in this country is a business which annually generates revenue of over $10 billion, but, except for the small press community, the major publishers do not seem to think in terms of saving significant amounts of money by applying modern technology to their own business.

Nolo Press in Berkeley, a publisher of legal textbooks, uses DTP, and so does Sandlight Press in San Diego. The March-April, 1987 issue of *Small Press* tells the story of Mercury House and how it has used desktop publishing to both save money and time with its books. North Point Press in San Francisco publishes trade books, but its commitment to desktop publishing is currently under review. A decision is expected by the end of 1988. There may be others, like Wadsworth Publishing Co. in Belmont, California, a leading publisher of college textbooks. This company proofs its books on an Apple LaserWriter, but sends text by modem to a service bureau for 1,250 dots per inch (dpi) output on a Linotronic L100 phototypesetter, but at a cost of $10 per page. With trade books, however, everything except printing and binding the books can be done in-house.

Mercury House, Inc. a San Francisco publisher of trade books (fiction and nonfiction) was one of the pioneers in the Bay Area. In 1986, it acquired a Genesis laser imaging printer from Tegra, Inc. It turns out camera-ready copy with a resolution of 1,000 dpi. At the same time, Mercury House acquired typesetting software, Magnatype, sold by Magna Computer Systems, Inc. Even earlier, Mercury House used a Dest PC Scan which "reads" an author's manuscript and creates a file in Multimate Advantage, word-processing software sold by Ashton-Tate. If Mercury House gets a "clean" manuscript from an author after line and copy editing, the capacity to "read" it with the Dest PC Scan, an optical character reader (OCR), saves about $3.00 per page of text. It costs this much to have the author's text re-keyboarded into a computer's file. The Dest PC Scan "reads" one page of 8½ x 11" paper with about 300 words in 21 seconds and transfers this text to Multimate Advantage, the wordprocessing software used by Mercury House. In Multimate Advantage as a file—each chapter is a separate file—the manuscript is copy edited for typos and other minor changes. Then, it is converted to ASCII text with Multimate Advantage's conversion feature and copied to a disk. From this same disk, the text is copied to Magnatype, typeset and sent to Tegra Inc.'s Genesis printer with output of camera- ready copy at a rate of 8 pages per minute. This output is then sent to Crane Duplicating Co. where it is printed and bound as "Uncorrected page proofs" which are sent to reviewers. The amount saved by this DTP combination is $14 to $18 per page of text in the book.

Typesetting software is essential to give the printed page that professional look with the left and right margins straight and not ragged. The software does this by kerning and tracking. A computer can take about 1,500 letter pairs and move the letters in each pair closer together or further apart. This is kerning. Tracking does the same thing with entire words. Thus, each line on each page is hyphenated and justified to produce that professional look. A few publishers will show books at trade conventions with ragged right pages. This means only that production editors have not really decided what typeface or font to use or whether line editing needs more attention. The final output will be hyphenated and justified. The software also produces headers and footers on each page along with chapter headings, and each page is consecutively numbered, all by computer. Mercury House has six different fonts or typefaces, and the computer does the point size and leading (the distance between lines). This book was typeset in *Bembo* with 11 point type and 13 point leading. Formats written for Magnatype control all this, and the Genesis can produce an output of camera-ready copy at a rate of eight pages per minute.

In 1986, Mercury House, using this combination of hardware and software, published ten trade books. In 1987, it published fifteen more and, in 1988, Mercury House has published about eighteen more trade books. It is not concerned about a graphics capability yet, since its books, with two exceptions, are all text. The two exceptions were Sanford Roth's *Portraits of the Fifties* and Joseph Cotten's autobiography, *Vanity Will Get You Somewhere.* Both contained many photographs. All but one of its trade books were printed by R.R. Donnelley & Sons, Inc., one of the largest commercial printers in the United States.

At the Seybold Seminar, R.R. Donnelly announced it had signed an agreement with Adobe Systems Inc., which developed a page descriptor language, PostScript, in 1984. As a result of this agreement, R.R. Donnelley is expected to market a do-it-yourself Customer Publishing System. For the moment, magazines are likely to be the early beneficiaries of this announcement, but publishers of trade books may be next in line. Essentially, users may mail a disk or telecommunicate text to R.R. Donnelley which will then print the magazine or book. No costs of this Customer Publishing System to users were announced.

Another feature of desktop publishing is telecommunication of text. Mercury House uses Crosstalk Mark 4 and a Hayes modem which sends and receives text of a book at 1,200 bits per second. In 1986, it acquired the U.S. rights to a book first published in West Germany, *The Martyr.* They were acquired at the International Book Fair in Frankfurt. The translator used lived in Boston. When the text was translated into English, he sent the text to San Francisco, using telecommunications software. It was captured to a disk at 1,200 bits per second, or about 47 minutes for the entire book. Five hours later the entire book had been typeset with an output of camera-ready copy.

This text was sent to Crane Duplicating Co. in Massachusetts for printing as "Uncorrected page proofs." These *Cranes* were sent to trade magazines like *Publishers Weekly* and *Library Journal* for reviews. They were also sent for reviews to print media like *The New York Times, The San Francisco Chronicle, The Chicago Tribune, The Philadelphia Enquirer, The Columbus Dispatch, The Denver Post, The Atlanta Constitution, The Washington Post* and *The Los Angeles Times.*

This procedure did not originate with Mercury House. For decades, most publishers have done the same thing, and their objective has been to somehow induce reviewers in the trade journals and print media to review the book sent as a *Crane*. A good review clearly helps sell books and, to bookstores using R.R. Bowker's CD-ROM, Books in Print With Reviews and Forthcoming Books, a good review helps a trade buyer for that bookstore make a "buy" decision. Recently, Mercury House has gotten some good reviews for some of its books. *Newsweek,* for example, ran an outstanding review of *Eve: Her Story,* and *The New York Times* ran an excellent review of Clarence Major's book, *Such Was the Season. The San Francisc Chronicle* ran a great review of *Chocolate Mouse* and *Kirkus Reviews* did another on *Poppies: The Odyssey of an Opium Eater.* Both *Poor Dear Charlotte* and *The Chinaberry Album* were well reviewed in *The New York Times* in the spring of 1988.

Now, with a program custom-designed by Mercury House, it can print such reviews and send them to *all* bookstores within the circulation area of the newspaper publishing it. If, for example, *The San Francisco Chronicle* or *The New Times* prints a good review, a copy of it can be mailed to bookstores within a few hours. The program will sort bookstores by state, cities within a state, SAN, zip code or even area code. In case of a San Francisco newspaper, mailing labels would be printed by area codes 415 to 805 (Santa Barbara), and about 460 bookstores would be included. A mailing label would look like this:

> Paul Yamazaki
> City Lights Bookstore
> 261 Columbus Avenue
> San Francisco, California 94133
>                    or
> Mahri Kerley
> Chaucer & Company Bookstore
> Loreto Plaza, 3321 State Street.
> Santa Barbara, Ca. 93105

Then, to do telemarketing, the same program will print out bookstores with the name of the trade buyer together with his or her area code and phone number, two examples of which appears below.

Books Plus Wilton Ct. Janice Whitney (203) 762-5553
or
The Haunted Bookshop, Inc. Joyce Whaley (602) 297-4843

This book, a mass market paperback, *Publishing in a Global Village,* could have been sent to over 4,500 general bookstores in the United States. Their names and addresses may be found by searching the "electronic yellow pages" of a database in Palo Alto, California, Dialog Information Services, Inc. Mailing labels for each one could have been printed out on a Hewlett-Packard *Laserjet Series II* printer. The cost of this search would be an estimated $750 in connect time. However, Mercury House got its own program, the use of which will save a significant amount of money, and it was written in-house using programming software written by DataEase International, Inc. With this software, a person with virtually no background in programming can write a custom-designed program.

Mercury House is a publisher that, early on, saw the potential of selling its own books via the Electronic Mall. It now offers a total of 36 books to CompuServe's 420,000 plus subscribers via an "electronic bookstore." These subscribers may dial in to the Mall using their own computers, "browse" through the Mercury House catalog, order what they want and charge the cost on any one of three credit cards.

The cost of Mall connect time continues to be a factor in determining "browsing" time in this kind of unique bookstore. This is the only reason why Mercury House offers subscribers a 35% discount on all its books. Unlike the conventional bookstore, "browsing" costs money. To reduce this cost, subscribers may download the entire Mercury House catalog as well as the "flap" copy about each book. Most telecommunications software programs have this capability. Crosstalk Mark 4, for example, allows a subscriber to capture text to a disk in the A drive, and CompuServe has developed and sells software which will download text. Text can also be printed out while on line. Using either method will reduce connect time charges by a significant amount and allows a subscriber to look at a Mercury House catalog at his or her leisure. The entire catalog can be saved in less than 4 minutes using a 1,200 bits per second modem. Conventional bookstores send their customers catalogs, and downloading the Mercury House catalog is essentially the same process.

Mercury House believes that when a subscriber keys in GO MER to access Mercury House, he or she is walking into a bookstore, albeit an "electronic" one. An option provided by the Electronic Mall's menu allows subscribers or "browsers" to "read" current reviews of each book offered by Mercury House. Good reviews help sell books. *Eve: Her Story* and *Chocolate Mouse* are the latest beneficiaries of great reviews, in *Newsweek* and *The San Francisco Chronicle,* respectively, and *The Day Nothing Happened* by Terence Clark got an excellent review on July 21, 1988 in this same newspaper. Earlier, *Such Was the Season* was another, this one in *The New York Times. Guest in the Jungle, Hubble Time* and *Shrinking* all got good reviews in newspapers around the United States from San Diego and Los Angeles to Chicago, Cleveland, Atlanta, St. Louis and Washington.

Mercury House can now track all bookstores placing orders for its titles, using its computer records. As a result, it can also sponsor a co-op mailing to *their* (the bookstore's) customers, a contemporary version of electronic marketing at a cost of less than $150 per mailing. Mercury House sent its first newsletter, *The Messenger* in May, 1988. Mercury was the messenger of the gods in mythology, after all. Its most recent newsletter was sent to bookstores in advance of a one-column advertisement in *The New Yorker* of July 25, 1988.

The program used prints out mailing labels to over 5,590 bookstores. They can be sorted by state, cities within each state and by zip code as well as by area code. *Such was the Season,* by Clarence Major, got a very good review in *The Washington Post.* A mailing to all bookstores in the *Post's* circulation area is simple, and other titles can be included in this direct mail marketing to the customers of those bookstores at no expense to them.

Also, with bookstores using compatible hardware and software, Mercury House can send reviews of its books to these bookstores with Crosstalk Mark 4 software. An IBM or compatible computer, a modem, a printer and comparable software now cost about $1,800, and the cost of this basic package can be recovered in less than a year. An off-the-shelf program for accounts receivable, for example, will easily save $2,000 in labor alone including the time lost doing about five or six hundred statements a month manually, instead of by computer. Sending reviews to a bookstore with a modem allows the manager to capture the text and read it at leisure, another time-saver. Mercury House has sent out a questionnaire to 5,690 bookstores. In general, this is a way of finding out which bookstores have (a) a computer, (b) a modem and (c) compatible applications software. Two new electronic ordering programs, BookBase and Pubnet, will be available for use by booksellers, publishers and their distributors, and Mercury House will use both.

In the near future, Mercury House expects to be able to accept orders for its books from bookstores and fulfill them. Electronic ordering is still another aspect of desktop publishing. Books published have to be sold. Pubnet, an electronic ordering system started by the American Association of Publishers, is expanding into the trade bookstores. It began as a system for use by college bookstores selling textbooks. The software costs only $300, and it's simple to use. By reducing the time between placing an order to shipping date from about two weeks to a few days, bookstores will be able to operate comfortably with less inventory. BookBase operates in very much the same way. It offers overnight processing of orders, sorts the books ordered and advises the publisher of each via modem. Both systems are expected to reduce the time between placing an order and fulfillment by more than 60% from current practices in the industry.

Furthermore, by 1992 or even earlier, Mercury House expects to see "publishing on demand." This means that a bookstore, or a regional printing service center, will be able to print and bind books in-house and on demand from a customer. It also means that a bookstore will need to have only a minimum inventory of books to display on its shelves. The savings are expected to be very large.

The revolution in electronic publishing begins with a type-written manuscript from an author. It's "read" into a word-processing program for editing, and each step in this process leaves an edit trail using Compare which checks the author's version with the editor's changes. It is then typeset by computer and sent to a commercial printer. This is not the end of the process, only the point at which distribution to booksellers begin in response to electronic ordering after commission reps have discussed titles with trade buyers. Electronic marketing, either by newsletters using conventional mail or electronic mail sent to booksellers with reviews, is the final step and should last until the book is no longer in print or returned to the publisher for credit. All this, at least the part using telecommunication, occurs at 2,400 bits, or about 300 words per second.

Mercury House expects to share in this revolution by making the text of all its titles available on a disk to bookstores, either by sending the text by telecommunications software upon request by a bookstore and tracking the number of copies actually printed or actually sending the disk and doing the same thing. Mercury House uses Taproot Accounting software and custom-designed software to track its inventory from the commercial printer to the distributor and the bookstore ordering its titles. By doing this, Mercury House knows where to concentrate its marketing by direct or electronic mail.

This is what the revolution in desktop publishing is all about. Some small presses have been riding the *Fourth Wave* for three or four years and for a relatively modest investment in technology of about $60,000. Most of this can be recovered in less than two years via savings plus depreciation and, when it was available, the investment tax credit. All this may still be referred to as desktop publishing, but the desks are now found in a richer environment, *Fortune 500* America.

# Chapter 2
# The Culture of Publishing: Literacy, Textbooks and Money

Publishing, while not often thought of as including textbooks, is big business, an estimated $3.9 billion per year in the 1990s, for textbooks alone. Professionals, including various teachers' colleges, are now saying that we have produced "a nation at risk," because too many textbooks used in the secondary and high schools have produced what may be described as "cultural illiteracy," particularly in the areas of history and social studies. Even reading skills are said to suffer, because young students are simply "turned off" by textbooks with little or no literary merit and put together by editors who don't know the subject matter. Formula writing and textbooks with a "low concept load" are the rule, not the exception.

An increasing number of critics have noted the disappearance of controversies, conflicts, colorful characters and tragedies in textbooks, the very stuff from which legends are created, but in fiction. Autobiographies and biographies, authorized or unauthorized, merely perpetuate legends. Textbooks about both American (or any other) history and social studies have been analyzed for accuracy, balance and representation, but not, until recently for their literary merit. If such textbooks are treated by teachers as crutches or read and forgotten, as boring, by their students, the resulting historical amnesia raises the specter of a wholesale loss of a national heritage. Even worse, this student *ennui* will almost certainly and adversely affect what students will read and enjoy when they are older. Small presses may want to take a hard look at publishing textbooks, since they use their own editors, not a committee of pseudo editors. Good authors are more likely to enjoy the finished product, rather than being the target of educational reformers.

From the Teachers College at Columbia University, *A Report of the Educational Excellence Network* (The Report), published in 1987, has examined and found wanting most American history textbooks. In its Introduction, the Report stated: "Perceptive studies as different as Francis FitzGerald's *America Revised* (1979) and Herbert London's *Why Are They Lying to Our Children?* (1984) have noted startling changes in tone, interpretation and selection of material. . . As citizens quarrel over the content of social studies and history, the nation's courts try to adjudicate among differing systems of belief and interpretation. . . State adoption policies and local selection practices discourage improvement of history textbooks. Publishers are increasingly in the business of appeasing willful interest groups." The Report, for example, gave Silver Burdett's *The United States and Its Neighbors* special attention. Silver Burdett is a subsidiary of Simon & Schuster, Inc., and this book was, the Report said: "a *de facto* approach [to] a national curriculum." An estimated one million fifth graders are required to read it each year. Its original cost had been recovered from the sale of earlier editions. Presumably, each revision was made to catch up with some national trauma like World War II and the civil rights struggles of the 1960s.

One may get some idea of the balance of this 502—page textbook by noting that World War II rated *four* pages, Abraham Lincoln was summarily dealt with in two paragraphs and Valley Forge was not even mentioned. In the last chapter, the text wandered "from topic to topic, . . [ranging] from the 1976 Bicentennial celebration [of the Declaration of Independence] to Theodore Roosevelt to synthetic fibers to automobiles to the Great Depression to Franklin Roosevelt to Martin Luther King, Jr., to human rights." As the Report noted, "[It was] easy to read, sentence by sentence; but, taken as a whole, incoherent." Finally, the Report described the writing style as one calculated to "produce a coma—like state of boredom." And, it said, ". . . the book's tone is generally lifeless, monotonic, without feeling; a bus schedule [to somewhere] and the Vikings are treated with equal passion."

However, the Report noted on page 13 that "A few boutique publishers *do* provide superior, literary texts, mainly to upper — end public and private high schools. The mass market textbook is developed, sold and consumed in a different scolastic universe." If, by boutique publishers, the Report meant the small presses of the United States, they should take note. A copy of this Report may be ordered for $4.00 from the Educational Excellence Network, Box 32, Teachers College, Columbia University, New York, New York 10027.

Simon & Schuster, Inc., the publisher of *The United States and Its Neighbors,* Time, Inc. and Harcourt Brace Jovanovich are the three largest publishers of textbooks in the United States. These three account for 27% of domestic and export sales of *all books of all types.* All this has come about as a result of mergers and acquisitions. There may be more of these in 1989 and 1990, but 1987 was a big year for publishing. Rupert Murdoch's News America Holdings, Inc., acquired Harper & Row Publishers, Inc., for $300 million, and Bertelsmann AG, a West German publisher, acquired Doubleday & Co., Inc. Harcourt Brace Jovanovich acquired the net assets of the Educational and Professional Publishing Division of CBS, Inc., for $500 million in cash and the assumption of certain liabilities.

The literary style or merit of textbooks has not been the only subject of notice. Jeffrey L. Pasley wrote an article for *The New Republic,* entitled "The Trouble With Textbooks." In it, he notes that "the treatment of religion as a force in U.S. history continues to receive short shrift." Textbooks do not seem to equate religion with the abolitionist, temperance or early women's movements. And they give Martin Luther King and the civil rights movement extended coverage, but without noting the importance of Christianity to King and his followers. What they believed in, nonviolence, had its origins in the Bible, and David Thoreau, as well as Gandhi, applied this principle to contemporary activism. Pasley explains all this by saying: "Textbook publishers aren't ideologues, but merely salesmen eager to please. 'The assumption is if you put religion in your textbook, it won't sell,' says one publisher. Until recently, textbook publishers were convinced it was just good business sense to steer clear of religion. People are afraid that, if they allude to religion, they'll get into a controversy over separation of church and state." Pasley cites a few examples of what can only be labeled as historical revisionism. One of them is *Triumph of the American Nation,* which was published in 1986 by Harcourt Brace Jovanovich. It completely "sanitized" the Mayflower Compact of 1640 by deleting all but one of the document's seven references to God and Christianity. As Pasley noted, "we discover that the Pilgrims 'celebrated their first year . . . by setting aside several days for recreation and thanksgiving.' The authors do not say Whom the Pilgrims were thanking." It is not surprising to find some publishers handling other controversial subjects as gingerly as they treat religion. An example cited by Pasley was *Land of Liberty,* a single—volume textbook for junior high school students, which "offers only the most anodyne view of social unrest in the 60's, concluding that 'the increase in anti-war and civil rights demonstations was deeply disturbing to many Americans.' " *Land of Liberty,* was published by Holt Rinehart & Winston, Inc., acquired by Harcourt Brace Jovanovich in December 1986 for $500 million in cash. In something of a role reversal, Random House acquired a British consortium, Chatto, Virago, Bodley Head and Jonathan Cape, Ltd. In 1986, Penguin Books, Ltd., of London acquired E. P. Dutton and New American Library.

Some people feel that in the wake of recent mergers and acquisitions, the cultural aspect has been replaced by a corporate mentality and a new emphasis on the "bottom line." They fear that these giants see books (including textbooks) as "product" rather than as something to be read and enjoyed, and the public will see fewer serious books as editors become less inclined to encourage unknown authors because they are told these books will not be commercial, i.e., they won't sell. At the giant publishers' offices, even quality—minded editors feel the pressure and tend to lose their independence.

Some people also believe that these trends toward publishing "giantism" herald the decline or end of the small presses which account for an estimated 50% of all books published. This need not be the case, if small presses are willing to invest in innovative technology, to attract talented and versatile editors, and to take advantage of new opportunities that open up as our world becomes a global village. In fact, the very technologies that have made us a global village — computers and telecommunications — can work to the advantage of small presses, as well as to the advantage of booksellers and readers.

With these new technologies, small presses can reduce editorial and production costs, streamline operations, and use the money saved to advertise and market serious books for the pleasure of literate readers.

And there is some evidence that the public's taste is turning from commercialized mediocrity and hyped "blockbusters" to more serious literature. Patricia Holt, Book Editor of the *San Francisco Chronicle,* observed in her article of May 31, 1987, on the American Booksellers Association: "At exhibits that used to be notorious for commercial bestsellers, fluff fiction and expensive gift books, editors were pushing serious novels and nonfiction works by unknown authors, often in new and affordable paperback formats. There was little or no overkill in it, either . . . no huge advertising budgets to glut bookstores with slow-starting books; few overprintings and much pride."

In her comments after the 1988 convention of the American Booksellers Association, Patricia Holt noted that the "hottest rumor circulating around the exhibit floor. . . . was that the Federal Trade Commission [was] about to serve letters of 'proposed complaint' against hardcover and paperback publishers in New York." It was not a rumor. On January 8, 1989, the Federal Trade Commission filed complaints naming Random House, Simon & Schuster, The Hearst Corporation and William Morrow, The Putnam Berkley Group, Harper & Row and Macmillan as respondents and alleging violations of the Federal Trade Commission Act and the Clayton Act. Basically, the Complaints naming each alleged that the respondents engaged in discriminatory pricing practices by giving Waldenbooks, B. Dalton Booksellers and Crown Books (favored purchasers) higher discounts than those given to "disfavored purchasers" for the same books, the effect of which "has been or may be to lessen competition. . . or to injure, destroy or prevent competition between favored and disfavored purchaers." According to the Complaints, "Disfavored purchasers include most, if not all, of the nation's independent bookstores, i.e., bookstores that are not owned by a large chain." The Complaint also stated that "Under respondents' pricing schedules for certain books, the price at which [they] sell or distribute these books is determined by the number of books in individual orders. On large orders, purchasers pay a lower price per book. On smaller orders, purchasers pay a higher price per book. Since respondents treat orders placed by bookstore chains as one order, even if the books are separately packed, itemized, and shipped to individual chain outlets, bookstore chains pay lower prices for their books than independent bookstores, even when the shipments to independent bookstores are as large as or larger than the shipments to individual chain outlets." Chairman Daniel Oliver filed a dissenting statement saying in part that "most if not all of the price differences are cost justified. . . and the respondents have been simply meeting the competition of other publishers." A hearing was scheduled before an administrative law judge on February 21, 1989.

If substantiated by proof, the small presses are likely to find the market for their books limited to a diminishing number of independent bookstores without the cease and desist order sought by the Federal Trade Commission. Moreover,unless discriminatory discounting is held as illegal by the Federal Trade Commission, the people who enjoy reading serious literature instead of "hyped blockbusters" will find their search for quality more difficult, but not impossible during the transition from the closing to the opening of the American mimd.

Small presses have a definite role to play in this transition. Their niche in the global village will be to bring quality fiction and non-fiction to a public that seems increasingly eager to receive it. Allan Bloom's bestseller, *The Closing of the American Mind,* is itself evidence that people want to find out what happened to the "liberal education" of the sixties, and the humanities taught by universities as part of it. As Allan Bloom noted: "I was convinced in the early sixties that what was wanted was a liberal education to give students the wherewithal to examine their lives and survey their potential. This was the one thing the universities were unequipped and unwilling to offer them. By the mid-sixties, universities were offering them [students] every concession other than education, but appeasement failed, and soon the whole experiment in excellence was washed away, leaving not a trace."

A few pages later, Bloom said: "Students now arrive at the university ignorant and cynical about our political heritage, lacking the wherewithal to be inspired by it or seriously critical of it." Notwithstanding the civil rights activists of the sixties, students, he said, seemed unaware that "the teachings of equality, the promise of the Declaration of Independence, the study of the Constitution, the knowledge of our history and many more things were the painstakingly earned and stored up capital that supported them." While he does not say so, Bloom seems to argue that after 1964, student activism focused on anti—war—in—Vietnam protests, but that the moral imperative of racial justice was left to the politicians and the courts. Bloom also seems to be saying that it's not too late for serious students to learn the foundation on which this "stored up capital" rests by reading *Democracy in America* by Alexis de Tocqueville. This two—volume book was written in Paris in 1835, first translated from the French in the same year, retranslated in 1862 and published in the United States in 1945 by Alfred A. Knopf, Inc., Both Volumes I and II were translated into Spanish, Danish, German, Italian, Russian and Serbian soon after their publication in France. In the Introduction to *Democracy in America,* Phillips Bradley wrote: "From the 1840's to the 1940's, it has remained an enduring source of insight and inspiration for each new generation in search of the fundamental criteria of and conditions for economic, social, and political democracy." Alfred A. Knopf, Inc. published a sixth printing of *Democracy in America* in 1953.

Many may and should criticize Bloom's basic premise as being too general and not admitting of any exceptions, but they should not dismiss it out of hand. Too many students of the early sixties, he said, who arrived at a university "had hardly heard the names of the writers [Descartes, Pascal, Voltaire and others] who were the daily fare of their counterparts across the Atlantic . . . ," an "intellectual obtuseness" which produced "an utter lack of engagement in the civilization's ongoing discourse." Had Allan Bloom been so inclined, he could logically have concluded that history and social studies textbooks in secondary and high schools produced this "utter lack of engagement" at the university level.

Another bestseller, *Cultural Literacy,* by E.D. Hirsch, Jr., was published by Houghton Mifflin Company. In its Preface, Hirsch wrote: "To be culturally literate is to possess the basic information needed to thrive in the modern world." What he seems to be saying is that we must reinstitute a policy of imparting common information in our schools, rather than relying on a "fragmented curriculum based on faulty educational theories." At the end of his book, Hirsch has attached an Appendix, listing, in 63 pages, all the words, dates, names and phrases a culturally literate person should know. By necessary implication, there may not be many who satisfy his criteria, presumably because they don't read enough of the right books. Alternatively, they read and were bored by history textbooks as students from the primary school level on through high school. Revised constantly by editors, these textbooks gave students little or no foundation for college life. It is not surprising that so many people now read books like *The Closing of the American Mind* and *Cultural Literacy.* They simply wanted to know what went wrong with their education or why we produced a "nation at risk." There can be little doubt that rampant revisionism in history textbooks was a major factor, along with their lack of any redeeming literary merit.

The evidence of historical revisionism in textbooks is overwhelming, but a few examples are worth noting. In 1967, *The Free and the Brave,* published by Rand McNally, had this to say about American involvement in Vietnam: "One thing was certain: although the United States and its South Vietnamese allies were stuck in a cruel war, the United States showed no signs of abandoning the fourteen million South Vietnamese." Not mentioned, of course, was the fact that President Lyndon Johnson often read about violent student protests as early as 1963. "Hey, hey, LBJ, how many people did you kill today?" Rand McNally, however, was stuck with this sentence until 1972 when it was deleted and replaced with a revised sentence which stated: "The cease-fire [negotiated by Secretary of State Henry Kissinger] did not hold. But at least the United States was out of the war...," led by President Richard M. Nixon who resigned for unrelated reasons in August, 1974—the Watergate crisis and the threat of impeachment.

Social studies textbooks are no better even though they purport to teach "values." In Kenneth Weeden's *Teaching Decision Making in Secondary School Studies,* the author, or his editor, asks: "What would you say to Nixon if you were his aide and discovered the [Watergate] cover-up in the winter of 1973?" The answer, if there was one then or now, was not given. The theory then was that such a question provided an opportunity for students in a badly overcrowded classroom to have a free and open exchange with the teacher. If the teacher were not familiar with concepts such as "executive privilege" and "obstruction of justice," the exchange was probably without much real content.

A future textbook might ask a more contemporary question. "What would you do as an aide to President Ronald Reagan if you discovered that Admiral John Poindexter was withholding from President Reagan the fact that funds from the sale of arms to Iran were being used, possibly illegally, to finance deliveries of arms to the *contras* in Nicaragua?" The teacher would have difficult questions to answer. One might be "Who are the *contras,* and why are they fighting the *Sandinistas?*" Depending on the teachers political orientation, he or she might say that the *contras* were fighting an extension of the Soviet Union's "evil empire" in Central American or that the *Sandinistas* were no worse than "agrarian reformers" frustrated by Yanqui "imperialism." Without a knowledgeable teacher, the student-teacher exchange would be devoid of any intellectual content and some form of the truth would be the only real casualty.

Finally, in 1974, Pantheon, a division of Random House, published a book intended as both a textbook and a trade book. Entitled *Mississippi: Conflict and Change,* it was written as a collaborative effort by both students and faculty of Tougaloo and Millsap Colleges in Mississippi. Racial conflict was discussed frankly as was the contribution blacks had made to the state. Most of the copies of this book never left the warehouse. The Mississippi State Textbook Purchasing Board refused to approve the text for use in state schools at public expense. Thus, the white ninth-grade students for whom it was intended were left in the dark about their own history.

All of this suggests that what we are reading today and will read into the 1990s will be determined by *money.* Money is shaping our reading habits and, to paraphrase Hannah Arendt, is perpetuating the banality of mediocrity which is well on the way to being "globalized" by some publishers. There are many exceptions — publishers like Random House and Harper & Row who seek quality — and it is here that the small presses may find their niche in the market place — literate books, both fiction and nonfiction, both of which should illuminate some aspect of the human condition and do it with compassion, understanding and accuracy.

It seems all too clear that what did happen at the universities and schools in the sixties and much earlier has had a very significant impact on what people read today, including commercialized mediocrity, some of which reflects a contemporary version of the life — style or counterculture of the sixties. According to Bloom, for example, all sexual restrictions imposed by tradition or disapproval were abandonned, and drugs became a regular part of life for many students of the sixties. Grade inflation, at least in the humanities, became routine, and the social sciences were not much better if one accepts what the author writes in an all too didactic style. And to Allan Bloom, the pre-MBA of today is an economics major motivated not by love of the science of economics, but by love of what it is concerned with — money —

and a way of insuring a lucrative living. "It is not," he said, "a mark of scholarly achievement. Wealth, as opposed to the science of wealth, is not the noblest of motivation, and there is nothing else quite like this perfect coincidence between science and cupidity elsewhere in the university." It is the MBAs who see the values being assigned to companies generally, and it doesn't take long for the same MBAs to assign comparable dollar values to publishing houses.

Small presses do not generally spend their time, energy and money in this way. Few, if any of them have the financial resources to hire MBAs. Talented editors are far more useful. Nor are they held captive to the costs that seem inherent in being a giant. Ted Solotaroff, a senior editor at Harper & Row, Inc., wrote in the June 8, 1987 issue of *The New Republic:* "Given the narrow profit margins of trade publishing, is it sound business to saddle it with the inflated salaries that corporate officers receive? They are four to five times those of senior editors and marketing people, who are willing to work in publishing for less money than they would earn in a more profitable business . . . Does a publishing house really need the towering midtown location office that pushes its overhead through the roof? Are the new breed of executives in the right to flood the market with non-books that may or may not increase their market share, but surely drive out genuine books and degrade the business?"

The pressure on an editor working for a publishing giant, he said, "affects the way he reads, judges and even edits man-uscripts." Without the characteristics which make it promotable, he added, " . . . he [the editor] becomes less and less willing or able to take the book on." This pressure inevitably pushes even a quality—minded editor toward the major or commercial authors and tends to "curtail his independence and compromise his editorial role and skills." The return— on—investment men-tality generates an erosion of good editorial judgment and a "heedless momentum in the direction of mediocrity and unre-ality" as the article noted.

There are many publishers with quality—minded editors who though unnamed, deserve credit for what they have done. The editor at Farrar Strauss & Giroux who worked with the author of *Presumed Innocent* is one. So is the editor who signed up the author of *Memoirs of an Invisible Man, The Hunt for Red October, The Prince of Tides* and *Bonfire of the Vanities*. Some of the best American publishers include Random House, Inc., Houghton Mifflin Co., The Putnam Publishing Group, Inc., Harper & Row Publishers, Inc., and Villard Books. There are many others, and they all have one thing in common. They must show a net profit to continue what they do best — publishing books. The pressure on editors has always been there, but it seems to have become greater with the recent growth of mega-publishing.

The high cost of publishing has created a frantic scramble to acquire and promote the blockbuster book. But when one or two of these "blockbusters" fail, as they always do, it is the quality books that must pick up the financial slack. Less money is spent to produce and promote them, and authors are left with little or nothing to sustain their careers.

Authors and literary agents are concerned that the profit motive of giantism will depersonalize publishing to the point that quality books by unknowns are rejected in favor of inferior books by established commercial authors. They are taking a closer look at small presses, where they feel appreciated and are treated as friends, and not just as commodities. Todd Walton had published three books with New York giants, but chose Mercury House, a small press in San Francisco, for his successful *Night Train,* because he felt the small press would recognize that "my work was something valuable and worthy of publication and sale."

In a *New York Times* article of April 5, 1987, Barney Rosset, who recently sold Grove Press, was quoted as saying: "To me publishing has been an expression of a point of view and it's still the same." He believed that publishing should always be a marginal business. If it is run with the commitment it deserves, he said, "I don't know how you earn back anything on your money." The "bottom liners" say that because they have a cash cushion from the big books or bestsellers to absorb occasional losses for quality's sake, they can and do print important, if not necessarily high profit books. Curiously, the "cash cushion" from textbook sales is rarely mentioned. Richard E. Snyder, President of Gulf & Western's Simon & Schuster division was quoted as saying: "The idea is to sell books. Publish good books and the best of them will become blockbusters."

These views in the *New York Times* article (editors versus bottom liners) are not necessarily irreconcilable. The adoption of more businesslike practices and better control of editorial and selling costs as well as cost of goods sold (books) will help, and still leave editorial judgment more freedom of expression.

Literate people who read for pleasure continue to be assaulted by commercialized mediocrity, and one may wonder why such books are published at all. The bottom line, of course, is profit for the publishers' shareholders. Accordingly, it may be useful to take a close look at the economics of publishing by one of the giants, Harcourt Brace Jovanovich (HBJ), to see what the "bottom line" is all about. The dust from the most recent attempt to "buy" into the American market by acquisition has now settled, but it has been in the news because of litigation initiated by British Printing & Communications Corporation PLC, the company which sought to acquire HBJ.

On May 18, 1987, by letter addressed to William Jovanovich, Robert Maxwell, who owns a controlling interest in British Printing & Communications Corporation Corporation PLC offered $44 per share for the 39 million outstanding shares of Harcourt Brace Jovanovich, Inc., one of the largest publishers of trade books, textbooks and periodicals in the United States. At $44 per share, this places a value of $1.7 billion on the offer. HBJ's Chairman, William Jovanovich, almost immediately rejected the offer as "preposterous, both as to intent and value," even though HBJ's stock was then selling at $29 per share on New York Stock Exchange. Moreover, as recently as December 31, 1986, HBJ's accountants reported a book value of $13.48 per share with 39,418,557 shares outstanding. On May 22, 1987, the stock closed at $43.375 per share on the New York Stock Exchange. According to HBJ's Form 10-K filed with the Securities and Exchange Commission (SEC) for 1986, William Jovanovich,

Chairman and President, owned about 1.5% of the outstanding common and received cash compensation of $867,744 for 1986. Peter Jovanovich, Executive Vice-President received cash compensation of $237,500 for the same period. All directors and officers as a group (33 individuals) collectively owned 5.6% of the outstanding shares. Directors receive annual compensation of $18,000 for their services. On May 26, 1987, HBJ's directors approved a complex recapitalization plan which would increase HBJ's total debt to $2.9 billion from $837 million on March 31, 1987. The directors also rejected Robert Maxwell's offer of $44 per share or $1.7 billion.

The rejection of this offer was followed by a Complaint filed by British Printing on June 1, 1987 in the U.S. District Court in New York. In less than two months, British Printing lost on all counts, and Robert Maxwell began to look at Macmillan, Inc. which he acquired in 1988. The recapitalization plan, however, left HBJ in debt to the tune of $2.9 billion, but it wasn't long before Time, Inc. and Warner Communications, Inc. announced a tax-free merger that dwarfed anything seen in publishing, even after the acquisitions of Doubleday Publishing, Inc., Harper & Row Publishers, Inc. and Macmillan, Inc.

On March 4, 1989, Time, Inc. and Warner Communications, Inc. announced a merger of their companies, the value of which is estimated to be $14 *billion*. This combination, if approved by the Department of Justice after a review of antitrust considerations, has converted Time Warner, Inc. into a global publishing and communications enterprise fully capable of competing with Robert Maxwell's British Communications, PLC and Australian Rupert Murdoch's global empire as well as Bertelsmann AG. The latter's ultimate owner, according to the *International Literary Market Place,* is Transworld Publishers (Australia) Pty. Ltd. Simon & Schuster, Random House, Inc. and Viking Penguin, Inc. have been more or less equal on a global scale, along with William Collins, PLC and McGraw-Hill, Inc. Time, Inc. and Warner Communications, Inc. have just decided, not only to join the party, but to host it. The combined net income before taxes of this combination is an estimated $1.5 *billion* from film for theaters as well as television programming, cable television, records and magazines. Publishers in the United States have been slow in recognizing the importance of global communications, but the merger just announced has more than made up for this temporary oversight.

Time Inc. acquired Little, Brown & Co. of Boston several years ago, and it also owns Time-Life Books. These two publishers account for an estimated 7% of Time, Inc.'s $792 million in net income before taxes, or $55.4 million annually. Warner Books, Inc. will account for an estimated $8 million of annual net income as a very aggressive mass market publisher of books. Perhaps equally important is the fact that the Book of the Month Club is a part of this combination which expects to operate on an international scale. Even though Little Brown & Company published only 411 books in all of 1988, it is expected to be far more aggressive than heretofore and will probably concentrate on commercial bestsellers. Warner Communications, Inc. published some 2,000 mass market paperbacks in all of 1988, and it may now concentrate on the hardcover-softcover deals that contribute most to the bottom line of this new combination.

Little Brown & Company has its own sales force, and it also distributes books from the American Association of Retired Persons, Atlantic Monthly Press and Time-Life Books. Warner Books, Inc. only recently began publishing hardcover books now distributed by the Random House sales force. Distribution of its mass market paperbacks goes through Ballentine/Del Rey/Fawcett, a division of Random House. Warner Publisher Services is a wholesaler for Ballentine's own mass market paperbacks, an arrangement that seems to limit profit potential for the new combination. It is not at all certain how long Time Warner, Inc. will allow this apparent profit dilution to continue. Little Brown & Company can easily show its new corporate parent the advantages of a single sales force.

When the dust settles, Time Warner, Inc. may also see other areas in which significant savings in costs can be made, such as a more aggressive returns policy, or even less generous discounting in favor of the chains. Market power on the scale represented by this merger has never really existed in the publishing industry of the United States, and this new combination has the annual revnue to, for example, acquire Waldenbooks from K Mart, its corporate parent. With about 1,200 retail outlets in early 1989, its acquisition would be consistent with a practice followed for years by some European countries, such as Spain, where many publishers also own bookstores. In view of the single market within the European Community by 1992, the acquisition by Time Warner Inc. of W. H. Smith & Co. in the United Kingdom would make even more sense. This bookstore chain has an estimated 800 outlets now, and vertically integrated operations on an international scale are clearly an option with economies to match. Time, Inc. has had a European issue of *Time* for at least 30 years, and it would be perfectly natural to publish books there, too.

Where does a combination on this scale leave the small presses of the United States? So far, they have survived the acquisitions of Harper & Row, Doubleday and Macmillan. The mega-publishers are expected to concentrate on the bottom line, while the small presses are expected to concentrate on midlist fiction. Literary agents may now find it more difficult to sell unknown authors to a diminishing number of the mega-publishers, and the small presses may be the ultimate beneficiaries of this trend. The advances paid are far less than those offered commercial authors, such as Robert Ludlum and Sydney Sheldon, and the operating costs of the small presses are a small fraction of those paid by mega-publishers, primarily because the small presses, entirely aside from the literary quality of their books, have been willing to experiment with contemporary technology, i.e., the computer.

Mercury House is a small press in San Francisco and has been in business for just over three years. Early on, a decision was made to invest in state-of-the art technology. When making such a decision, one must be aware that its benefits often fail to show up when measured by traditional financial formulas. Too many small companies rely on a return-on-investment technique, and these rates are usually well in excess of the actual cost of capital.

Even a discounted cash flow technique does not adequately measure the value today of tangible benefits or payments to be received at a later date. In the case of computer—assisted—publishing (CAP) technology, these benefits translate into greater flexibility, lower editorial and book production costs, and acceleration of the entire process, such as the ability to move quickly.

The publishing giants with the "return-on-investment" mentality, by using the same hardware, could reduce their editorial and book production costs by an estimated 35%. Instead, the search continues for the "blockbuster" without much thought for the gross profit margin for that book. Harper & Row, Inc., is one of the exceptions, having begun the installation of the Penta International System a little over three years ago. Now it's owned by Rupert Murdoch who may or may not complete the entire system at a cost of about $7 million.

Small presses have been on the cutting edge of these new technologies, simply because they must in order to survive with only modest funding. Mercury House, for example, does a budget for each title published using a program worked out with Lotus 123. It shows net income for each title assuming the optimum print run and the best cover price and accounts for marketing, editorial and administrative costs allocated to that title.

The publishing giants have big-time overheads including six-figure salaries for the officers, skyscraper rents and $18,000 a year for directors' fees. They can also pay six and seven figure advances to commercial authors. With a first time author, the struggle to get that book published can be debilitating for both the author and the editor. Even after an editor has convinced his publisher to publish such a book, he or she must still fight tooth and nail for a substantial advertising budget. Many authors resent this and look for a publisher where an editor treats him as a friend. As Todd Walton, with three earlier books published by large presses, said: "Each book purchased [by a small press] is a significant investment. The author must be treated with respect, since money is not the primary bond . . . . At a small house, the creation itself is usually the highest priority, not the system."

One cannot help but agree with Ted Solotaroff when he says: "Envy and greed lead one to think big. Respect and care lead one to think small. Thinking small pays attention, in Paul Goodman's words, to 'the object, the function, the program, the task, the need,' while thinking big pays 'immense attention to the role, procedure, prestige and profit.' " Near the end of his article, Solotaroff noted the small press by saying: "It continues to lead its dispersed, precarious, seminal life. Like a surprise witness at a trial, shrewd and reasonably well-funded presses such as North Point, Ardis, and David R. Godine testify that the future of independent trade publishing may well lie in regional centers like Berkeley, Ann Arbor, Atlanta and Cambridge."

The small presses must somehow find their market niche and expand it in a way which saves time and reduces costs. They can do this in two ways: Give talented and versatile editors more independence and trust, and prepare to give them the technology to work with. For an investment of about $60,000, this combination should produce a modest profit in less than three years.

First rate editorial judgment, however, is not a substitute for using time in cost-effective ways. Archaic and costly practices, such as manual editing and conventional book production, should be the first to be abandoned in favor of the computer and what it will do for survival. Production time for a trade book (camera — ready copy) can be reduced to about five hours from as many weeks. And the small presses can also look for authors first published outside the United States. Text and graphics, for example, can now be sent from Munich and London to New York or San Francisco via satellite for about 10% of what it costs to pay "offset" fees ($2 or more per page) to a European publisher.

U.S. publishers have been slow to recognize what the computer has done to revolutionize their world, and computer systems developers, until quite recently, have been slow to focus on publishers as a market for their hardware and software.   Even now, with the right hardware and software, a small press publisher can save an estimated $6,000 per book. For the IBM or a compatible, Penta Systems International offers its new EditMaster or EditMaster Plus. Both offer a split screen with simultaneous access to two files for editing drafts. Aldus Corporation offers PageMaker which integrates text and graphics. This does for the IBM and compatibles what Page One does for Apple's Macintosh.

Magnatype, sold by Magna Computer Systems, Inc., offers both typesetting and automatic pagination. For about $7,500, a small press, using Ventura Publishing, can produce camera ready copy as output from the Tegra, Inc. printer with both text and graphics. The Genesis printer from Tegra, Inc. will then output both scanned and electronically created line art and halftones on plain paper.

In 1985, both Harper & Row and McGraw-Hill, Inc., made a commitment to a total publishing system. The cost of these systems is very high, so the small press has had to look at hardware and software that are within a limited budget. Nolo Press in Berkeley, Mercury House in San Francisco and Sandlight Publications in San Diego all use one or more features of "desktop publishing" and make significant savings in editing time and production costs. At Nolo Press, Associate Publisher Carol Pladsen estimates that her company saves several weeks and thousands of dollars in the production of each title by using a desktop publishing system. Nolo Press is one of the nation's leading publishers of legal self-help books. "The information in our books changes very quickly," she said. "We need to make changes at the last minute and revise text between reprints. Using the Mac and Laserwriter makes it much, much easier and less expensive. We are saving at least $5,000 to $6,000 on the production of a book," she claimed, "and that doesn't include staff time savings and the increased revenue from having the book out earlier."

According to William Sanders, President of Sandlight Publications, "The single biggest expense in a small print run is typesetting. A small publisher who can save $2,000 per title can publish more books and make more money." Sandlight uses

Apple Computer's Macintosh and Pagemaker software. Streamlining the book production enables publishers to put out books while interest in their subjects is high. In 1985, Sanders recalled, four of his friends prepared a book in about two months, using a desktop system and published it themselves. The title: *Who Is This Guy Halley and How Did He Get His Own Comet?*

Composition and book design software systems with a graphics capability all have one thing in common—more flexibility for the publisher and its editors. Word processing software also helps the author.

Many authors, for example, send in manuscripts on a disk from word processing software. Unfortunately, too many such authors are not completely familiar with all the capabilities of the software they use. The internal coding, eg., paragraph indents, is not the same in all word processing software. The text must be converted to ASCII before being sent to a publisher. Unless it is so converted, a publisher will have to send it out for conversion, a cost add—on it can do without. An author who knows this can now use Software Bridge, a translation program which can convert text and codes in one word processing program into text and codes usable by another.

Some authors can send their manuscripts using telecommunications software, such as Crosstalk Mark 4, with an XM protocol. Text can be compressed using Archive software to about 50% of its original length and decompressed by the publisher. Line charges tend to be much less with this method, and it all saves money. Using an Everex 2400B modem (2400 bps), about 350 manuscript pages, with each chapter as a separate file, can be sent from San Francisco or Sydney to London in about 16 minutes.

Authors who can actually do their own page layout on, for example, an Apple with page composition software, will get much more attention from a publisher. Every chapter is typeset and laid out. For an author, this can mean a higher advance against royalties, a substantial advertising budget or both. If the cost of the appropriate hardware and software is too high for page layout, a local service bureau can do the same thing for around $7 per page. Quadratype in San Francisco, for example, uses a Kurzweil optical scanner to "read" a manuscript and output camera — ready copy at $7 per page. The June 1987 issue of *Small Press* published an article entitled "Preparing Electronic Manuscripts for Authors and Publishers" excerpted from the University of Chicago Press's book on this subject. In Chapter I, "Instructions to Authors," the Chicago Guide defines an "electronic manuscript" as everything an author has typed and stored on his or her computer in the process of creating the electronic version of the book's text.

A manuscript, no matter how it gets to the publisher, is only the beginning. At Mercury House, line and copy editors turn out a finished manuscript which it then typesets in-house before it is sent to a commercial printer for printing and binding. All this must be carefully coordinated with the production editor as well as an art director who is responsible for dustcover design and the copy which appears on it as "flap copy." When all this is finished, the book is turned over to a distributor and its sales representatives. They can make or break a small press. A distributor likes an advertising budget and schedule of ads to make certain that books are in the bookstores when and where the ads appear. By itself, this is not enough. A distributor *must* have enough sales representatives to get books into the bookstores.

There are, of course, other considerations. Will a book get good reviews? To ensure that a book is reviewed at all, and not all of them are, many publishers turn to Crane Duplicating Co. in Massuchusetts. This company prints what is essentially a paperback of the book some author hopes will make him a fortune. These, for obvious reasons, are known as *Cranes,* and they carry a note which labels them as "Uncorrected Page Proofs." It is these which are sent to all reviewers in trade journals such as *Publishers Weekly, Kirkus Reviews, American Bookseller* and *Library Journal* as well as other print media such as *The New York Times, The San Francisco Chronicle, The New York Review of Books, The Los Angeles Times, The Washington Post, The New Yorker* and many others.

Book fairs and conventions also represent opportunities for the small presses. The American Booksellers Association Convention is held once a year. It is here where owners of bookstores do some of their buying from publishers. The London Book Fair occurs in April of each year, and the International Book Fair has been held in Frankfurt, West Germany, in October each year since 1947. In all of these gatherings, subsidiary rights to books are bought and sold by publishers, eg., a U.S. publisher will buy the rights to translate and publish a French, German or Italian novel in the United States, either as a trade or mass market book. Mercury House has acquired the rights to some of its books this way, e.g., Alain Gerber's French bestseller, *Rumor of an Elephant* which got a great review from *Publishers Weekly* in its May 29 issue. "This is an outrageous and funny book, its humor sharp as a spike."

There is a very simple point to all this. The small pressses have to publish books and sell enough of them to make a net profit on each one to survive. Distribution, whether national or regional, is essential. A good review is not enough, even though it helps. Computer assisted publishing (CAP) saves both time and money and allows editors to be more flexible. Marketing, whether conventional or done via telecommunication, is also essential. The point is to cut costs in a manner consistent with quality book production and sell the idea that the small presses support the books they publish. This sits well with the bookstores who order from a publisher's catalog which must be designed to sell those books. Costs at every level should be reduced constantly, and they can be. Computer hardware and software becomes more sophisticated and less expensive with the passage of time, and there are real savings to be made at every level of the publishing process.

With the savings realized from typesetting and other sources, the small presses must make a commitment to authors to market their books. This means an advertising budget appropriate for a small press. This also helps bookstores, since they know that a good ad will help sell the books they do buy. Like any other buyer, the Tecolete Book Shop, an independent in Santa Barbara, California, buys books from a publisher's catalog and very often from *Advance,* a monthly publication of Ingram Book Company, a very large book wholesaler in Nashville, Tennessee. The *Advance* annotations and order form were designed to help the bookstore to select and order books. Its Best of the Best section always indicates the "hottest" forthcoming titles, each one of which has six or eight lines of copy about the book. All of this underscores the importance of a really good catalog designed by a small press publisher and the enthusiasm with which its titles are "sold" by a distributor's sales representatives.

There are plenty of knowledgeable people who will sell first and second serial rights as well as hardcover and paperback rights in Europe or elsewhere for small presses in the United States. Literary agents or representatives in London, Madrid, Zurich, Munich and Paris work on a commission basis. They do not get paid except as a percentage of the amount received for the rights sold, about 10%. Mercuruy House has sold foreign rights to some of its books, and has bought the U.S. rights to books written in four different languages, including British. In one case, it made the mistake of trying to convert British spelling into the American version of the same words. It was a moderately costly mistake and not worth the time it took. Some authors, however, will write for the American market. John LeCarré is probably better known in the United States than in the U. K., and Sydney Sheldon is well known in at least four European countries. So-called "sub rights," i.e., paperback rights, represent an important source of revenue for publishers. It is almost axiomatic in the publishing business that trade (hardcover) books alone do not sell well enough to support a publisher unless it has one or more bestsellers.

Eventually, the consumer becomes the final arbiter of which books sell well or even become bestsellers. Not many of them do out of 52,000 new books published each year. A great many of the publishing giants have substantial advertising budgets for print media, authors' tours and radio or television shows. A publisher who has paid an author a high six figure advance and announced its first print run will be 1,000,000 copies is determined to at least recover the advance and, if possible, make a substantial gross profit on that book. Overhead costs continue, and all publishers dread the day when bookstores "return" unsold books which are usually sold to "remainder" dealers for less than the cost of printing them in the first place. The notion that bookstores can return books began in the 1930s, probably because of the Great Depression. No other retail establishment returns anything except damaged goods. Merchandise that is not defective and can't be sold at the sticker price is marked down until someone does buy it. Books are different. They are taken essentially on consignment and returned if unsold within a relatively short time. Unless a book is a bestseller, its shelf life is about three to six months.

Independent bookstores and small presses have much in common, and it is in the interests of both to develop close and continuing contacts. This is why Mercury House has decided to send its newsletter, *The Messenger,* to as many bookstores as possible. They, in turn, may want to advise their customers of good reviews or recommend Mercury House titles to *their* mailing list. Independent bookstores and small chains account for more than 60% of all domestic book sales. The acquisition of B. Dalton by Barnes & Noble, and the expansion of Waldenbooks (4,200 outlets by 1992) represent a parallel to the acquisitions among the giant publishers.

Some publishers see this same trend as an opportunity to sell more and more books. Gulf & Western owns Simon & Schuster. Waldenbooks was acquired by K mart Corporation in August of 1984 for $300 million. The latter is the largest bookstore chain in the United States and does an excellent job in selling more books to more people. So do Barnes & Noble and Crown Books. These media giants and the large chains were guided by the quest for improvement in the "bottom line." Bookstores exist to sell books published by both the giants and the small presses. The small presses had to be technologically innovative to survive. They also have to get their books into more bookstores for the same reason.

Small press publishers can cooperate with the 4,000 or more independent bookstores by offering better discounts on small orders in exchange for no returns. Better and more cost—

effective distribution by telecommunications of catalog artwork and copy plus current reviews of their books will also help. Computer technology has come a long way in a very few years. A small press can now send its entire catalog to a bookstore with compatible hardware and software in color or monochrome. A Dest PC Scan, using PC Paintbrush Plus, can "read" the catalog graphics and copy, store it in a file and telecommunicate both to a bookstore whose buyer may print it out or read it on his monitor at leisure.

This is electronic marketing of books by a publisher and helps the bookstore manager make "buy" decisions before a distributor's sales representatives make their semi-annual visits to that store. Publishers' traditional practice of offering Spring and Fall lists may disappear in favor of a publishing "season" lasting 365 days a year, thereby reducing the costs of distribution and the semi-annual production of catalogs by both publishers and distributors. Ingrams, a wholesale jobber of books, offers Laser-Search, which allows a bookstore to find a book for its customers. Market research shows that the customer will almost always buy this book from the bookstore which found it. Seeing the telecommunicated catalog artwork and copy in color or monochrome will almost guarantee a sale via Imgrams, thereby making its job easier. Baker & Taylor, another large wholesaler, offers a comparable service.

Many features of "desktop publishing" are being applied on a global scale, at least as it is used for books in the English language. Telecommunication of text is only one of them. For this and other reasons, a small press should not overlook the sale of foreign language rights to its books using agents in Paris, Milan or Munich. These sales represent an expansion of the market for books published by the small press community. The revenue from such sales is not substantial in most cases, but it can make the difference between a small net profit and one which may be higher.

Editors, however, are beginning to find out that editing on a computer with word processing software is faster and more effective than manual editing. Moreover, they can leave an edit trail with CompareWrite software. This is a program that instantly compares two drafts of a manuscript and highlights the differences between them. The program is called The Instant Redliner for good reason and keeps an accurate record of the changes from one draft to another and it's *fast*. It also works with just about any word processing software and has a directory feature which will find text in one file and compare it with text in another. It should be an editor's dream and costs $130.

The basic objective of all publishers should be and, in some cases is, to cut editing and book production time by at least 50% and use the money saved to market the quality book. One or more color imaging systems can help, and a few of them are currently available at a reasonable cost. They represent a new form of electronic marketing.

Mercury House believes in a love of books and a diversity of voices, and encourages its editors to recommend for publication serious books which will be read and enjoyed by literate readers. Its publisher believes in its editors and supports them. It also supports its books and authors by using technology — computers and telecommunications — to reduce its editorial and production costs of making books available for sale in bookstores. Keeping pace with the changes in a global village as they apply to publishing is an exciting challenge. Making money doing this is an even greater challenge, but it all seems well worth the effort.

# Chapter 3
## The Bookstore–A Publisher's Best Customer

The Gutenberg Bible made its first appearance in 1456 at Mainz, Germany, not far from where the International Book Fair is now held every year in October. With the possible exceptions of the webb and offset high speed printing presses and the computer, no invention has spread so rapidly. Within about 25 years, there were printers in France, Italy, Spain and England. Within about 100 years, there were also printers in the United States. At a very early date, the danger of an uncontrolled press was recognized in both England and its American colonies. In 1695, King James II wrote to his governor in New York that "no person keep any press for printing, nor that of any book. . . without your special leave and license first obtained." Printers operated under this dictate from London until shortly before the American Revolution, and there was absolutely no conception of a free press until the Bill of Rights ratified in 1791. The printers were also publishers, ant it was not until seven years earlier that the colonial settlers had even a rudimentary system of booksellers from which the present system of mass retailing of books grew fairly rapidly.

Mathew Carey, in 1784, was the first American publisher as we know them today. He was also one of the first booksellers, having developed the idea of book exchanges in small village centers. Over time, these "centers" became bookstores as we see them around us today in big cities as well as small villages — 205 years later. Carey's early contributions to what is now widespread, included both a Catholic and a Protestant Bible. He also did a great deal with reprints and their distribution, and the first regular trade book catalog was issued in 1804. In 1801, Carey sent out circulars to publishers and booksellers inviting them to assemble in New York, to buy, sell or exchange their books. Today, the American Booksellers Association meets annually allowing publishers to exhibit their books to the trade buyers of American booksellers. Publishing and bookselling has become a very big business in the United States, and Mathew Carey deserves most of the credit for laying the foundations on which it rests.

During 1986, Walden Book Company, Inc., operated Waldenbooks' 994 bookstores in all 50 states. The number of bookstores is expected to more than double by 1990. In 1988, the number of bookstores opening increased to an estimated 1,200 from the 1986 figure. Waldenbooks is one of the nation's largest retail bookstore chains and has its corporate offices in Stamford, Connecticut. Walden Book Company, Inc., is a wholly owned subsidiary of K mart Corporation which acquired Waldenbooks in August 1984 from Carter Hawley Hale Stores, Inc. for $300 million.

Waldenbooks 994 stores typically occupy about 3,000 square feet in regional or local shopping malls. Many of its bookstores may be found in the retail floors of a city's high rise office buildings, an ideal location with a great deal of foot traffic. "Location," say most experts in retail selling, "is everything." In addition to books, its stores offer video and audio tapes and computer software. Waldenbooks maintains a wide selection of titles and can quickly obtain for customers any title not in stock through its Quicktrac, a computerized special order system. If a customer wants a particular title, store personnel will look it up using microfiche and key in the code for that book on the cash register— the ISBN and title— which is then telecommunicated to its regional distributor, Ingrams or Baker & Taylor, both of which have warehouses in Nevada and elsewhere in the United States.

Since K mart Corporation operates three other specialty retail operations (Pay Less Drug Stores, Bargain Harold's and Builders Square), it's difficult to separate the annual sales of Waldenbooks from those of the other specialty retail operations. All of its specialty retail operations accounted for $2.504 billion in sales for the year ending January 28, 1987, and showed an operating profit of $37 million. Waldenbooks accounted for an estimated 69% of this group's operating profit, or $25.5 million on estimated sales of $1.73 billion for the year ending on January 28, 1987.

Any one of the approximately 4,900 independent bookstores in the United States would immediately agree with this rough estimate. Hardly anybody believes that gross profit margins in their bookstores, to put it into perspective, are all that great. All too few of them, however, seem willing to make the investment in computers and telecommunications to increase those margins. In 1986, for example, the American Booksellers Association (ABA) to which most of the independents belong, abandoned its pilot project to do just that. It was the Booksellers Ordering Service (BOS) which was discontinued on November 1, 1986.

PUBNET may soon replace BOS. Using the PUBNET system publishers, on a daily basis, update a database of titles (80,000 in early 1988) that includes information about their availability. In this respect, it operates something like R. R. Bowker's *Books in Print with Reviews Plus,* namely forthcoming titles. A bookstore with this information on a CD–ROM (750,000 titles), may electronically order one or more titles from either the publisher or a wholesaler. PUBNET, however, differs from the service offered by R.R. Bowker — cost. To own this and use a CD–ROM "player," a bookstore has to spend about $1,900 in the first year and about $1,000 a year thereafter. PUBNET's basic service costs $50 a month, and the startup fee is about $900. To use PUBNET, a bookseller must have a modem and a compatible personal computer (PC). With these, a bookseller may order a title and get an acknowledgment within 24 hours. Limited to college bookstores initially, PUBNET is planning to expand into the trade book field soon. Trade titles may already be ordered from participating publishers. These include Random House, Macmillan, Simon & Schuster and Viking Penguin. More, including Mercury House will be on line soon. Richard Bates, PUBNET's managing director had this to say about its service: "We see the major change (from current ordering systems) being that the bookstore buyer sits down with the sales rep at a PC rather than over paper (a catalog)." He also noted that PUBNET "grew out of the inadequacy of publishers' customer-service departments and the desire of stores and publishers to have better service." Another major change expected from the expanded use of PUBNET is a standard order form, making it simpler and faster to order titles. All a bookstore need really know is the book's ISBN. Finally, Bates said that an additional advantage to publishers is the system's ability to send electronic mail. "This," he said, "could be used as a marketing tool" by sending out an announcement that a title "had hit the *Times* bestseller list." This feature, combined with the program used by Mercury House, would also allow publishers to send an announcement of a good review in, say the Denver Post, to all bookstores within its circulation area, which includes most of Colorado. The only word so far on cost savings to booksellers is that it's too early to tell. One user in a metropolitan area college bookstore commented that: "In general, we've found it neither to be expensive, nor are we saving a great deal of money. The whole idea is for us to provide better service to the textbook faculty community."

Many, if not most bookstores know the rough economics of operating and the slim profit margins of doing so. Aside from rent, the owner must count on spending $12 to $15 a square foot for utilities and interior amenities, another $9 to $12 a square foot for display shelves, work space and some form of a cash register. In a more or less typical bookstore of 1,000 square feet, this means an annual expense of $24,000. An initial book inventory will cost about $35,000 or more according to Ingram Book Company's Recommended Opening Store Inventory (ROSI). The bookstore should have annual sales of $180 per square foot, or $180,000. A modest advertising and mailing budget will be about $3,000, and working capital for at least two months will run to about $9,000. Hardly anyone wonders why bookstores, both old and new, don't invest in a computer, a printer and a modem plus book inventory, general ledger and telecommunications software. This does save money and time, the second of which allows personnel to serve customers instead of waiting for someone to answer the telephone and take an order for more books. BOS was both expensive and difficult to use even though the concept was right. Current systems, like PUBNET, are simpler and less expensive. They use telecommunications by dialing a local number via a computer plus modem. A computer, however, performs functions which tend to simplify life for the bookstore owner and give him or her more time. A cash register, for example, not only records sales, but it also reduces the inventory by the number of books sold as part of the entire transaction. It will also alert the buyer to re-order books before they're all sold.

In September 1986, BOS had about 95 member stores in 106 locations on line for this electronic ordering system. "Electronic ordering," said a spokesman for WordStock's computerized book inventory system, "is directly related to the rate at which bookstores computerize," and for most booksellers, that computerization will not take place unless the store's owner can sit down with an accountant and hear him say, "This will pay for itself in three years."

Bookstores seem curiously reluctant to take the step toward electronic ordering to increase their gross profit margins. Their European counterparts did this several years ago. While the book industry in the Netherlands functions as a cartel, with all publishers stocking their titles in one central location, it would not serve as a model for electronic ordering in the United States. In Great Britain, however, Teleordering, a centralized electronic ordering system has been operating for over seven years. It is owned by a private consortium which includes J. Whitaker & Son, W.H. Smith, the country's largest book retailing chain and Thorne-EMI, an entertainment-computer company that owns 60% of Teleordering. J. Whitaker & Son owns the database known as British Books in Print (Dialog) in Palo Alto has a BIP database like it) and also publishes *The Bookseller,* the British equivalent of *American Bookseller.* For 1985, the last year for which figures are available, Teleordering had a profit on operations of $150,000. A British publisher pays a one time entry fee of

$10,000 and between $5,000 and $6,000 per year to receive orders electronically. This is a significant investment for a small press, so an American version should probably require an initial entry fee based on annual sales and do the same for the right to receive electronic orders from bookstores. In Great Britain, they pay a one-time charge of about $300 on joining and about $30 a month thereafter. Were the same or essentially the same system organized in the United States, it could incorporate the Dialog database or those now operated by Ingrams and Baker & Taylor with a strong show of support from the American Booksellers Association. The name of the game is to sell more books and to do it using telecommunications and computers in order to increase gross margins. While it's not in the book business, McKesson Corporation is in the business of selling drugs to more than 14,000 drugstores. The electronic ordering system it started in 1975, ECONOMOST now operates 24 hours a day to fill orders from 14,000 customers. The independent drugstores can now match or do better than the big drug chains like Rexall's on price and availability. McKesson Corporation's ECONO-PLAN, for example, assists its retailer-customers with inventory management and display allocation on shelves, two problems common to bookstores. While bookstores may move in the right direction, some of them are intimidated by the cost of doing so. In most of them, inventory management software would save time and money and pay for itself in a very short time.

Book inventory software, however, is not for everyone because of cost. Depending on the number of titles in inventory, Word-Stock or Cat's Pajamas may cost as much as $4,000 or more. Personnel needs to be trained in how to use it efficiently, but the hard work is over once every title has been logged. Ohlson's Bookstore in Washington, D.C.'s Georgetown area has all of its books on inventory software as does the University Bookstore in Madison, Wisconsin. Each has an inventory estimated at over 30,000 titles. On the computer's monitor, the number of a particular title will show up as well as the discount as a percent of the cover price, and, naturally, the cost of buying it in the first place. The moment one of these books is sold, the amount received and a sales tax will show up on the same monitor. Using this system, operated in tandem with book inventory software, a bookseller will know his gross and net profit on sales at the end of each day. He will also know when to re-order books which, using FIRSTcall, Baker & Taylor's electronic ordering service, can be delivered within 24 hours from the time the order is sent by telecommunications software.

The FIRSTcall system requires an IBM or compatible computer with a minimum of one disk drive and 64K of memory, as well as a modem. There is a one time charge of $19.95 for software. To use the system, a bookseller enters ISBNs and quantities of desired titles into the computer, then transmits the order to Baker & Taylor on its toll-free line. This toll-free number is incorporated into the software for simplicity of operation.

In contrast, Ingrams, another major book wholesaler, offers FLASHBACK software to bookstores free. However, it works in essentially the same way as FIRSTcall, and the same hardware and software are required. Ingrams also offers LaserSearch for a rental of $215 per month. This includes all the hardware and software needed to operate the system. All of these systems incorporate identification codes as well as account numbers to prevent unauthorized orders.

A bookseller may wish to consider using CrossTalk XVI telecommunications software, or the most recent version of Crosstalk known as Mark 4 sold by Digital Communications in Atlanta, Georgia. In this way, a bookseller may use the Setup option on the menu offered by the software after it has been copied to a hard disk with at least 10MB of memory. Any local systems consultant can show him very quickly how to create so-called batch files with each one listing a publisher who can take electronic orders, print them out and send the printout to its fulfillment division or, in the case of a small press, its distributor.

Development for the order confirmation facet of FIRSTcall was completed in early 1986, a feature not included in BataPhone software. First offered in 1984, this service is still used by about 19,000 public libraries in the United States. They seemed to have dealt with this problem by searching a data base, a feature offered so far only by LaserSearch, Ingrams software. However, a bookstore will need a compact disk player working with an IBM or compatible computer with a hard disk. LaserSearch has a data base of about 750,000 titles.

Electronic ordering systems like FIRSTcall and FLASH-BACK are clearly the wave of the future. According to James Ulsamer, vice president for marketing for Baker & Taylor, the number of electronic orders received by it in 1987 "is not that significant, probably in the range of ten percent." He predicts, however, that "within two or three years, the majority of orders will be electronic." He also added that FIRSTcall was an affordable system, noting, "I don't think we've excluded anyone. If they have enough volume to afford an IBM PC, then this system makes sense for them." Currently, a bookstore can buy an IBM compatible computer, monochrome monitor, a Hayes compatible modem and telecommunications software for about $1,300. Inventory control systems come higher, and electronic ordering works much better when used in tandem with such a system.

A basic IBID system, for example, costs $16,500, and includes an Altos computer, a point--of-sale station, with terminal, cash drawer and receipt printer; one backroom station, with terminal and 132-column printer; a 2400 bps modem; software and start-up supplies. The cost of a more modest system now starts at $9,000. Not every bookstore, however, needs a system as elaborate as this one. Booklog is a more affordable system at $1,950 for the software. It requires only an IBM or compatible computer. The history of the computer business is important. Each year, the software and hardware become more sophisticated and less expensive. General ledger software now costs about $1,700, and inventory control system software is probably around $1,200. With quite a few booksellers, there is much less reluctance to the use of computers. One bookseller noted, "If I don't have a computer, I won't have the competitive edge to run my store well." Another, in St. Petersburg, Florida, is Andy Haslam of Haslam's Book Store, He said, "You'll be able to stay in business without a computer, but you won't have as many days off."

Time is important. In addition to the flow of information available from databases like Dialog in Palo Alto, California (Books in Print), and Newsnet (just about anything), bookstores receive printed material, too. Most of the 4,400 independent bookstores in the United States have at least one thing in common — they all receive a barrage of mail. Foremost among these is *Publishers Weekly* which is considered by most people as the bible of publishing. The Fall Announcement issue contained 365 pages, and publishers paid an estimated $800,000 to advertise books scheduled for publication in late 1987. A typical issue of *Publishers Weekly* contains Features-articles of current interest, e.g., "Fourth Quarter Sales: 1987 Strongest Since '83," Announcements, Trade News, News of the Week, PW Interviews, Bookselling & Merchandising and Forecasts, reviews of fiction, non-fiction, paperbacks and children's books scheduled for publication. It will also contain columns with an abundance of trade news.

*American Bookseller* is on very much the same frequency as *Publishers Weekly,* although it's considered in the trade more as a "how to" magazine for bookstores. A more or less typical monthly issue contains articles such as University Press Books, The Challenge of Marketing to the Trade, as well as a section entitled Departments with shorter articles of current interest to bookstores.

Baker & Taylor, Inc. and Ingrams are the two largest book wholesalers in the United States. Each one publishes a magazine of interest to bookstores. Baker & Taylor's *Forecast* and Ingrams *Advance* reach almost the same people in bookstores. Of more than passing interest to bookstores is *Forecast's* "Publicity News," a listing of authors' tours which demonstrably sell more books, national TV appearances, movie tie-ins, TV tie-ins, serial rights (who bought them and the title of the book) and Book Club sales. Baker & Taylor also publishes *BookAlert,* its monthly preview of forthcoming titles that goes to bookstores and public libraries.

*Advance,* a monthly publication of Ingrams has a slightly different format but reaches essentially the same bookstores as

*Forecast.* Both Ingrams and Baker & Taylor are in a unique position to publish information needed and wanted by bookstores. Except for those books sold to them by a publisher's sales representatives or by national and regional distributors, these wholesalers buy books in advance of the publication date. Their sales to bookstores reflect a trend which is now tracked by computer. Evidence of a pickup in sales alerts bookstores to a public demand for such books, so bookstores order more of them from the two wholesalers. Bookstores must be alert to trends, mostly because they often operate on a small gross margin for each book sold, even bestsellers. To move these faster, some bookstores will start discounting bestsellers within two months or less after a bestseller makes the "list."

*Cultural Literacy,* by E. D. Hirsh, Jr., became a bestseller in June, 1987. It had a cover price of $17.95 and was sold to small bookstores at a discount of 40%, or $10.77 per copy. Waldenbooks, because it orders so many copies of a book like this, probably got a discount of as much as 48%, or $9.33 per copy. Depending on the number of copies ordered, a bookstore may be able to negotiate a Freight Pass Through price which represents a discount of .05% more than it would ordinarily pay.

Another bestseller, *The Closing of the American Mind,* by Allan Bloom, had a first print run of 10,000 copies and had a cover price of $19.95. The cost of printing and binding this book (the production cost) was an estimated $2.00 per copy. The publisher's gross profit on each copy of this book, at least from the first print run, was an estimated $9.50 per copy. At the time of publication, hardly anyone except the author knew or even hoped it would turn into a bestseller. The rest is history, and this book will be bought by at least 500,000 people at $19.95 a copy. The cost of second and third printings of a book like this drops to about $1.60 per copy from the original production cost of about $2.00 per copy. When it goes into paperback, as it surely will, the production cost will be about $0.90 a copy for 100,000 copies and around $0.58 for 500,000 copies. Both *The Closing of the American Mind* and *Culturall Literacy* had moved to the paperback bestseller list by May 1988.

With a book like this, a bookstore will make a gross profit of between $7.98 and $9.58 per copy in hardcover and between $3.00 and $5.00 in paperback. These estimates depend on several factors, one of which is the cost of paper used by a commercial printer. How a book becomes a bestseller in the first place is sometimes a function of media "hype" and expectations of the publisher. In the case of *The Closing of the American Mind,* the promotion of the book and the message in its advertising touched a sensitive nerve in the nation's psyche—What happened to the liberal education I was supposed to get in college? Another the factor which helps sell books is the way they are displayed in a bookstore. Like "location," how a book is displayed is quite literally the cornerstone of publishing and marketing of books by bookstores. Most customers walk into a bookstore with no fixed idea of what book they want to buy, and the bookstores know this. In the well-designed bookstore, new releases and bestsellers are prominently displayed so a customer, often an impulse buyer, will see these first and very often buy them. Now, however, the way a book is displayed is threatened by state laws making it either a misdemeanor or a criminal offense to display a book with sexually explicit material "harmful to minors" in a place accessible to minors. The American Booksellers Association has been in the forefront of organizations challenging these state laws as a violation of rights guaranteed under the First Amendment, freedom of speech and the press. In most of these cases, local bookstores have been plaintiffs along with the ABA.

In American Booksellers Association v. Commonwealth of Virginia, for example, Ampersand Books and Books Unlimited, Inc., both located in Alexandria, Virginia, are plaintiffs, along with the Association of American Publishers and the National Association of College Stores, Inc. The state law challenged was amended in 1985 to provide in part that "It shall be unlawful for any person knowingly to sell or loan to a juvenile, *or to knowingly display for comercial purposes in a manner whereby juveniles may examine or peruse . . . .* " any sexually explicit material. A "juvenile" was defined as "a person less than eighteen years of age."

Ampersand Books was a member of the American Booksellers Association and carried 12,000-15,000 different titles at any one time, with multiple copies of most titles. The books were arranged in sections according to subject matter, including children's books, science fiction, mystery, fiction, romance, art, health, photography and bestsellers. Children often shopped at Ampersand Books, frequently with their parents, and children's books accounted for about 10% of Ampersand's sales. In terms of its size, design and customer profile, Ampersand was similar to many other northern Virginia bookstores. Books Unlimited, Inc., was also a member of the American Booksellers Association. This bookstore, however, was atypical in that it relied more heavily on sales of children's books than other area bookstores. Between 10% and 15% of its books could not be displayed under the 1985 amendment to the state law. Its books were displayed in a manner similar to those in Ampersand Books and also arranged by subject matter.

The U.S. District Court found in part as follows: "In all bookstores, the display of a particular book, and the manner in which it is displayed play a critical role in determining how many copies the bookstore will sell. Customers often become familiar with a book, and desire to purchase it only after browsing and looking through the shelves. Customers are generally hesitant about asking for help in locating books, and they are especially reluctant to ask for books that have a strong sexual content. Therefore, at least one copy of every title carried by Ampersand Books is on display. The books that fall within the restrictions (harmful to minors) come from a wide variety of subject matters, such as romance, fiction, photography, bestsellers, science fiction and health." The Court also found that from 10% to 25% of all books so displayed in northern Virginia bookstores fell within the category of books "harmful to minors." The Court held that "In promoting the morals of its youth by restricting their access to certain communications, the state may not create barriers which simultaneously place substantial restrictions upon an adult's access to those same protected materials." Affirmed by the U.S. Court of Appeals for the Fourth Circuit, this case was argued before the U.S. Supreme Court in its session beginning in October 1987. A number of states in this country have laws substantially the same as that challenged in Virginia. Unless successfully challenged, these laws will unquestionably determine what books will be published and just how, if at all, they will be displayed.

# Chapter 4
# American Booksellers Association v.
# Commonwealth of Virgina

In the October Term, 1987, the Supreme Court of the United States heard and decided the issues presented by Commonwealth of Virginia v. American Booksellers Association, et al, Docket No. 86–1034. Those interested in reading the Court's opinion may find it at 484 U.S.___, 98 L.Ed. 2d 782. Oral argument was heard on November 4, 1987. In the first paragraph of the opinion, the Court provided a short history of the Virginia statute. It stated: "In 1968, this Court held constitutional a state prohibition on the sale to those under 17 of materials 'harmful to juveniles.' Ginsburg v. New York, 390 U.S. 629 . . . . The next year, Virginia enacted a similar statute. The Virginia Code's definition of 'harmful to juveniles' is a modification of the Miller definition of obscenity, adapted for juveniles . . . . In 1985, Virginia amended its law to make it also a crime to 'knowingly display for commercial purposes in a manner whereby juveniles may 'examine and peruse' the aforementioned materials, even if these materials are not actually sold to any juvenile." Plaintiffs made a facial challenge to the 1985 amendment, asserting that it was fundamentally different from the prior statute in that it burdened the First Amendment rights of adults, as to whom at least some of the works covered by the Virginia statute were not obscene. Plaintiffs argued at the trial that the statute effectively restricted access to the entire population. Juveniles would either be barred from the bookstore or from an "adults only" section, and adults would feel stigmatized by being seen to enter an "adults only" bookstore or section of that bookstore. "In effect, the plaintiffs argued, "the law reduces the adult population to reading and viewing only works for children." The Supreme Court has repeatedly held such statutes as a First Amendment

66

violation. Even though the Court noted that it rarely reviewed a construction of state law agreed upon by the two lower courts (the Court of Appeals affirmed the judgment of the District Court). " . . . . this case," it said, "presents the rare situation in which we cannot rely on the construction and findings below."

Unfortunately, the Supreme Court did not resolve all the issues in this very important case. Instead, it certified two questions to the Supreme Court of Virginia. Docket No.86–1034 was an appeal from a decision of the United States Court of Appeals for the Fourth Circuit. In that case, the Court of Appeals affirmed a judgment of of the United States District, Northern District of Virginia, enjoining enforcement of the "display" of books law passed by the state legislature in 1985.

On January 25, 1988, the Supreme Court concluded that the "unique factual and procedural setting in this case leads us to conclude that an authoritative construction of the Virginia statute by the Virginia Supreme Court would substantially aid our review of this constitutional holding, and might well determine the case entirely." In the trial transcript, the District Court judge had ruled that it was "not an appropriate case for this Court to abstain, because there is no peculiar state law that needs interpreting by a state judge. And he won't have any more advantage than I have in trying to come to grips with this" (abstention is a doctrine allowing a federal court to defer to a state court in certain matters). However, the Supreme Court effectively did what the District Court declined to do in a First Amendment case. It certified two questions as follows:

1. Does the phrase 'harmful to juveniles' as used [in the Virginia Code challenged in the District Court], properly construed, encompass any of the books introduced as plaintiffs' exhibits below, and what general standard should be used to determine the statute's reach in light of juveniles' differing ages and levels of maturity?

2. What meaning is to be given to the provision of [the] Virginia Code . . . making it unlawful to 'knowingly display for commercial purposes in a manner whereby juveniles may examine or peruse' certain materials? Specifically,

> is the provision complied with by a plaintiff bookseller who
> has a policy of not permitting juveniles to examine or
> peruse materials covered by the statute and who prohibits
> such conduct when observed, but otherwise takes no action
> regarding the display of restricted material? If not, would
> the statute be complied with if the store's policy were
> announced or otherwise manifested to the public?"

Justice Stevens, concurring in part and dissenting in part,
expressed the view that the certified question seeking construction of the phrase "harmful to juveniles" should be modified to ask the state court which, if any, of the books introduced
into evidence was covered by the 1985 amendment. It seems
clear from the Supreme Court's opinion that the Justices concurring with Justice Brennan may have missed a major point familiar to almost all booksellers. A bookstore buyer must, but rarely
does, read each book ordered from a publisher *before* placing an
order for one or more books. Under such circumstances, the
buyer cannot possibly decide whether books not read will be
treated by the police as "restricted material" making it unlawful
to "knowingly display [that book] for commercial purposes in a
manner whereby juveniles may examine or peruse it."

In almost the same breath, the Supreme Court recognized that
plaintiffs had standing to sue (injury in fact), i.e., booksellers
"will have to take significant and costly compliance measures or
risk criminal prosecution." It added that "the alleged danger of
this statute is, in large measure, one of self-censorship; a harm
that can be realized even without an actual prosecution."

Moreover, as Justice Brennan, writing for the Court, noted:
"There is no reliable evidence in the record supporting the
District Court's holding that the statute reaches up to 25 percent
of a typical bookstore inventory, since the two bookstore owners
who testified were unfamiliar with the statutory definition of
'harmful to juveniles.' " In fact, the U.S. Court of Appeals (802
F.2nd 691) criticized the basis of the District Court's holding, but
gave no alternative basis for its own determination. It seems quite
clear that the Supreme Court found that the 16 books admitted
in evidence at trial were inadequate to support plaintiffs' First

A Role for the Small Press 69

Amendment claim on two grounds. First, the books were not sexually explicit enough to fall within the statutory standard, and, second, the bookseller plaintiffs testified under a mistaken impression as to the reach of the statute insofar as it defined "harmful to juveniles" (persons under 18 years of age).

This phrase was defined in the Virginia Code as follows:

"Harmful to Juveniles means that quality of any description or representation, in whatsoever form, or nudity, sexual conduct, sexual excitement, or sadomasochistic abuse, when (a) predominantly appeals to the prurient, shameful or morbid interest of juveniles, (b) is patently offensive to prevailing standards in the *adult* community as a whole with respect to what is suitable material for juveniles, and (c) is, when taken as a whole, lacking in serious literary, artistic, political or scientific value for *juveniles*.

This language underscore the burden cast on booksellers and emphasizes what the Supreme Court meant by the "significant and costly compliance measures" they would have to follow to avoid the risk of criminal prosecution. Virginia booksellers would actually have to *read* most trade books *before* placing orders for any of them from publishers. A publisher's catalog shown to the book buyer for that bookstore by a publisher's sales rep would no longer suffice, unless the phrase "knowingly display for commercial purposes" is strictly construed by the Supreme Court of Virginia. This imposes on book buyers the burden of self-censorship when the books are placed on shelves or "displayed," a constitutionally protected form of speech. Moreover, even then, the bookseller does not enjoy immunity from criminal prosecution. Local police, with a search warrant issued for probable cause (display of books containing restricted material), may search and seize some books as evidence in a criminal prosecution, if some local citizen were to disagree with the book buyer's judgment in displaying them in a place accessible to juveniles and where juveniles "examined or perused" them.

There can be little doubt that the Virginia statute governing the "display" of books "restricted" as to juveniles will also substantially restrict access to adults. Literal compliance with the

Virginia statute would be economically devastating. Adults are reluctant to enter an "adults only" bookstore as conduct likely to stigmatize them as having "a prurient bent" or "a morbid interest in sex." The Virginia statute is a legislative aberation which the Supreme Court should have found was a violation of the First Amendment guarantee of free speech. Once again, it has plunged into a legal thicket by certifying two questions to a state court, the Supreme Court of Virginia. Along with publishers, the American Booksellers Association and its members in other states have every right to be concerned.

However, on September 23, 1988 the Supreme Court of Virginia, per Justice Charles Marshall, seems to have given booksellers some hope for relief from criminal enforcement of the 1985 amendment of the Virginia statute. In his opinion, Justice Marshall answered the first certified question in the negative. This means that 16 books admitted in evidence at the trial were not found to be in violation of the 1985 amendment. The second certified question was answered in the affirmative. This seems to mean that a bookseller with a policy of not permitting juveniles to examine and peruse materials covered by the statute and prohibits such perusal when observed may be in compliance with the statute. In its Slip Opinion, the Supreme Court of Virginia concluded that "if a work is found to have a serious literary, artistic, political or scientific value for a lefitimate minority of normal, older adolescents, then it cannot be said to lack such value for the entire class of juveniles taken as a whole."

Later in the Slip Opinion, Justice Rusell wrote that "The thrust of the [1985] Amendment . . . was directed at the perusal of harmful materials by juvenile readers on bookstores, not at the method chosen by booksellers to display their wares for adults." Accordingly, Justice Rusell wrote that a juvenile cannot stand in a bookstore and read a book "harmful to juveniles," a book he would be unable to buy. Thus, in a criminal prosecution, a prosecutor would have a heavy burden of proof to carry. He must show beyond a reasonable doubt "that the defendant bookseller knowingly afforded juveniles an opportunity to peruse harmful materials, or took no reasonable steps to prevent such perusal when the juvenile's opportunity was reasonably apparent to the bookseller."

This may be considered a heavy burden by some prosecutors, but there are still some unanswered questions. Is every bookseller, for example, charged with general knowledge of character and content of the books offered for sale? Is every bookseller to be made the judge of whether a given book is "harmful to juveniles" in all cases? Trade book buyers seldom, if ever, actually read the books they order from publishers or distributors, and not many booksellers, even after reading a book, could possibly decide whether it was "harmful to juveniles" within the test to be applied by a jury. Additionally, how does one decide whether there is a serious literary, artistic, political or scientific value for "a legitimate minority of *normal, older adolescents . . ."?* What is a "normal, older adolescent? These are all complex questions which must still be addressed by the U.S. Supreme Court.

Even though the injunction enjoining enforcement of the Virginia statute will remain in force pending review by the Supreme Court of Virginia and any further proceedings in the Supreme Court of the United States, publishers and booksellers have further cause for concern. In mid–August of 1987, a federal grand jury in Virginia indicted several individuals and a magazine, Educational Books, Inc., in the first case ever brought under the Racketeer Influenced and Corrupt Organizations Act, usually referred to as RICO. Henry Hudson, the United States Attorney for the Eastern District of Virginia stated that: "Educational Books has been convicted 15 times for violating the Virginia obscenity dtatute since 1981 and still conducts business as usual." Hudson also said that the case would be prosecuted by his office and the National Obscenity Enforcement Unit of the Department of Justice. This was established by Attorney General Edwin Meese 3rd earlier in 1987. He himself is the subject of an investigation arising out of his alleged involvement in the scandal–plagued Wadtech kickback case and the Iraqi pipeline case.

Pursuant to the provisions of 18 U.S.C. 1963(a)(3) of RICO, a District Court may require the defendants to "forfeit to the United States all property . . . " described in the indictment, including real property and, of course, all books found to be in violation of the Virginia statute. With the exception of the "display" amendment of 1985, this statute is essentially the same as the one involved in American Booksellers Association vs. Commonwealth of Virginia. It seems clear that the Attorney General is determined to stamp out all explicit sex in books, just as Hitler did in Nazi Germany during the 1930s unless books were of pure Aryan origin.

In United States vs. Educational Books, Inc. et al (Docket No. Criminal 87-00208-A), the defendants were tried and convicted in the United States District Court and an Order of Forfeiture was entered. Defendants filed a timely Notice of Appeal of their criminal conviction with the United States Court of Appeals for the Fourth Circuit. They also moved for an order staying the forfeiture of property which included an office building owned by defendants. The motion for a stay of the order pending the outcome of the appeal was denied by the U.S. District Court. During the pendency of the appeal, the United States Marshall plan to sell at auction both the real property and some video tapes found at the trial to be "obscene."

# Chapter 5
## Some Law About Publishing
## What Can Be Published or Disclosed?

The answer, or at least a partial answer to this question lies in the Constitution. The First Amendment, Article I, Section 8, Clause 8, and Article III, Section 1. The latter vests "The judicial power of the United States . . . in one Supreme Court, and in such inferior courts as the Congress may from time to time ordain and establish . . . "

Section 2 provides that:

> The judicial power shall extend to all cases, in law and equity, arising under this Constitution, the laws of the United States . . .; to which the United States shall be a party . . .

The First Amendment to the Constitution, ratified on December 15, 1791, is entitled "Restrictions on Powers of Congress." It states:

> Congress shall make no law respecting an establishment of religion, or prohibiting the free exercise thererof; or abridging the freedom of speech, or of the press; or the right of the people peaceably to assemble, and to petition the Government for a redress of grievances.

Article I, Section 8, Clause 8 of the Constitution spells out "Powers Granted to Congress." It gives Congress the right:

> 8. To promote the progress of science and useful arts, by securing for limited times to authors and inventors the exclusive right to their respective writings and discoveries."

In 1976, Congress enacted The Copyright Act of 1976 and four years later, it enacted The Software Protection Act of 1980. Section 102 of the 1976 Act provided that "(a) Copyright protection subsists...in original works of authorship fixed in any tangible medium of expression, now known or later developed, from which they can be perceived, reproduced, or otherwise communicated, either directly or with the aid of a machine or device. Works of authorship include the following categories:

> (1) literary works; (2) musical works, including any accompanying words; (3) dramatic works, including any accompanying music;(4) pantomines and choreographic works;(5) pictorial, graphic, and sculptural works;(6) motion pictures and other audio-visual works; and (7) sound recordings."

In 1980, Congress amended the 1976 Act to extend copyright protection to computer programs. It defined a "computer program" as "a set of statements or instructions for use directly or indirectly in a computer to produce a certain result." This definition has spawned litigation, such as Whelan Associates, Inc. v. Jaslow Dental Laboratory, Inc., 797 F.2nd 1222 (3rd Cir. 1986) and its progeny, leaving in the dark the question of what features of a computer program, if any, are entitled to copyright protection.

Whelan held that the "structure, sequence and organization" of a computer program was entitled to copyright protection. This "look and feel" rule was extended to visual displays generated by a computer program in Broderbund Software, Inc. v. Unison World, Inc., 648 F. Supp. 1127 (N.D. Cal. 1986). Now, Apple Computer, Inc. has initiated copyright litigation to protect its widely known graphics programs such as MacDraw and Mac-Paint. Naming Microsoft Corporation and Hewlett-Packard Company as defendants in a suit filed on March 18, 1988, Apple has focused on the use of graphic interface programs (screen display) to communicate with other personal computers. IBM and other third-party developers have all endorsed such user interface programs, principally to establish a standard for all such programs, and enormous sums have been spent on the hardware and software to support them. For its part, Microsoft Corporation has filed a cross complaint charging Apple with slander (trade libel), breach of contract and unfair business practices.

IBM competes with Apple in the market for business computers, and Microsoft makes the OS/2, the new operating system IBM uses in its new line of personal computers. Hardly anyone expects IBM to be a disinterested spectator of this litigation. The entire situation literally invites congressional attention and an amendment to the Software Protection Act of 1980. Without an amendment allowing the creation of a uniform standard and antitrust immunity for agreeing on one, purchasers of personal computers will be left in the dark without any standard.

In a case of great interest to lawyers nationally, West Publishing Company v. Mead Data Central, Inc., 799 F.2nd 1219 (8th Cir. 1986) has raised novel questions of copyright protection for computerized search programs used by Mead Data Central, Inc., such as Lexis. West Publishing Company offers a search program, Westlaw, which competes with Lexis, and searches for case citations in volumes printed and bound by West Publishing, as does Lexis. It secured a preliminary injunction enjoining the use by Lexis of the same page numbers as those used by West Publishing in the printed and bound volumes of all state and federal cases decided by all courts. A judicial opinion, however, is not entitled to copyright protection, but West Publishing claimed that its "arrangement of cases" was "original" and represented an intellectual creation of its editors. The opinion of the Court did not even mention the 1980 amendment to the Copyright Act of 1976 and showed no knowledge of how computerized search programs worked. Eventually, the case will be heard by the Supreme Court, because it involves important issues under the Copyright Act of 1976 as amended in 1980 (The Software Protection Act), and Section 2 of the Sherman Act (monopoly).

It seems clear that a publisher may publish any "literary work(s)" it pleases according to the language of Section 102 of the 1976 Act. However, what a publisher may not do, notwithstanding the language of the First Amendment, is to publish a literary work which is libelous or otherwise prohibited by law. Mead Data Central, Inc., for example, has stated that West Publishing Company has engaged in anti-competitive trade practices and censorship which has the effect of limiting public access to the courts in violation of the First Amendment.

In a number of recent cases, the Supreme Court has decided that the First Amendment does not necessarily allow the publication of all *literary work(s)*. The italicised language reflects a limitation on what some people can write at all, if they were working for an agency of the United States and use classified or non-public information. In 1980, for example, the Supreme Court held that an ex-CIA agent's publication of a book about the Central Intelligence Agency without its prior approval, was a breach of his fiduciary duty (Snepp v. United States). The Court found that Frank Snepp, the author, had voluntarily agreed in 1968 "not to publish any information or material relating to the Agency . . . . without specific prior approval by the Agency." By not getting pre-publication clearance from the Central Intelligence Agency, Snepp, according to the Court, had breached a valid contract. The U.S. District Court had imposed a constructive trust on all profits he mighht earn from publishing his book, *Decent Interval*. His publisher, Random House, Inc., had paid him an advance of about $60,000, and his agreement with Random House called for the payment of royalties and other potential profits such as the sale of paperback and film rights to third parties.

In an earlier case decided by the U.S. Court of Appeals, Victor Marchetti, also an ex-CIA agent was enjoined from publishing a proposed book in violation of the same agreement that Snepp had signed. The Court of Appeals held only that Marchetti could not disclose *classified* material or information obtained by him during the course of his employment. In Snepp v. United States, the government did not contend that Snepp's book contained classified or non-public material.

Accordingly, an author who happens to have been an ex-CIA agent is no longer free to exercise even his First Amendment right to speak or write about the Central Intelligence Agency, or even to criticize it as any other citizen might do. As Justice Stevens, in a dissenting opinion in which Justice Brennan and Justice Marshall joined, wrote that "The Court seems unaware of the fact that its drastic new remedy (a constructive trust on profits) has been fashioned to enforce a species of prior restraint on a citizen's right to criticize his government." In the 1971 Pentagon Papers case (New York Times Co. v. United States), the Supreme Court held that, under the First Amendment, the press must be left free to publish news, whatever the source, without censorship, injunctions or prior restraint. The United States governent had sought to enjoin publication by *The New York Times* of the contents of a classified study entitled "History of U.S. Decision-Making Process on Vietnam Policy." The Supreme Court affirmed denial of injunctive relief, because, it said, the government had not met its heavy burden of showing justification of a prior restraint of expression. The Pentagon Papers were published by the *New York Times,* and no discernible damage to national security occurred.

On April 2, 1982, President Reagan went even further in imposing prior restraints in Executive Order No. 12356, ostensibly to safeguard "national security information." The Order prescribed a uniform system for classifying, declassifying and safeguarding national security information. In an Order of May 7, 1982, the President designated certain officials authorized to classify information. Those authorized to classify information as Top Secret included the Director, Office of Management and Budget, and the Adminstrator of General Services. Those authorized to classify information as Secret included the Chairman, Council of Economic Advisers, the Secretaries of Commerce and Transportation, and the Administrator, Agency for International Development. The Administrator, Environmental Protection Agency was treated in rather cavalier fashion. He was authorized to classify information as Confidential only. For about five years, acid rain has fallen on and destroyed areas classified as Confidential. To delegate this classification authority, Agency heads need only ensure that subordinates "have a demonstrable and continuing need to exercise this authority." This clearly means that Congress has no meaningful right to know how federal funds are spent, or what policies of the executive branch of the government it is asked to finance with public funds. In the meantime, bureaucratic ineptitude and incompetence seem to flourish behind a veil of secrecy.

Almost from the date on which Ronald Reagan became President of the United States (January 20, 1981), he has shown an obsessive concern with secrecy in government. Executive Order No. 12356 was merely the first step toward expressing this concern by making it Reagan Administration policy. Its text is set forth in 50 U.S.C. 401, and began with the phrase "by the authority vested in me as President by the Constitution and laws of the United States . . . . it is hereby ordered as follows: "

Ever since 1951, when the Supreme Court decided Youngstown Sheet & Tube Co. v. Sawyer, there have been restrictions on Presidential power. There, the Court enjoined enforcement of Executive Order No. 10340 which allowed the Secretary of Commerce to seize and operate the nation's steel mills. This power, said Justice Black, writing for the Court, could not be sustained as an exercise of the President's power as commander in chief of the armed forces. Nor could it be sustained on the basis of constitutional provisions granting executive powers to the President–his power to see that the laws be faithfully executed. There was no statute expressly allowing the seizure of the steel mills. There is no statute expressly authorizing the President to deny persons their rights under the First Amendment as Executive Order No. 12356 clearly does. He repealed a section in a predecessor order which authorized the certain officials to declassify information noting in Section 3-3 of Executive Order No. 12065 (1978) that "in some cases, however, the need to protect such information may be outweighed by the public interest in disclosure of the information, and in these cases the information should be declassified . . . . That official will determine whether the public interest in disclosure outweighs the damage to national security that might reasonably be expected from disclosure."

In signing Executive Order No. 12356 on April 2, 1982, President Reagan repealed this section which allowed the courts to "balance" the value of disclosure in the public interest against any damage to national security that might reasonably be expected from such disclosure. See Afshar v. Department of State, 702 F.2d 1125, 1135 (D.C. Cir. 1983), where the Court said: "After oral argument in this appeal, President Reagan issued a new Executive Order, which, *inter alia,* repealed the balancing provision of E. O. 12,065." Since the Supreme Court's decision in Snepp v. United States, which held that the CIA could, consistent with the First Amendment, recover damages for breach of a secrecy agreement requiring pre–publication review of material to be included in a book by a retired CIA employee, most authors or their publishers have sought such review as in McGehee v. Casey, 718 F.2d 1136 (D.C. Cir. 1983). There, the Court noted that: "Unlike the former order (12065), which required an articulation of 'identifiable damage' to justify a 'confidential' classification, the new order [12356] requires only a finding of unspecified 'damage' "

In McGehee v. Casey, pre-publication review was sought by McGehee for an article he proposed to submit for publication, but the CIA's definition of "national security" prevailed, and portions of McGehee's manuscript which had been submitted were excised for reasons of national security. His article, with some deletions, appeared in *The Nation* magazine. McGehee then asked for declaratory relief in the U.S. District Court and raised questions under the First Amendment relating to the CIA's classification and censorship scheme. Relying on Snepp v. United States, the Court of Appeals held that the CIA censorship of "secret" writings obtained by former agents did not violate the First Amendment. McGehee had argued that the classification scheme—"information, the unauthorized disclosure of which reasonably could be expected to cause identifiable damage to the national security"—should be invalidated as being "too broad and vague to satisfy the First Amendment." The Court summarily rejected this argument, noting that McGehee lacked standing to assert overbreadth and vagueness challenges to a "confidential" classification, since the censored portions of his article were classified as secret. However, the Court of Appeals did concede that Executive Order No. 12065 could "touch constitutionally protected speech," noting the phrase "identifiable damage" might include a minimal amount of harm which may not be sufficient in all cases to justify suppression of speech. Executive Order No. 12356, requiring only a finding of unspecified "damage" to the national security removed the last vestige of any protection under the First Amendment.

Thus, *any damage,* however minimal, will now be seen as sufficient to support an indictment alleging unauthorized disclosure of classified information to a person not entitled to receive it, including the press. Congress needs to address the ongoing problem of secrecy in government. Otherwise the free flow of information important to the public interest will quite simply come to an end, leaving the public to deal with executive absolutism if it can.

While the phrase "national security" has absolutely no statutory definition, its use in cases and classification systems has gone virtually unchallenged. The Cold War rhetoric of the Reagan Administration has effectively pre-empted any attempt to define this phrase with more precision. Congress and the courts have almost unquestionably adopted a military definition of "national security." Specifically, the Joint Chiefs of Staff offer their definition as "(a) a military or defense advantage over any foreign nation or group of nations, (b) a favorable foreign relations position, or (c) a defense posture capable of successfully resisting hostile action from within or without, overt or covert." This definition has the inevitable result of requiring an enormously expensive search for "security" by making our potential enemies more insecure. This is a prescription for more or less permanent war, and it is clearly the rationale for most, if not all classification systems since the enactment by Congress of the National Security Act of 1947. In March, 1988, *The New Yorker Magazine,* in an article by Richard Barnet, offered a new definition as "a desired state of physical safety, economic development, and social stability within which there is space for individuals to participate in building an American community free of both foreign coercion and manipulation by government." Parenthetically, Barnet recognized that citizens could not be secure if the strategy for keeping foreign enemies at bay caused the government to treat dissent as something to be suppressed or otherwise treated dissenting citizens as enemies to be watched. Unfortunately, this has already happened.

On April 8, 1988, the Court of Appeals, in United States v. Morison, converted 18 U.S.C. 793 (e) and (d)–The Espionage Act of 1917, as amended in 1950–into an Official Secrets Act, contrary to congressional intent. Congress has always been sensitive to the importance of not unduly restricting the constitutionally protected freedom of the press under the First Amendment. In 1917, its attention had focused on two provisions which would have punished the mere publication of certain designated types of defense information, but without any intent to aid the enemy. Both provisions were deleted, since Section 494(b) of the Espionage Act did require proof that publication by a newspaper that the information was intended to reach the enemy. It seems quite unlikely that Congress ever intended Section 793(e) to apply to newspapers. Moreover, United States v. New York Times, decided in 1971, certainly stands for the proposition that the First Amendment granted special protection to the press against a prior restraint on publication. It also stands for the proposition that the free flow of information to the public is essential in a democracy to check governmental power.

In United States v. Morison, a different issue was presented to the Court of Appeals. Broadly, the issue may be stated as follows: Notwithstanding a non-disclosure agreement, clearly a prior restraint, does a classification system imposed by Executive Order No. 12356 allow the government to punish the release to the press of classified information without judicial review of the propriety of the classification itself by invoking Sections 493(d) and (e) of the Espionage Act? This is not to say that all government employees with a high security clearance remain free to disclose information which does in fact or could reasonably be expected to cause damage to the national defense. Clearly, some information must remain classified, such as "military plans, weapons, or operations" and "intelligence activities." The national security interest in secrecy must always be balanced against a public interest in disclosure of information. Even severe injury to national security interests should not in all cases trigger criminal punishment until this balancing is carried out by the courts. In a few cases, the government has declined to prosecute persons whose conduct was thought to violate a criminal statute, because evidence necessary to convict might compromise national security—the disclose or dismiss dilemma.

To resolve this problem, Congress enacted the Classified Information Procedures Act (18 U.S.C. App. 1) in 1980. This was essentially a law specifying the procedures to be used by a defendant in a criminal trial of classified information. It reflected a congressional intent to resolve disputes over whether disclosure requirements infringe legitimate executive interests by allowing the judiciary to examine documents *in camera*. Congress felt that a trial court judge had to know *why* certain material was classified in order to decide questions of admissibility or relevance of evidence submitted by either the prosecution or the defendant.

The Classified Information Procedures Act will apply to the trials of Admiral John Poindexter and Lieutenant Oliver North. U.S. District Court Judge Gerhard A. Gesell has already demanded that some 300,000 pages of classified documents be made available to their attorneys, much of it withheld from some members of Congress during the televised Iran-Contra hearings. The Act itself provides for proceedings *in camera* in which the defense must identify what classified information it will use at the trial. If relevant and admissible as evidence, Judge Gesell must allow its release, or he may require a summary of the contents from the prosecution, in this case, the special prosecutor, Lawrence E. Walsh. If neither alternative is acceptable to the prosecution, the case must be dismissed by Judge Gesell. This is the classic "disclose or dismiss" dilemma for the prosecution. Rather than run the risk that disclosure of highly classified information may implicate the White House itself, President Reagan may exercise his constitutional right to pardon both Poindexter and North.

Entirely aside from the legitimate interest of protecting from disclosure information which could "reasonably be expected to cause damage to the national security," President Reagan also had an obsessive concern with "leaks" to the press. Even officers at cabinet level, however, leaked to reporters bits and pieces of information about defense and foreign policy, many of them classified as secret. These leaks sometimes occurred with the blessing of the Administration itself to promote its policies. Unauthorized leaks very often exposed waste, fraud and abuse of bureaucratic power. In 1972, for example, Assistant Attorney General William Rehnquist, now Chief Justice of the Supreme Court, was appointed by President Nixon to serve as chairman of a committee to examine the classification system as it existed then. In the Moorhead Hearings, pt. 3, at 791, he told a House subcommittee that virtually every member of his committee believed there was a tendency in the Government to overclassify information. One expert, William Florence, asserted that probably 99.5% of all classified material held by the Defense Department alone could be released without predjudicing the national security. Moorhead Hearings, pt. 1, at 97. In the deposition of Max Frankel taken as part of the discovery proceedings in The Pentagon Papers case, he stated that it was quite commonplace for middle level officials to attempt to change conditions in their own agency by passing secret information either to the press or to members of Congress. In *The Craft of Intelligence*, A. Dulles recited the example of an Air Force general who leaked proposals to place more reliance on conventional forces than on nuclear forces to discredit the policy.

It is against this background of leaks and growing executive paranoia that the Department of Justice decided to prosecute Samuel L. Morison for violations of the Espionage Law [18 U.S.C. 793 (d) and (e)], first enacted in 1917. Morison was also charged with a violation of 18 U.S.C. 641. The defendant was tried and convicted by a jury in the U.S. District Court in Maryland, and an appeal was taken to the United States Court of Appeals for the Fourth Circuit. On April 8, 1988 the Court of Appeals affirmed the judgment of conviction with an opinion by

Judge Russell and two separate concurring opinions, __ F.2nd
__(4th Cir. 1988.) At this writing, it is not known whether a
petition for a hearing *en banc* by all the judges of the Fourth
Circuit had been filed by attorneys for Samuel Morison.

The facts, briefly summarized, show that Morison was
employed at the Naval Intelligence Support Center (NISC)
from 1974 to 1984. At the time of the violations for which he was
convicted, he had a security clearance of "Top Secret–Sensitive
Compartmented Information." In connection with his security
clearance, Morison had signed a Non-Disclosure Agreement
which stated in part that "direct or indirect unauthorized disclosure, unauthorized retention . . . . by me could cause irrepar-
able injury to the United States or be used to advantage by a
foreign nation . . . ."

During the time of his employment by NISC, Morison had
done some off-duty work for *Jane's Fighting Ships,* an annual
British publication which provided current information on
naval operations internationally. This arrangement had been
submitted to and approved by the Navy subject to Morison's
agreement that "he would not obtain and supply any classified
material on the *U.S. Navy* or extract unclassified data on any
subject and forward it to *Jane's."*

Notwithstanding his Non–Disclosure Agreement and his
agreement with the Navy, Morison took "certain glossy photographs of a *Soviet* aircraft carrier under construction in a Black
Sea shipyard" and sent them to Derek Wood, editor–in–chief of
*Jane's Defence Weekly,* a periodical where Morison had sought
employment. The photographs had been taken by a "KH-11
reconnaissance satellite . . . . and stamped 'Secret' " with a
"Notice: Intelligence Sources or Methods Involved."

At this point, the NISC could probably have successfully
invoked the Sanctions set forth in Section 5.4 (3)(c) of Executive
Order No. 12356. These sanctions "may include reprimand,
suspension without pay, removal, termination of classification
authority, loss or denial of access to classified information, *or other
sanctions in accordance with applicable law and agency regulation."*

"Whether pure 'information' constitutes property which may

be the subject of statutory protection under Section 641, "according to Judge Russell, ". . . . is not, however, involved here. We are dealing with specific, identifiable tangible property, which will qualify as such for larceny or embezzlement under any possible definition of theft." See Slip Opinion, pp.46–47. "The mere fact that one has stolen a document in order that he may deliver it to the press . . . . will not immunize him from responsibility for his criminal act. To use the first amendment for such a purpose would be "to convert the first amendment into a warrant for thievery." The Court cited Branzburg v. Hayes, 408 U.S. 665, for this extravagant proposition.

That case involved a single issue — the obligation of reporters to respond to grand jury subpoenas and answer questions relevant to the commission of a crime. The Supreme Court held only that the First Amendment accords a reporter no privilege against appearing before a grand jury and answering questions as to either the identity of his news sources or information which he has received in confidence. The citation of Branzburg, however, seems to be a blunt reminder to all reporters that they will now have to rely on canned handouts from government agencies instead of doing investigative reporting by talking to or interviewing informed sources on a not-for-attribution basis. Fear of accountability to a grand jury will cause publishers, editors, and critics of governmental ineptitude to write with more restrained pens. Government policies are now far more likely to be determined without the public debate which serves as a check on executive absolutism.

The Court's affirmance of the judgment of conviction under the Espionage Act raises far more troubling questions for publishers in general, and it is no coincidence that *The Washington Post, CBS, Inc., National Broadcasting Company, Inc., Capital Cities/ ABC, Time, Inc., Newsweek, U.S. News & World Report, The Wall Street Journal, The New York Times* and many others, including the American Booksellers Association, Inc. filed *amicus curiae,* (friend of the court) briefs, all of them supporting reversal of Morison's conviction on First Amendment grounds. At the trial, the jury was instructed that Morison could be convicted of espionage only if the information he disclosed was *"potentially damaging* to the United States or might be useful to an enemy." In a separate concurring opinion, Judge Wilkinson noted that this instruction would "restrain the possibility that the broad language of this statute would ever be used as a means of punishing mere incompetence and corruption in the government...the strictures of these limiting instructions confine prosecution to cases of *serious consequence* to our national security." Judge Phillips, concurring with Judge Wilkinson, agreed that "the limiting instruction which required proof that the information leaked was either 'potentially damaging to the United States or might be useful to an enemy' sufficiently remedied the facial vice (of 'relating to the national defense')." He said this phrase was "both constitutionally overbroad and vague." Finally, on page 71, Slip Opinion, Judge Phillips said: "I observe that jury instructions on a case-by-case basis are a slender reed upon which to rely for constitutional application of these critical statutes; . . . . and surely press to the limit the judiciary's right and obligation to narrow, without 'reconstructing,' statutes whose constitutionality is drawn in question."

Both of these critical sections are quoted here in part:

> (d) Whoever, lawfully having possession of . . . . a photograph . . . . relating to the national defense . . . . or information relating to the national defense which information the possessor has reason to believe could be used to the injury of the United States or to the advantage of any foreign nation, willfully communicates [it] . . . . to any person not entitled to receive it; or
>
> (e) Whoever having unauthorized possession of . . . . a photograph . . . . relating to the national defense, or information relating to the national defense which information the possesor has reason to believe could be used to the injury of the United States or to the advantage of any foreign nation, willfully communicates [it] . . . . to any person not entitled to receive it . . . . Shall be fined not more than $10,000 or imprisoned not more than ten years, or both.

At all times, it must be noted, the photographs were of a Soviet carrier under construction in a Black Sea shipyard, construction that Moscow clearly knew about. One of Morison's witnesses testified that in his opinion, the materials in question "had not told the Soviets anything they did not already know"...and that they "did not reveal anything about our intelligence collection capabilities that was not otherwise known to the public." The Court of Appeals seems to have ignored this patently obvious fact and applied a "literal" construction of the provisions of both sections. It did so in the face of Supreme Court authority holding that in "exceptional circumstances," where a literal reading of the statute will produce a result demonstrably at odds with the intentions of its drafters, or where acceptance of that meaning would lead to absurd results or would thwart the obvious purpose of the statute, or where an absolutely literal reading of a statutory provision is irreconcilably at war with the clear congressional purpose, a less literal construction may be considered. The Court of Appeals dismissed these "exceptional" conditions, saying there "was no warrant for looking to the legislative history of sections 793 (d) and (e)."

Instead of a careful analysis of the history of secrecy in government and attempts to deal with it in a manner consistent with the First Amendment, the Court of Appeals looked to Section 794 which prohibits disclosure of such information an "agent . . . . of a foreign government . . . .", describing this section as one that dealt with "classic spying." Then, on page 23 (Slip Opinion), the Court of Appeals said: "Actually we do not perceive any First Amendment rights to be implicated here. This certainly is no prior restraint such as New York Times v. United States . . . . and United States v. Progressive, Inc." Beyond a precisely defined "national security" or "national defense," there is, indeed, a prior restraint in the language of Executive Order No. 12356, the language of which was not analyzed by the Court of Appeals. Its reliance on McGehee v. Casey, 718 F.2nd 1137 (D.C. Cir. 1983) is misplaced, as already noted. Judge Wald, in a separate opinion, noted that Executive Order No. 12356 had superseded Executive Order No. 12,069 of 1978. The lattter had contained a "balancing" provision deleted from the former. He said:

> It would of course be extremely difficult for judges to 'balance' the public's right to know against an acknowledged national security risk, and I do not believe we are currently authorized to do so.

Judge Wald was correct, and the Presidentially authorized deletion makes Executive Order No. 12356 constitutionally suspect, since it restricts judicial review of any case with First Amendment implications and leaves the executive free to exclude the courts from any review of classification procedures or any determination that information had been properly classified in the first place. No release or disclosure of any classified information was authorized except at the sole discretion of the classifying officer under the language of Executive Order No. 12356. In United States v. Reynolds, 345 U.S. 1, the Supreme Court declared in a "state secrets" case, that judicial control over the evidence in a case "cannot be abdicated to the caprice of executive officers." See also Ellsberg v. Mitchell, 709 F.2nd 51 (D.C. Cir. 1983) and 91 Yale Law Journal 570 (1982) and an article there entitled The Military and State Secrets Privilege: Protection for the National Security or Immunity for the Executive? Courts, said its authors, could and should apply a straight sensitivity test to classified information as to which pretrial discovery is sought. Instead of dismissing a case where even nonsensitive material was withheld, courts "should not consider information privileged solely because of its potential predjudicial impact; instead, they should determine whether the danger from discovery conducted under conditions imposed by the court warrants withholding the information despite its disclosure value." Given the unfettered discretion of Executive Order No. 12356, the executive would have the right to withhold information Congress said was available when it enacted The Freedom of Information Act, subject only to the exemptions therein.

Section 1.6 of Executive Order No. 12356 provides in part that: "In no case shall information be classified . . . . to prevent or delay the release of information that does not require protection in the interest of national security." Without the trial transcript, it is impossible to tell whether Morison challenged the propriety of the classification of the satellite photographs, the delivery of which to a person "not entitled to receive" them was the basis of his conviction. A KH–11 satellite is an intelligence "source," but Morison communicated the "result" of using this source which was not compromised in any way, since the fact of its existence has been in the public domain for years.

An obsessive concern with secrecy, executive paranoia, led to the prosecution of Morison, and, upon a proper evidentiary showing, an action for declaratory relief should be considered by those parties who filed *amicus curiae* briefs in the Court of Appeals challenging Executive Order No. 12356 under the First Amendment. In the meantime, publishers, editors and authors need to be concerned with this trend toward secrecy in government.

With some obvious and permissible limitations, Executive Order No. 12356 went further than the Supreme Court did in the Pentagon Papers case. Its language would clearly prohibit the disclosure to Congress of information it must have in order to appropriate money and authorize its expenditure. It is clear that secrecy in government is fundamentally undemocratic and tends to perpetuate bureaucratic errors. Open debate and discussion of public issues are vital to our national health. This was recognized by James Madison who introduced the Bill of Rights in the House of Representatives in 1789, saying: "I believe that the great mass of the people who opposed the Constitution disliked it because it did not contain effectual provisions against the encroachments on particular rights . . . . " Madison also said: "If they (the first ten amendments) are incorporated into the Constitution, independent tribunals of justice will consider themselves in a peculiar manner the guardians of those rights; they will be an impenetrable bulwark against every assumption of power in the Legislature or Executive; they will be naturally led to resist every encroachment upon rights expressly stipulated for in the Constitution by the declaration of rights." I Annals of Congress 421, 433, 434 and 439. Whatever happened to the "inpenetrable bulwark [of the courts] against every assumption of power in the Legislature or Executive. . . ?"

# Chapter 6
## What Can We Read
## or Write Without Fear?

Until the Supreme Court defines "national security" more precisely or until Congress provides a classification system meeting First Amendment requirements, publishers, editors and authors will face a classic dilemma. What can be written without fear of criminal prosecution under the Espionage Act? In another First Amendment area—state regulation of obscenity and libel—this administration has whittled away at the right of free speech and freedom of the press. While he may not have meant to do so, Alexis de Tocqueville wrote in terms applicable to these areas. In *Democracy in America* he had something to say about speech as it treated the trade of literature, including by implication, obscenity. He said that "among democratic nations a writer may flatter himself that he will obtain at a cheap rate a moderate reputation and a large fortune. For this purpose he need not be admired; it is enough that he is liked. The ever increasing crowd of readers and their continual craving for something new ensure the sale of books that *nobody much esteems.*" This includes books and magazines which the Supreme Court has struggled to define as "obscene" ever since it held in Roth v. United States that "obscenity" was not protected by the First Amendment. Ever since 1957, the Supreme Court has struggled to define the undefinable. It should abandon this exercise in futility and let people decide for themselves what characteristics make a book something "nobody much esteems." It is clear, however, that the freedom of speech guaranteed by the First Amendment includes the right to publish what de Tocqueville would condemn as a book that "nobody much esteems," subject only to those laws which were designed to protect persons offended by sexually explicit material in books,

91

i.e., the Attorney General, or from having their reputations maligned by false and defamatory statements.

In 13 of the 14 states which had ratified the Constitution by 1789, laws did provide for the prosecution of libel, and all of them made either blasphemy, profanity or both, statutory crimes.

Today, no publisher interested in solvency can afford to go without insurance against perils of this kind. Juries have awarded plaintiffs five and six figure judgments in libel cases. And even though about 80% of these are reversed on appeal, the costs of defense are a major consideration to publishers. Some publishers will not include authors in their policies on the ground that authors will then be less careful in doing their research. Literary agents may have to bargain for such coverage, so their author-clients may not be paid the huge advances of the past.

Libel is defined broadly as including unprivileged communications exposing a person to hatred, contempt, ridicule or obloquy, or which causes him to be shunned or avoided, or which has a tendency to injure him in his business or occupation. This definition has been held to include almost any language which, on its face, has a natural tendency to injure a person's reputation, either generally or with respect to his occupation. However, a statement need not charge a crime or sexual misbehaviour or lower a person's business reputation in order to be libelous. An imputation that the plaintiff was publicly intoxicated and had acted boorishly was libelous per se.

Different factual material can sometimes lead to anomalous results, since truth is a defense in most cases. When a plaintiff is a public official or public figure, proof of truth is unquestionably a constitutionally mandated bar to the imposition of liability for libel. However, if a plaintiff is a private individual, the status of truth as a constitutional defense is undetermined. In a case decided in 1974, the Supreme Court held that where a private individual was the object of defamatory statements, there can be no recovery for presumed or punitive damages unless the libelous statement was false (Gertz v. Robert Welch, Inc.). The opinion stated in part: "We hold that so long as they do not impose liability without fault, the States may define for themselves the appropriate standard of liability for a publisher or broadcaster of defamatory falsehood injurious to a private individual."

Gertz was a reputable attorney retained to represent the family of a man shot and killed by a Chicago policeman. The State of Illinois prosecuted the policeman for the homicide and ultimately obtained a conviction for murder in the second degree. Robert Welch, Inc. published *American Opinion,* a monthly outlet for the views of the John Birch Society. In 1969, it published an article saying that the state's prosecution was part of the Communist campaign against the police and that Gertz was an architect of the policeman's "frame-up," a "Leninist" and a "Communist fronter."

The article contained serious inaccuracies and an implication that Gertz had a criminal record was false. The managing editor of *American Opinion* made no effort to verify or substantiate the charges against Gertz. The principal issue in the case was whether *American Opinion* or any other magazine publishing defamatory falsehoods about a private individual may claim a constitutional privilege against liability for the injury.

In Gertz v. Robert Welch, Inc., the Supreme Court laid down broad ground rules of general application to private individuals who have been defamed. These ground rules recognized that public officials and public figures usually enjoyed greater access to the channels of effective communication and hence a more realistic opportunity to counteract false statements than private individuals enjoy. The latter are therefore more vulnerable to injury and the interest of the state in protecting them is correspondingly greater. Moreover, an individual who decides to seek public office must accept certain necessary consequences of that involvement in public affairs. He runs the risk of closer public scrutiny than might otherwise be the case. A private individual has not accepted public office or assumed an influential role in ordering society. Moreover, he has relinquished no part of his interest in the protection of his good name, and consequently, he has a more compelling call on the courts for redress of injury inflicted by defamatory falsehoods.

Having said all this, the Supreme Court held that the standard of New York Times Co. v. Sullivan (actual malice) was not applicable, and remanded the case for a new trial on the basis of its new ground rules. In a separate concurring opinion, Justice Blackmun noted that Rosenbloom v. Metromedia, Inc. extending the New York Times standard to an event of public or general interest was logical and inevitable.

In the Metromedia Inc. case, defendant broadcaster made allegedly defamatory comments about a distributor selling obscene material. Rosenbloom, a distributor of nudist magazines, was arrested for selling allegedly obscene material while making a delivery to a retail dealer. He sought and obtained an injunction prohibiting police interference with his business. On appeal, the U.S. Court of Appeals reversed, and the Supreme Court affirmed the judgment.

Its rationale was not at all clear, since five different opinions were written, none of which got more than three votes. In all of them, it seems clear that reconciling the law of defamation with the First Amendment was a question the Court wanted to decide to avoid future review of libel on a case-by-case basis. In an earlier case, New York Times Co. v. Sullivan, the Court had held that "all discussion and communication involving matters of public or general concern [in this case, a political advertisement endorsing civil rights demonstrations by black students in Alabama], warrant the protection from liability for defamation. It said:

> The consitutional guaranties require, we think, a federal rule that prohibits a public official from recovering damages for a defamatory falsehood related to his official conduct unless he proves that the statement was made with "actual malice" — that is, with knowledge that it was false or with reckless disregard of whether it was false or not.

In Gertz, the Supreme Court was able to resolve a question which had troubled it in the wake of the Sullivan standard. Curtis Publishing Co. v. Butts and Associated Press v. Walker, both decided in 1967, extended the Sullivan standard to "public figures" as distinguished from "public officials." In Rosenbloom, the Supreme Court extended the Sullivan standard to private persons "if the defamatory statements concerned matters of general or public interest." In his opinion for the plurality, Justice Brennan said: "If a matter is a subject of public or general interest, it cannot suddenly become less so merely because a private individual is involved, or because in some sense the individual did not 'voluntarily' choose to become involved."

It is clear that, in Gertz, the Supreme Court declined to extend the Sullivan standard to private individuals not involved in a matter of general or public interest. Instead, the plurality opinions showed an effort to balance the needs of publishers and the individual's claim to compensation for wrongful injury. It left fully protected whatever First Amendment values transcended the legitimate state interest in protecting the particular plaintiff who prevailed. The Court concluded that the states should retain substantial latitude in their efforts to enforce a legal remedy injurious to the reputation of a private individual. It held that a new trial was necessary, reversed the judgment for respondent (Robert Welch, Inc.) and remanded the case for further proceedings, saying, "the jury was allowed to impose liability without fault and was permitted to presume damages without proof of injury."

In his concurring opinion, Justice Blackmun, noted that "the Court's opinion departs from the rationale of the Rosenbloom plurality, in that the Court now conditions a libel action by a private person upon a showing of negligence as contrasted with a showing of willful or reckless disregard [for the truth],"

Amongst other states which have adopted the rationale in Gertz, California is one. In 1986, the California Supreme Court, per Chief Justice Bird for a unanimous court, held that the average reader of a newspaper column must have reasonably understood an alleged defamatory statement to be one of fact, not opinion (Baker v. Los Angeles Herald Examiner, 42 C3rd 254), citing Gertz with approval.

In her opinion, Chief Justice Bird, unfortunately recalled by the voters of California in 1986, used the following quotation:

"Under the First Amendment there is no such thing as a false idea. However pernicious an opinion may seem, we depend for its correction not on the conscience of judges and juries but on the competition of other ideas."

Accordingly, the Supreme Court seems to have deferred to the states to allow "substantial latitude in their efforts to enforce a legal remedy injurious to the reputation of a private individual." It is within this context that both publishers and authors must decide what is permissible under the First Amendment. Both must carefully distinguish fact from opinion. Whether an allegedly defamatory statement was one of fact or opinion is a question of law to be decided by a court.

For various reasons, California has developed a "totality of circumstances" test to determine whether an allegedly defamatory statement is one of fact or opinion.

"First," the Supreme Court of California said in Baker, "the language of the statement is examined. For words to be defamatory, they must be understood in a defamatory sense. Where the language of the statement is 'cautiously phrased in terms of apparency,' the statement is less likely to be reasonably understood as a statement of fact rather than opinion. Next, the context in which the statement was made must be considered. Since "a word is not a crystal, transparent and unchanged, but is the skin of a living thought and may vary greatly in color and content according to the circumstances and the time in which it is used, the facts surrounding the publication must also be carefully considered."

In cases involving the Copyright Revision Act of 1976 as amended in 1980, the same distinction between an idea and its expression has been carefully preserved. Section 102(b) provides that: "In no case does copyright protection for an original work of authorship extend to any idea, . . . . concept, principle, or discovery, regardless of the form in which it is described, explained, illustrated, or embodied in such work." Section 107, however, carves out an exception, "the fair use of a copyrighted work . . . . for purposes such as criticism, comment, news reporting . . . . or research." Factors to be considered in a "fair use" case include "the purpose and character of the use, including whether such use is of a commercial nature or is for nonprofit educational purposes" and "the amount and substantiality of the portion used in relation to the copyrighted work as a whole; and the effect of the use upon the potential market for or value of the copyrighted work."

It is within this context that the Supreme Court of the United States decided Harper & Row, Publishers, Inc. v. Nation Enterprises in 1985. In a 6-3 decision, it held that *The Nation Magazine's* unauthorized publication of quotations from former President Ford's unpublished memoirs was an infringement of Harper & Row's copyright. President Ford, in 1977, contracted with Harper & Row to publish his as yet unwritten memoirs including his account of the Watergate crisis and his pardon of former President Nixon and the Watergate crisis. Harper & Row licensed Time, Inc. to publish 7,500 words from this account in advance of publication of the book (first serial rights). Shortly before release of the article in *Time Magazine,* an unauthorized source provided the *Nation Magazine* with the unpublished Ford manuscript. Working from this, an editor of The Nation produced a 2,250 word article, at least 300 or 400 words of which consisted of verbatim quotes of copyrighted material taken from the manuscript.

The Supreme Court held this was not a permissible "fair use" of copyrighted material. In her opinion, Justice O'Connor stated:

> In using generous verbatim excerpts of Mr. Ford's unpublished manuscript to lend authenticity to its account of the forthcoming memoirs, *The Nation* effectively arrogated to itself the right of first publication, an important marketable subsidiary right . . . . we find that the use . . . . even stripped to the verbatim quotes conceded by The Nation to be copyrighted expression, was not a fair use within the meaning of the Copyright Act.

In the dissenting opinion by Justice Brennan, in which Justices White and Marshall joined, he took sharp issue with the majority's narrow construction of "fair use." The quotation of 300 words from an unpublished 200,000 word manuscript infringed the copyright "even though the quotations related to a historical event of undoubted significance — the resignation of President Nixon."

Essentially, the dissent relied on the fact that the quotations appearing in *The Nation* represented information — concepts, ideas or facts — which had value as news of historical significance. Moreover, it did not believe Congress intended to give publishers an unlimited monopoly of ideas as distinguished from expression of those ideas. Copyright protection should not preclude others from using the ideas or information revealed by an author's work. Protection should be controlled by the literary form in which that author expressed intellectual concepts. Were an author allowed to prevent others from using concepts, ideas or facts appearing in his work, the creative process–"the promotion of science and the useful arts"– would probably wither, and scholars would be forced into unproductive replication of the research of their predecessors. It, the dissenting opinion, is clearly an argument in favor of history and what it might reveal to students. Without such knowledge, they would find, to paraphrase Allan Bloom, that their minds were closed even further than ever.

In another area, judicial regulation of obscenity, courts as recently as 30 years ago found books obscene on grounds that seem utterly incomprehensible in the 1980s. In Roth, the Supreme court held that "obscenity [was] not within the area of constitutionally protected speech or press." The trial judge had instructed the jury that "the words 'obscene, lewd, and lascivious' . . . . signify that form of immorality which has relation to sexual impurity and has a tendency to excite lustful *thoughts*."Ever since Roth v. United States, the Supreme Court has had a problem in dealing with a definition of obscenity. In his opinion for a 7-2 majority, Justice Brennan noted that "the dispositive question is whether obscenity is utterance within the area of protected speech and press." Citing a long line of cases, he said the Court had assumed that obscenity was not protected by the First Amendment, but that the question had not previously been squarely presented. An early standard of obscenity was: "whether, to the average person, applying contemporary community standards, the dominant theme of the material taken as a whole appeals to a prurient interest." In United States v. One Book Called 'Ulysses,' this standard was applied to the book written by James Joyce. He sought "to make a serious experiment in a new, if not wholly novel literary genre," according to the opinion of the district court admitting this book to the United States.

Post-Roth v. United States cases continue to struggle with the standard to be applied. In Memoirs v. Massachusetts (1966), the plurality opinion established a three-part test, one of which required a court to find that the material "was utterly without redeeming social value." In Miller v. California (1973), the Supreme Court noted that the trier of fact had to determine "whether the work taken as a whole, lacks serious literary, artistic, political, or scientific value."

In 1977, the Supreme Court (Smith v. United States) citing Miller, stated the three part test to be: "(a) whether the 'average person applying contemporary community standards,' would find that the work, taken as a whole, appeals to the prurient interest; (b) whether the work depicts or describes, in a patently offensively offensive way, sexual conduct specifically defined by the applicable state law; and (c) whether the work, taken as a whole, lacks serious literary, artistic, political, or scientific value."

In 1987, the Supreme Court was still struggling with a related question. Do instructions to a jury—the trier of facts—on the application of contemporary community standards so confuse the jury that they make a constitutionally impermissible finding? Thus, in Pope v. Illinois, the Supreme Court, per Justice White, plunged even further into a legal thicket. He said that, " . . . . the first and second prongs of the Miller test—appeal to a prurient interest and patent offensiveness—are issues of fact for the jury to determine applying contemporary community standards."

But, Justice White then added: " . . . . unlike prurient appeal and patent offensiveness, 'literary, artistic, political or scientific value' . . . . [was] not discussed in Miller in terms of contemporary community standards." Instead, he said: "The proper inquiry is not whether an ordinary number of any given community would find serious literary, artistic, political, or scientific value in allegedly obscene material, but whether a reasonable person would find such value in the material, taken as a whole. The instruction at issue in this case was therefore unconstitutional."

Taken as a whole, the Miller standard may probably not be applied in any reasonable way by 12 reasonable people. It seems clear that censorship is not the appropriate response to the problem of obscenity or pornography. People who read or watch television must be educated to become critical consumers of imagery so they can learn to see through the myths of female submissiveness and degradation which pornography portrays. *The Final Report of the Attorney General's Commission on Pornography* (Rutledge Hill Press), concluded, for example, there is a causal link between the use of pornography and the commission of sex crimes. The Meese Commission was sponsored by a conservative Republican administration, and its agenda was set by the radical Christian right: "Those whose traditional values are perceived as most threatened by the wholesale dissemination of pornography."

In a case decided in 1986, the American Booksellers Association came down on the side of its members in a case, American Booksellers Association, Inc. v. Webb. There plaintiffs challenged a Georgia statute making it a criminal offense to display, in a place accessible to minors, any material deemed "harmful to minors." As the district court noted: "This variable standard [harmful to minors but protected speech with respect to adults] is not novel. Indeed, nearly twenty years ago, the United States Supreme Court held that a state may, without violating the First Amendment, employ a variable standard of obscenity to bar the sale of sexually explicit materials to minors." Plaintiffs, however, challenged the display provisions of the Georgia statute, since there was undisputed evidence in the trial record that "in-store display of books is the cornerstone of the industry's marketing practices." The district court also accepted the opinion of a Vice-President and General Counsel of Bantam Books, Inc. She said that "the predominant amount of all of the adult reading material, fiction and nonfiction, could arguably be encompassed within the terms of the Georgia Act." The court found the display provision of the Georgia Act unconstitutional, because it unduly hampered an adult's access to protected material. Final disposition of this case appears to have been deferred pending the outcome in American Booksellers Association v. Virginia. In that case, the U.S. Supreme Court certified two questions to the Supreme Court of Virginia, and, at this writing, that court had not given its answers to the questions.

The court also found that most books are purchased by bookstores based on a synopsis provided by a publisher's catalog and that booksellers would be unable to predict the percentage of new inventory which would be displayed. "There is," said the court, "no question that a state government has an interest in shielding minors from some sexually explicit materials which are not considered obscene as to adults." However, in Upper Midwest Booksellers v. City of Minneapolis (1985), a U.S. Court of Appeals held that a local ordinance requiring an opaque (not transparent) wrapping was constitutionally permissible to shield minors from sexually explicit books. The dissenting opinion, noting that the Minneapolis ordinance was "paternalistic censorship by government in a free society," said the ordinance was unconstitutional on its face as regulating the manner in which certain books were displayed.

It is difficult, if not impossible for adults to see books by authors such as Sidney Sheldon, Judith Krantz and Harold Robbins and many more, if they are shrink-wrapped by either publishers or bookstores to insulate themselves from possible penalties. Before ordering proscribed books for sale, buyers for bookstores sush as Waldenbooks (1,200 retail outlets), Barnes & Noble, Crown Books and Doubleday Bookstores would have to read most of them for content (about 50% to 60% of inventory would be covered). The proprietors of approximately 4,500 independent bookstores in all 50 states would have to do likewise. All those ordering books would also have to make an independent judgment, taking each book "as a whole" that they contained material obscene enough as to minors to be regulated or displayed within the definition of "obscene" found in Miller v. California.

Noting that display was significantly closer to pure speech than the activities at issue in New York v. Ferber (child pornography), the district court left in place a preliminary injunction enjoining enforcement of the Georgia statute, and it held that the statute was unconstitutional "because it unduly hampered an adult's access to protected expression (free speech)." The judgment enjoining enforcement was stayed pending appeal. Along with an appeal from the Alabama district court's opinion ("secular humanism" is a religion), the U.S. Supreme Court is very likely to hear and determine both cases in its next term. Both involve the First Amendment as it applies to trade books (sexually explicit content of fiction and nonfiction) and omission of textbook content (religion).

Publishers avoid the discussion of religion in textbooks as being too controversial. However, these same publishers and the electronic media have come down on the side of the First Amendment, namely, that censorship is far more dangerous than any idea or image could ever be. Publishers, however, need to be concerned, because in most agreements with authors, writers warrant and represent that there is nothing obscene or defamatory in the books they submit and get published.

On January 13, 1988, the Supreme Court of the United States struck out at high school publishers in Hazelwood School District v. Kuhlmeier. It allowed a high school principal to delete from a school-sponsored newspaper some articles he considered objectionable against a claim by the newspaper's "publishers" that their First Amendment rights were abridged. In a 5-3 decision, Justices Brennan, Marshall and Blackmun dissenting, Justice White, writing for the Court, said:

> We have nonetheless recognized that the First Amendment rights of students in the public schools "are not automatically coextensive with the rights of adults in other settings," and must be "applied in light of the special characteristics of the school environment." A school need not tolerate student speech that is inconsistent with its "basic educational mission. . . . even though the government could not censor similar speech outside the school."

This logic flies in the face of policy guidelines adopted by the Hazelwood School Board itself. Board Policy 348.51, for example, stated in part that "school- sponsored student publications will not restrict free expression or diverse viewpoints within the rules of responsible journalism." The Court's opinion conceded that students were permitted to exercise some authority over the contents of *Spectrum,* the school newspaper. This, the Court held, did not convert a curricular newspaper into a public forum, even though the Journalism II class presumably taught student "responsible journalism." Skills learned in the classroom were intended to be used in publishing a newspaper outside that classroom. However, said the Court, "A decision to teach leadership skills in the context of a classroom activity hardly implies a decision to relinquish control over that activity." If not, just where will these "leadership skills" be used in a practical way? One paragraph seems to sum up what the Court has held. "Instead, we hold that educators do not offend the First Amendment by exercising editorial control over the style and content of student speech in school-sponsored expressive activities so long as their actions are reasonably related to legitimate pedagogical concerns." This clearly means the "educational function" of a school which seems limited to a classroom environment. Justice Brennan, with whom Justices Marshall and Blackmun joined in dissent, stated:

> This case arose when the Hazelwood East administration breached its own promise (in Board Policy 348.51), dashing its students' expectations. The school principal, without any prior consultation or explanation, excised six—comprising two full pages–of the May 13, 1983, issue of *Spectrum.* He did so not because any of the articles would "materially and substantially interfere with the requirements of appropriate discipline," but simply because he considered two of the six articles "inappropriate, personal, sensitive and unsuitable" for student consumption.
>
> In my view the principal broke more than just a promise. He violated the First Amendment's prohibition against censorship of any student expression that neither disrupts classwork nor invades the rights of others, and against any censorship that is not narrowly tailored to serve its purpose.

Some civics lesson in a public high school! The presence or absence of religion in the public schools is another source of controversy. The fundamentalists seem determined to force their own views on students, but in a way somewhat different from that used by the school principal in the Hazelwood School District case, but still representing an erosion of First Amendment rights under the Establishment Clause of the First Amendment.

The actual contents of public school textbooks has rarely, if ever been challenged on the basis of what they have omitted as a violation of the First Amendment's Establishment Clause. However, in 1968, the Supreme Court dealt with a state statute proscribing the teaching of evolution in textbooks. In Epperson v. Arkansas, a 1928 state statute adopted by a voter initiative made it an offense to use a textbook teaching evolution (Darwinism) As Justice Fortas said, writing an opinion for himself and six other members of the Court, "The statute was a product of the upsurge of 'fundamentalist' religious fervor of the twenties."

Until the 1965-66 academic year in a Little Rock high school used a biology textbook which did not even mention the Darwinian theory. Then, the school administration, upon recommendation of biology teachers, adopted and prescribed a textbook which did deal with Darwinian theory. A biology teacher (Epperson) asked for declaratory relief and an injunction enjoining her dismissal for using this textbook, an offense under the state statute. The Chancery Court found for plaintiff Epperson but was reversed by the Arkansas Supreme Court. In a per curiam opinion, it said only that the statute was "a valid execise of the state's power to specify the curriculum in its public schools. The court expresses no opinion on the question whether the Act prohibits any explanation of the theory of evolution or merely prohibits teaching that the theory is true; the answer not being necessary to decision in the case, and the issue not being raised."

On appeal to the U.S. Supreme Court, the lower court's opinion was reversed. Justice Fortas concluded that: "Plainly, the law is contrary to the mandate of the First, and in violation of the Fourteenth Amendment to the Constitution." By contemporary standards, going beyond the issues presented in the case, this opinion would be treated as a form of judicial activism now condemned by the fundamentalist religious right. Justice Fortas also noted that the voters of Arkansas had sought to prevent its teachers from discussing the theory of evolution because it was contrary to the belief of some that Bible's Book of Genesis must be the exclusive source of doctrine as to the origin of man.

Since 1968 and the Supreme Court's opinion in Epperson, the approximately 14 publishers whose textbooks were enjoined from being used in Alabama's public schools have been on notice as to textbook content. They include Macmillan Publishing Company, Charles E. Merrill Publishing Company, Houghton Mifflin Company and Holt Rinehart & Winston. In December, 1986 the latter was acquired by Harcourt Brace Jovanovich, one of whose textbooks was also enjoined by the U.S. District Court in Smith v. Board of School Commissioners. Notwithstanding their notice that the states had the constitutional power to control curriculum and textbook content within First Amendment parameters, these publishers appear to have continued to sell textbooks virtually free of more than vague references to religion and the role it played in American history. School boards have also played a part in producing the result appearing in Smith v. Board of School Commissioners. At the trial, the Board's witnesses contended there was a clear secular purpose on the part of the state insofar as the curriculum was concerned. The reason seems clear. In cases arising under the Establishment Clause of the First Amendment, the Supreme Court has tried to be consistent in at least one respect. In a case decided in 1973 (Committee for Public Education v. Nyquist), it cited Epperson with approval. The opinion stated in part: "For the now well-defined three-part test that has emerged from our decisions is a product derived from the full sweep of the Establishment Clause cases. Taken together, these decisions dictate that to pass muster under the Establishment Clause the law in question, first, reflects a clearly secular legislative purpose, e.g., Epperson v. Arkansas . . . . second, must have a primary effect that neither advances nor inhibits religion, e.g., McGowan v. Maryland, and, third, must avoid excessive entanglement with religion, e.g., Walz v. Tax Commission. . . . "School boards and teachers have an abiding interest in the education of students, but that interest seems to be expressed via textbook selection in the least obtrusive (controversial) manner to avoid litigation as to textbook content. Publishers of such textbooks seem to have the same perspective.

The result of this overt coincidence has been least common denominator education for altogether too many students. Very few textbook publishers seem to be willing to offer books that state unequivocally that religion has played a role in all history, including that of the United States. Smith v. Board of School Commissioners may not be the last case challenging textbook content. For the moment, it's only the most outrageous one. The misunderstood rationale of the Supreme Court's "benevolent neutrality" in cases involving the Establishment Clause of the First Amendment today may be the literary decline of tomorrow. If this is what happens, all books, textbooks, fiction and nonfiction, may be the victims of this decline. Once again, the competing interests of money (revenue from the sale of textbooks) and the judicial requirement that a secular legislative interest be served via the selection process of textbooks have combined to produce a conflict between these two interests. Quality in textbooks is no less or more important than quality in what are known as trade books, fiction and nonfiction, by authors who want to contribute to "public enlightenment" and publishers who share their interest in doing so.

# Chapter 7
## What Got Published--Twice!

Parody. A writing in which the language or style of an author or work is closely imitated for comic effect or ridicule often with certain peculiarities greatly heightened or exaggerated.

Satire. A usually topical literary composition holding up human or individual vices, folly, abuses , or shortcomings to censure by means of ridicule, derision, burlesque, irony, or other method sometimes with an intent to bring about improvement.

Fiction. The act of creating something imaginary: a convenient assumption that overlooks known facts in order to achieve an immediate goal.

To place these definitions in a more or less contemporary perspective, it seems that one must decide what is not libelous as being constitutionally protected opinion. In 1968, Los Angeles Mayor, Sam Yorty, publicly expressed interest in being appointed Secretary of Defense by President-elect Richard Nixon. The *Los Angeles Times* was aware of this and published on its editorial page a cartoon and caption. The cartoon showed Mayor Yorty seated at his desk and talking on the telephone. Four white-coated orderlies with doleful expressions were standing by the desk, with one of them holding a straight-jacket behind his back while another was beckoning the Mayor to come with them. The caption read, "I've got to go now . . . . I've been appointed Secretary of Defense and the Secret Service men are here!"

Mayor Yorty alleged, in his complaint for libel, that the defendant newspaper, in publishing the cartoon and caption, intended to insinuate to its readers that he was unfit to serve as Secretary of Defense. In believing he was so qualified, he, Yorty, was shown as insane. The California trial court ruled that the cartoon was not libelous. The Court of Appeal agreed with the trial court, saying that " . . . . even the most careless reader must have perceived that the cartoon was no more than rhetorical hyperbole, a vigorous expression of opinion by those who considered Mayor Yorty's aspiration for high national office preposterous." The Court of Appeal also noted that, had the *Los Angeles Times* published a false report that he was in fact insane, the publication would unquestionably have been found libelous. It cited Goldwater v. Ginzburg which had found a false report that Senator Goldwater was "mentally unbalanced," a "dangerous lunatic" and "a compensated schizophrenic" to be libelous. That case was decided in 1969, and the U.S. Supreme Court declined to hear an appeal by the publisher. In *A History of American Graphic Humor,* compiled by William Murrell, there is a cartoon by William Charles, a widely acclaimed American political cartoonist. Entitled "A Fallen Pillar of the Kirk," it showed a bare-bosomed young woman bouncing on a clergyman's knee with a caption saying "Oh, Lord, what good things dost thou provide for us men!" The cartoon was published in Scotland in 1806, and Charles found it expedient to leave, probably for his own safety. *Dunnesbury,* a well known comic strip by Gary Trudeau, has more recently satirized the Reverend Pat Robertson's direct line to divine inspiration.

The threat that people will no longer be allowed to enjoy *"The Ungentlemanly Art, a History of American Political Cartoons,"* and books which satirize public figures is real. However, it is now being masked behind the idea that the individual public figure may have been somehow suffered "emotional distress" intentionally inflicted by a publisher. And those who enjoy either parody, satire or both may be denied these simple pleasures if the Reverend Jerry Falwell and the Moral Majority have anything to say about it, even though the publication involved was clearly labelled fiction and was "not to be taken seriously." They have already come out ahead in two appellate courts. On February 24, 1988, the Supreme Court of the United States reversed the Court of Appeals, noting that:

> This case presents us with a novel question involving First
> Amendment limitations upon a state's authority to protect

its citizens from the intentional infliction of emotional distress. We must decide whether a public figure may recover damages for emotional harm caused by the publication of an ad parody offensive to him, and doubtless gross and repugnant in the eyes of most. Respondent would have us find that a state's interest in protecting public figures from emotional distress is sufficient to deny First Amendment protection to speech that is patently offensive and is intended to inflict emotional injury, even when that speech could not reasonably have been interpreted as stating actual facts about the public figure involved. This we decline to do.

The opinion was written by Chief Justice Rehnquist and joined by all Justices, except for Justice White who wrote a separate concurring opinion. Justice Kennedy did not take part in the case. The rationale for this important decision appears as follows:

> At the heart of the First Amendment is the recognition of the fundamental importance of the free flow of ideas and opinions on matters of public interest and concern. "The freedom to speak one's mind is not only an aspect of individual liberty–and thus a good unto itself–but is also is essential to the common quest for truth and the vitality of society." We have therefore been particularly vigilant to ensure that individual expressions of ideas remain free from governmentally imposed sanctions . . . .
>
> The sort of robust political debate encouraged by the First Amendment is bound to produce speech that is critical of those who hold public office or those public figures who are "intimately involved in the resolution of important public questions or, by reason of their fame, shape events in areas of concern to society at large" . . . . Such criticism inevitably, will not always be reasoned or moderate; public figures as well as public officials will be subject to "vehement, caustic and sometimes unpleasantly sharp attacks."

The importance of the case to publishers and authors cannot be overstated. Prior to oral argument the Supreme Court had granted five motions for leave to file briefs *amicus curiae* (friend of the court) to include Reporters Committee for Freedom of the Press, Richmond Newspapers, Inc., the Authors League of America, the American Editorial Cartoonists and Volunteer Lawyers for the Arts. Entirely aside from the actual legal issues involved-they are complex-what books get published in the future is at stake.

The case arose out of an advertisement parody or satire which appeared in *Hustler Magazine* in November 1983, and again in March 1984. The subject of the ad was the Reverend Jerry Falwell, and it attempts to satirize an advertising campaign for Campari, a bittersweet aperitif. In the real Campari advertising campaign, celebrities talk about their "first time," meaning the first time they had enjoyed drinking this aperitif. In the *Hustler* ad parody, however, the "celebrity" was the Reverend Jerry Falwell who, when "interviewed," described an incestuous rendezvous with his mother in an outhouse in Virginia. His mother was portrayed as a drunken and immoral woman, and Falwell himself appeared as a hypocrite and habitual drunkard. At the bottom of the page was a disclaimer which stated "Ad parody-not to be taken seriously." The ad was listed in the table of contents as "Fiction; Ad and Personality Parody."

Soon after publication of the ad in *Hustler,* Falwell filed suit in the U.S. District Court for the Western District of Virginia. He alleged three theories of liability: libel, invasion of privacy and intentional infliction of emotional distress. At the close of evidence, the District Court dismissed the claim for invasion of privacy, and the jury found for defendant *Hustler* on the libel theory on the grounds that no reasonable man would believe that the parody was describing actual facts about plaintiff Falwell. On the claim for intentional infliction of emotional distress, the jury found for plaintiff Falwell, awarding him $100,000 in actual damages, $50,000 in punitive damages against Larry Flynt, *Hustler's* publisher, and $50,000 in punitive damages against *Hustler Magazine.*

Defendants *Hustler Magazine* and Flynt filed an appeal, and Falwell appealed from the judgment entered on the claim of libel. Before trial in Virginia, on November 15, 1983, Moral

Majority, Inc., a conservative political lobbying organization, sent out two mailings signed by the Reverend Jerry Falwell. One of them went to 26,900 "major donors" to Moral Majority, Inc. This mailing requested money to help finance his suit against *Hustler Magazine*. On November 18, 1983, Old Time Gospel Hour, a corporate sponsor of religious television and radio broadcasts, mailed letters soliciting money to 750,000 supporters of its programs. The mailing included a copy of the ad parody, and it was signed by Falwell. In a very short time major donors sent in about $45,000 to Moral Majority, Inc. and the Old Time Gospel Hour received about $672,000 as a result of its mailing. Finally, in December, 1983, Falwell displayed the ad parody during two nationwide television broadcasts of his weekly sermon on the Old Time Gospel Hour. The money raised as a result was not in the trial record.

On August 4, 1984, Hustler Magazine sued Falwell and Old Time Gospel Hour for infringement of its copyrights. Defendants interposed a defense of "fair use" found in Section 107 of the Copyright Act of 1976. Relying in part on the decision of the U.S. Supreme Court in Harper & Row Publishers, Inc. v. Nation Enterprises, the U.S. Court of Appeals for the Ninth Circuit held that Falwell's use of the "Ad Parody-Not to be Taken Seriously" was a "fair use" as that phrase appears in the Copyright Act of 1976.

Neither the fact of the mailings nor Falwell's appearance on television to raise money for his defense were part of the record in the trial in Virginia. If either had been called to the attention of the jury, it could arguably have reached a different result on the claim of intentional infliction of emotional distress. Viewers of television are not necessarily limited to members of Moral Majority, Inc., nor can the Old Time Gospel Hour's television program be said to reach only those people considering themselves as agreeing with all or part of the objectives of this conservative lobbying group. Accordingly, Falwell's voluntary exposure of himself as a target of satire undermines his motive in republishing the Ad Parody at all, even to raise money for his defense.

In his dissenting opinion in Hustler Magazine, Inc. v. Moral Majority, Inc., Judge Poole stated: "Quite clearly, the only reason for copying the entire parody would be to increase the chances that the parody would arouse such moral indignation that the members would be more likely to send in financial contributions to help Falwell. . . . " Judge Poole went on to say that "the legal conclusions by the majority that 'the public interest in allowing an individual to defend himself against. . . . derogatory personal attacks serves to rebut the presumption of unfairness.' " He found this to be a sweeping generalization finding no support in the law or the purposes underlying the "fair use" defense.

A third opinion serves to further illustrate the complexities of this case. When a person appeals and the judgment of the trial court is affirmed, he may apply for a rehearing *en banc*. If the application is granted, all judges of the Fourth Circuit would hear and reconsider the opinion affirming the judgment, not just a three judge panel. In the appeal from the jury verdict in Virginia, Hustler Magazine, Inc. petitioned for a rehearing *en banc*. With four judges out of nine voting to rehear the case. Since a majority voted against a rehearing, it was denied in an opinion dated November 4, 1986.

However offensive or even repulsive speech may be—and the Ad Parody was speech protected by the First Amendment—it enjoys immunity provided it does not violate those standards found in New York Times v. Sullivan. As the jury found by necessary implication, the Ad Parody did not violate those standards, since it found for *Hustler Magazine* on the claim for damages under a theory of libel. In its opinion of February 24th, the Supreme Court, in referring to the New York Times standard, said that " . . . . this does not mean that a literal application of the actual malice rule is appropriate in the context of an emotional distress claim . . . . "

The Court of Appeals, per Judge Poole, said in dissent, that its "recognition of the tort of emotional distress now threatens to disrupt our historic reliance" on a marketplace where a multitude of voices may be heard. The market cannot effectively regulate all forms of speech. So, New York Times v. Sullivan recognized libelous statements made with actual malice as a permissible exception to the rule of the marketplace. There is, of course, no constitutional value in false statements of fact. If individuals could freely publish knowing or reckless falsehoods injurious to reputations, the market would be forced to view all factual statements with growing suspicion, a suspicion that would seriously impede the give and take of political discourse.

The Reverend Jerry Falwell is at the forefront of political debates; he enjoys the most intimate access to the highest circles of power; he possesses a forum for presenting his views on television and establishing his character; he has sought and relished the give and take of political combat. To recover for intentional infliction of emotional distress, he need show only the defendant's intention to publish something he should have known would cause emotional distress; conduct that offended the generally accepted standards of decency and morality; severe emotional distress; and a causal connection between the act of publication and the emotional distress.

It is clear, however, that one cannot subject a parody of a political figure such as Jerry Falwell to a cause of action for emotional distress. Political satire and parody *aim* to distress. This literary genre of commentary depends on distortion and discomfiture for its effect. A writer's nightmare may be that the intended victim of all his insult and ridicule *fails* to cause emotional distress, but instead finds the whole thing merely crude, not worthy of attention or uses the media to reply. While the *Hustler's* coarse Ad Parody is unworthy of this or any tradition, the precedent created by the cause of action against this defendant could one day have come to stifle the finer forms of this genre.

Satire is particularly relevant to political figures because, amongst other things, it unmasks hypocrisy. In the case of the Reverend Jerry Falwell, the Ad Parody was no more than a coarse attempt to expose him to ridicule for selling salvation through his television ministry, a form of hypocrisy which earned millions and has yet to show it saved man from the power and effects of sin.

In Virginia, where the trial occurred, the essential elements to be proved in an action for intentional infliction of emotional distress are defined in terms of the wrongdoer's conduct. It must (1) be intentional or reckless; (2) offend generally accepted standards of decency or morality; (3) be causally connected with the plaintiff's emotional distress, and (4) have caused emotional distress that was severe. In construing these requirements, the majority opinion of the Court of Appeals stated: "An action for intentional infliction of emotional distress concerns itself with intentional or reckless conduct which is outrageous and proximately causes severe emotional distress, not with statements per se."

It's all right, for example, for an alleged wrongdoer to have an opinion that a public figure is no better than a cynical television minster who raises millions by selling salvation. However, the moment he publishes his opinion as an Ad Parody, his act loses First Amendment protection, even though no one could possibly believe the contents of the offending Ad Parody were true. On the contrary, the jury found that a reader could not reasonably believe the parody was describing actual facts about the Reverend Jerry Falwell. Just as Don Quixote was a parody of the exaggerated romances of chilvalry, Flynt's ad in *Hustler Magazine* was a parody of the exaggerated benefits of selling salvation directed at Falwell, one of its public salesmen. The ability to put ridicule into the mouth of the person being ridiculed is the most deadly arrow in the quiver of satire.

# Chapter 8
## The Publishers

For the last three years, Gulf & Western, Inc. has been growing by internal expansion. In addition to Simon & Schuster, Inc., acquired a number of years ago, it made the following acquisitions: Prentice-Hall, Inc. for $710 million (1984); Ginn & Company for about $110 million (1985); and Silver Burdett Company for about $110 million (1986). Prentice-Hall is a publisher of college textbooks and business and professional materials. Ginn & Company is an elementary and high school textbook publisher, and Silver Burdett publishes textbooks for elementary schools. Gulf & Western's Publishing and Information Services (Simon & Schuster) is organized into six operating units: School, Higher Education, Professional Information, Trade, Reference and International,

The Trade unit publishes and distributes hardcover, mass market paperbacks and trade paperback books. It sells its hardcover (trade) books principally under the Simon & Schuster, Linden, Summit and Poseidon imprints. Its trade paperbacks are published under the Fireside and Touchstone imprints,and its mass market paperbacks are sold under the imprints of Pocket Books, Wallaby, Archway Paperbacks and Washington Square Press. Under the Wanderer imprint, it sells books for young adults and juveniles. Simon & Schuster acts as a distributor for imprints of other publishers and has exclusive distribution rights in the United States for the Harlequin and Silhouette romance novels. It also produces and sells mass market audio-cassette titles.

Gulf & Western's International unit has publishing operations in Canada, the United Kingdom, Australia, Brazil, Mexico, Singapore and India. For its fiscal year ending on October 31,

1986, revenue from Publishing and Information Services was $949 million, almost triple the figure for 1984.

School textbook operations made the largest contribution to the 1986 increase, benefiting from the acquisition of the Silver Burdett Company. Revenues from the higher education operations increased primarily from sales of college books and technical publications, while the professional information group benefited from acquired product lines and other improvements. Higher sales in Canada and the United Kingdom increased the revenues of the International unit of Simon & Schuster.

Operating income from Gulf & Western's Entertainment unit, which, amongst other things, includes Paramount Pictures Corporation, increased in 1986. The substantial improvement in revenues from theatrical releases was primarily attributable to the blockbuster performance of *Top Gun, Ferris Bueller's Day Off* and *Crocodile Dundee.* During 1987, the Entertainment unit's operations are expected to receive substantial revenues from *The Untouchables* and *Beverly Hills Cop II.*

By any relevant standard, Gulf & Western's Publishing and Information unit (Simon & Schuster) is a publishing giant. Gulf & Western's Consolidated Balance Sheet for the fiscal year ending October 31, 1986 showed cash and other Assets of $9.269 billion. Founded in 1958, the company has become a broadly diversified, multi-industry enterprise in less than 30 years. Because it can pay authors five and six-figure advances, it attracts the most prominent and popular writers which gives, or tends to give Simon & Schuster and its authors a brand identity—on a novel, biography or reference book—frequently with extended sales potential. Its new computer system allows Simon & Schuster to fill an order for books in Canada or the United States within three days through one of its six distribution centers.

The School and Higher Education unit, also operated by Simon & Schuster, publishes high school and elementary textbooks and related materials as well as audio-visual products and vocational and technical materials. Some of imprints include Prentice-Hall, Silver Burdett & Company, Allyn & Bacon, Globe, Modern Curriculum Press, Coronet/ MTI and

Cambridge. Elementary and high school textbooks, local school districts in 22 states can be purchased *only* from lists reflecting state approval of certain textbooks (Alabama is one of them). A textbook that makes a states's approved list may be sold in that state for the duration of the adoption cycle, typically five or six years. In California, for example, the country's largest market for textbooks and the largest adoption state, seven of Simon & Schuster's line of textbooks were on the approved state list in five curriculum areas — reading, social studies, language arts, science and music.

In 28 other states, known as "open states," textbooks are sold directly to local public school systems. Simon & Schuster has about 1,700 sales representatives who are assigned to all its different product lines. At colleges and universities, too, the textbooks selected for student use reflect individual institutional preference. A university bookstore can usually sell 100% of such textbooks. One of the buyers for the University Book Store in Madison, Wisconsin said that all he had to know was the textbook selected for a history lecture course and the number of students signed up to take that course from the professor who teaches it and selected the textbook. With this information, he could sell 100% of the books ordered.

Publishing, like entertainment, seem to be "profit centers" for Gulf & Western, Inc. Its Entertainment unit, which includes Paramount Pictures Corporation, sells videocassettes for the home video market featuring its film and television library. Paramount also owns one third of the USA Network, a national advertiser-supported cable television network, in a joint venture with Time, Incorporated and MCA, Inc. Gulf & Western also owns a subsidiary, Madison Square Garden (MSG) in New York City. MSG operates the New York Knicks, a professional basketball team, and the New York Rangers, a National Hockey League team. MSG provides television of its own events for both over-the-air and cable television distribution through the Madison Square Garden Network. This network is linked to 82 basic cable systems in three states and is expected to increase its subscriber total from more than 2 million now to between 3 and

4 million subscribers when all of New York City's five boroughs have been fully wired, probably by 1990.

For the general consumer market, Simon & Schuster publishes 800 to 900 new titles each year, averaging 25 bestselles annually. In this market, the growth of large national book chains such as Waldenbooks, Barnes & Noble and others has helped expand book sales. It's easy to understand why Bertelsmann AG acquired Doubleday Publishing Co., Inc. and why Australia's Rupert Murdoch acquired Harper & Row Publishers, Inc. The United States is the world's biggest market for books in English.

When Simon & Schuster publishes a potential bestseller like Allan Bloom's *The Closing of the American Mind,* its marketing strategy includes aggressive advertising and publicity efforts, participation in the chains' merchandising programs, including discounting in-store displays, cooperative advertising and sales to specialized book clubs or to the Book of the Month Club as a main or alternate selection. Farrar Strauss Giroux is currenty doing the same thing with its bestseller *Presumed Innocent.* About 1,000,000 copies of both will probably be sold to readers. Simon & Schuster's revenues from such consumer sales was $949 million for fiscal 1986, an increase of $150.8 million in 1985.

The ability of Simon & Schuster to move quickly showed up with Allan Bloom's *The Closing of the American Mind* which had a publication date in March, 1987. By mid-June, it was on the bestseller list of *The New York Times, the Washington Post, the Los Angeles Times, The Chicago Tribune* and *The San Francisco Chronicle-Examiner.* No one was more surprised than the author himself who said: "It's a little as though I had made a home movie and ended up winning the Academy Award." His editor, Robert Asahina, said "This may be the the one book right now that speaks to the intelligent general reader we in publishing always talk about." Initially, only 10,000 copies were printed, but, since its early reviews were good, Simon & Schuster has been printing 25,000 copies a week. "It was," said its sales director, "reviews-driven all the way." *The Closing of the American Mind* seems to have gotten its initial momentum in the independent bookstores, probably because the early readers lived in eastern cities, major markets for books and a great many people associate books with New York as the center of the publishing universe. However, by closely tracking sales in the chains and the wholesalers such as Baker & Taylor and Ingrams, Simon & Schuster made a quick decision that this book was headed toward bestseller lists and acted accordingly by spending money on advertising, over $100,000, Now, both the author and his publisher are smiling all the way to the bank. So are bookstores such as Waldenbooks, A Clean Well Lighted Place in San Francisco, The Tattered Cover in Denver all the way to the Francis Scott Key Book Store in Washington, D.C., not to mention all those in between such as The Haunted Bookstore in Tuscon, the Tecolote Book Store in Santa Barbara and Hunter's Book Store in Beverly Hills.

Small presses in the United States simply do not have the resources to advertise their books, and $100,000 is a lot more than any one of them is likely to spend on book production costs in one year by publishing about *five* books. Editorial costs, advances to authors and advertising only in trade journals, along with the costs of distribution, might be budgeted at this amount for about four books by first-time authors. A small press that has invested in computers and telecommunications technology can react to a situation just as quickly as Simon & Schuster did with *The Closing of the American Mind* and another publisher did with the *Tower Commission Report*. The hearings before the joint Senate-House Committee on the arms for hostages sales to Iran and the diversion of funds to finance the *contras* in Nicaragua should provide enough material for dozens of novels and non-fiction for just about any small press. While the publishing giants are competing with each other for the rights to publish Oliver North's story or Admiral Poindexter's recollection, the small press can find good first-time authors to write about this whole sorry episode on the basis of actual experience in Central America. As *SMALL PRESS,* the magazine for independent, in-house desktop publishing noted in its March/ April issue, "Of the more than 700 books published on Central America since 1979, no more than 50 have come from mainstream publishers." Anne Winkler, Director of the Central American Resource Center in

Minneapolis, stated, "It is clear that as long as the large main-stream publishers prefer to publish material that (a) contains the proper dose of Hollywood adventurism, or (b) is written by insulated academics, or (c) mirrors the State Department line, small publishers must continue their work to bring fresh and vital information, historical and current, to the attention of the American public. Much depends on it."

During July of 1987, Americans were watching television and the Iran-Contra hearings bring them new reports of the lies and deceit which have caused President Reagan to lose credibility with both Americans and Europeans not to mention more than a few Arab states. At the National Security Council level, paranoia seems to have become institutionalized and shredding of documents is routine, just to give the President "plausible deniability." Where does the mentality come from that we hear North's secretary say "Sometimes we have to do things above the written law?" People watching these hearings must indeed wonder what's *really* going on? Winkler cites books published by the Ecumenical Program for Interamerican Communication in Action (*The Caribbean: Survival, Struggle, and Sovereignty*) and Bergin & Garvey (*The Nicaraguan Revolution in Health*). She also notes that Southend Press has published *Under the Big Stick,* by Karl Bermann, which provides a comprehensive history of U.S. involvement in Nicaragua since 1848 and that Curbstone Press has published a number of noteworthy volumes of poetry from Central America which, in their own words, "engage the reader in social and political issues" rather than in what might be called purely aesthetic art. In its own way, Mercury House has moved in the direction suggested by publishing books by European writers such as Alain Gerber, Enzo Siciliano and Jurgen Petschull, or about events in Europe, for instance, *Lovers and Fugitives,* by Gabriella Mautner. In 1988, Mercury House will publish *Judgment Day Archives,* a novel by Andrei Moscovit, a Soviet emigré.In fact, Mercury House follows a practice which originated in Europe, editorial grading of manuscripts. An editor evaluates a manuscript submitted and gives it a grade, A, B, C or D. If two or three editors give a submission an A, the publisher reads it. The editors are talented, so a highly-rated book usually gets published. Very little attention, if any, is given to the question whether the book will be "commercial." It's enough if the book is well written, has something to say and illuminates some facet of the human condition with understanding and compassion or humor. At the same time, however, Mercury House commits itself to market that book within a modest budget, and the author understands this budgetary limitation. Joseph Cotten's autobiography, *Vanity Will Get You Somewhere,* was published with this tacit understanding and so will Beulah Roth's *Portraits of Paris,* to be published in the fall of 1988. Her late husband, Sanford Roth, was a world famous photographer for *Time, Life* and other magazines.

Mercury House has a full time Executive Editor and an Administrative Assistant. There are five freelance editors who enjoy the trust and confidence of the publisher. In the near future, the editorial office in Marin County, across the Bay from San Francisco, will be connected to the corporate office in San Francisco by telecommunications software driven by low cost IBM computers and a modem. In this way, drafts of a book to be published by Mercury House may be sent to the corporate office, or vice versa, to the editorial office for comment or corrections. The text is captured by disk and, more often than not, transferred from disk to word processing software, or in the case of a final draft, to typesetting software to produce camera ready copy for the commercial printer. All this must be sent to Crane Duplicating Company in Massachusetts in order to print "Uncorrected Page Proofs" in paperback form. These "Cranes" go to reviewers well in advance of a book's publication date, where it is hoped all of the books will get good reviews. It doesn't always work out that way, since reviewers have minds of their own, fortunately. A freelance production editor handles all the details of getting "Cranes" to reviewers and the final, corrected camera ready copy to R.R. Donnelly & Sons, Inc., the commercial printer. When these books are printed and bound with a four color dustjacket, they are sent to a distributor's warehouse.

However, with all the activity in acquisitions and mergers, distribution has become a very competitive business with more and more small presses springing up just about everywhere. In 1987, almost 52,000 books were published, an estimated 50% of them by small presses. The problem, of course, is acute, since each book is unique. They can be ordered — or not ordered — on the basis of dustjacket design, pressure from sales representatives of distributors or some other completely subjective criteria, even whim. Unless enough books get into the chains or independent bookstores, the publisher will not survive for very long. Mercury House has its own catalog with artwork by the same artists who designed the dustjacket and text written by one of its editors. Most distributors also have their own catalogs as well, with as many as 400 books listed, so Mercury House prints its own and asks sales representatives to work with both catalogs and sends as many of its own to the independent bookstores as well as the chains. Because it's easier and less expensive to telecommunicate artwork (graphics) and copy to bookstores with compatible hardware and software, Mercury House has developed an in-house capability which allows it to do this. Facsimile technology has been around for quite some time, but now facsimile transmission (fax) has become easier and relatively inexpensive, and the basic software costs about $1,000. If a bookstore does not have a Fax machine — currently about $2,000 — Mercury House can send text and graphics to a bookstore's computer where both can be captured to a disk and viewed at leisure on a monochrome monitor or printed out on a dot matrix printer. With the cost of catalogs escalating — currently about $3.50 each for 5,000 copies — it makes much more sense to do all this by telecommunication software and use the money saved to market and advertise Mercury House books. In 1986, Mercury House paid its distributor almost $39,000 for its services on sales of almost $170,000 from books during its first full year of operations. Its sales during 1987 were more than double those in 1986, and 1988 sales are expected to be even better than 1987. Cost control has become almost obsessive, since no small press considers itself a philantrophic enterprise. Harper & Row, recently acquired by

Australia's Rupert Murdoch, is doing the same thing. It plans to cut back on the 35 publishers for whom it serves as a distributor. It is taking a close look at direct costs related to each account — its contribution to overhead, space utility, monthly inventory, indirect costs in collection of accounts receivable and accounting costs. Mercury House doesn't dislike paying a distributor for getting its books into bookstores, but it has preliminarily decided it might be less expensive to give traditional distributing a shot on the arm with available technology. Sales representatives calling on bookstores and order fulfillment plus warehousing of its books will continue to be essential, unless trade bookstores find that *PUBNET* tends to see commission reps as being less necessary, ie., booksellers will save money with electronic ordering.

## Chapter 9
# Computers and a Brief History of Publishing

In 1982, Leonard Shatzkin wrote a book entitled *In Cold Type: Overcoming the Book Crisis*. In it, he described the sorry condition of trade publishing, and he provides some remedies so logical that they are certain not to be adopted. Trade books are sold primarily through bookstores that order them from the publisher at various discounts (from 40% to 47%) or from the book wholesalers, such as Ingrams Book Company, Nashville, Tennessee, or Baker & Taylor, Inc. in Bridgewater, New Jersey. In the United States, books may be returned if they are not sold within a certain time, usually less than a year. The shelf life of a book is less than twelve months and, if they are returned, they will be remaindered at less than it costs to print and bind them. Everyone loses, including the author who gets no royalties on remaindered books. The practice of remaindering is hopelessly inefficient and self-defeating. Books that are remaindered flood the market for those books, so no bookstore can sell its own stock of the same book.

Twice a year, a bookstore owner is confronted with about 26,000 new titles (52,000 new titles were published in 1987). He must make a "buy" decision for books he hasn't read, because they're not yet available for inspection. Many of them are not even printed, bound and shipped to a distributor's warehouse at the time of sale or order for them. His decisions are based on the representations of commission salesmen or sales reps from either the publisher or a distributor. Both offer catalogs with artwork (sometimes) and text, usually a brief synopsis and always written to get the book buyer's attention.

Often, these sales reps have not even read the books they're selling. They know little or nothing about book content, having been coached in semi-annual sessions by a publisher's editor who rarely has more than ten minutes to describe the merits of a book and inspire the sales reps to read the books the publisher is pitching. Some of the best sales reps actually read the books published by the small presses which are handed out in paperback form and labelled as "Uncorrected Page Proofs." A catalog from Simon & Schuster or Random House, however, may have as many as 200 to 300 titles. A salesman can't possibly read more than a small percent of them. Random House, mindful of the time it takes a bookseller to key in all the data on books ordered, now offers "frontlist on floppy" disk, and a bookstore can copy all this data in less than two minutes, if it uses inventory software. Mercury House will follow suit within the year.

Bookstore owners or buyers make their decisions twice a year as a stream of sales reps come calling, each of them under economic pressure (they get as much as 10% of the book's cover price as a commission) to get large advance orders for what a publisher hopes will be a bestseller, i.e., it's commercial and has an author with a brand name. Each sales rep also hopes the bookstore will order and stock a few copies of some of the other books in the catalog. What a bookstore must know is to what extent a publisher will support each of its books with advertising and promotion. They rarely do except in the case of the book chains, such as Waldenbooks, Crown Book Stores and Barnes & Noble, as well as Doubleday Book Stores.

If a large publisher, such as Simon & Schuster, gets enough large advance orders from bookstores, it can make substantially more money from the sale of subsidiary rights, such as paperback, first serial, foreign, condensation and even film rights. Inefficient distribution of books ordered by bookstores and displayed there, however, often results in the anomaly of going to reprint to satisfy the needs of some stores only to find returns of books which remain unsold elsewhere. Many of the small presses are looking at backlists (books published a year or more earlier). North Point Press in San Francisco did very well with such a book, Beryl Markham's delightful and well written story about herself, *West With the Night*. It became a trade paperback bestseller almost immediately and may do even better with a title recently published by North Point Press.

Returns however, continue to be a major problem even for the large publishers. In 1986, for example, Harcourt Brace Jovanovich had returns amounting to about $31.1 million, even though it will find some consolation in the future tax benefits, presumably from selling books returned as remainders. Some distributors use books returned to fulfill later orders for the same title, but only if it's in mint, not hurt (damaged) condition.

To deal with one aspect of this problem, Ingrams Book Company recently prepared a Recommended Opening Store Inventory (ROSI). Results of this approach are not yet in, probably because not too many new bookstores are opening.

According to R. R. Bowker's *American Book Trade Directory* for 1987/1988, there are 21,819 book retailers in the United States. They range from 1,257 Antiquarian retailers to 1,111 Used book retailers. There are, for example, 3,100 College retailers and 3,871 retailers classified as Religious and 6,581 General book retailers. By searching Dun's Electronic Yellow Pages — Retailers in a California database, Dialog, it was possible to assemble a mailing list of 1,855 bookstores. There were a total of 13,633 records for retailers assigned a primary standard industrial classification of 5,942 (retail bookstores). Bookstores specializing in used, antiquarian or rare books were not selected for the list. The 13,633-record starting set was restricted to stores which had taken large listings in the local yellow pages and which had some form of the word "book" in the company name. Key words were used to eliminate most religious, "adult," foreign language, comic, and college/university book stores from the set. This reduced the final list to 1,855 entries. At this point, certain assumptions became necessary. Some college/ university bookstores, for example, sell so-called trade books. The R. R. Bowker list of General retailers — 6,581 — seems to include chain bookstores such as Waldenbooks, Crown and Barnes & Noble. These cannot be classified as independent retailers. Additionally, retailers have been surveyed by gross annual sales. Of the 23,902 survey forms sent out by R. R. Bowker, 9,315 were returned. Those with gross sales of from $50,000 to $100,000, 34% (3,167) fell into this category, and 18% (1,677) fell into the category of retailers with gross sales of from $100,000 to $250,000. From these figures, it is possible to assume that an estimated *4,844* book retailers may be classified as "independent" bookstores, ie., not one of the chain bookstores. The 3,100 college/ university bookstores, while not really classified as "independent," may be added to this total, since most, if not all of them sell trade books. Accordingly, 7,944 retailers may be dealt with as retail outlets for books from all publishers, including the small presses. Mercury House now has a computer program, which, amongst other things, will print out mailing labels for 5,200 bookstores in all 50 states and uses these to send its newsletter with excerpts of good book reviews to all of these bookstores.

It is these independent bookstores which still try to turn over inventory of trade books four to five times a year, a solid and profitable objective but not too easy to generate. Another aspect of the problem of inefficient distribution might be to encourage publishers and book wholesalers to make some — not all — placement decisions for trade books. In this way, small regular shipments become the principal strategy for enhancing merchandise turnover as titles moved through the bookstores. Their owners or buyers would then have to track sales, so they would know when to reorder and when to ship returns. Bookstores might be willing to do this if they could track sales accurately enough and use electronic ordering hardware to replenish inventory. However, book inventory management software is expensive now, even though the unit price is very likely to decline with the sale of more units to a larger market — the estimated 7,944 independent bookstores — not all of whom offer a full line as distinguished from specialized bookstores, e.g., religious or technical books.

Morse Data Corporation in Chicago has designed a system for publishers to track their sales but not those of bookstores. Morse Data offers a computerized inventory and sales management system specifically designed to crunch numbers for the benefit of publishers' book sale managers. Designed essentially for pub-

lishers, however, Morse Data's system can track sales to bookstores, the reorder point, monthly sales and monthly "returns"
for each title. Its system knows the cost of inventory, too. It
counts and evaluates each book in inventory, using either FIFO
or LIFO accounting standards. In effect, the Morse Data system,
with slight modifications, would allow a publisher to do the
bookkeeping for bookstores, but only for the titles of that publisher, not those sold by some other publishers' titles. Ideas like
this tend to move in all directions except the right one — bookstores are a publisher's best friend and customer — and eventually
bookstores may decide demand publishing is the only and best
way to operate efficiently and profitably. The history of publishing in the United Kingdom suggests this objective is virtually
inevitable. The parallel in the United States, while far from a
mirror image, has some startling similarities.

It's not entirely necessary to note that from very early times
there have been books "printed" on either stone tablets or
parchment. Almost 4,000 years ago, the *Book of the Dead* was
"published" in Egypt. It never became a bestseller, since the only
copies were either bought by mourners at funerals or placed in
the tomb of the decedent to serve as his passport to an after-life.
Effectively, the *Book of the Dead* was a "limited edition." Much
later, the Greeks and then the Romans "printed" either parch-
ments or maunusripts like Caesar's Commentaries.Centers of
learning and scholarship in England began with trips to and
from Rome, and the travellers returned with manuscripts or
parchment for the great abbeys of Wearmouth and Jarrow, the
first of which was founded in 764 and the second in 682. This
began a new age to replace the remnants of intellectual life
destroyed by the Anglo-Saxons in the 5th century and that had,
up to then been preserved by a small handful of scholars and the
monastic schools in Wales and Cornwall. Adam Bede was an
early author and kept many copiers at work in places as far away
as Rome. His *History* and a few other books seemed to have been
written in a monastic cell. When he died, the seat of learning
seems to have passed from an abbey to Ælbert's famous library in
York, which became the center of learning and education in

Western Europe. This library maintained what is probably the earliest book list or catalog ever reduced to writing. The contemporary version of this list is the Books in Print database maintained by Dialog in Palo Alto, California. Another is sold by R.R. Bowker on a CD-ROM disk. It has some 750,000 titles, and, in 1988, it offered reviews and forthcoming titles.

Like libraries everwhere, Ælbert's was a treasure of learning, and distribution was never a problem. Scholars travelled to it. Under William the Conqueror, the *Doomsday Book* was "published," and all titles to real property in England were reduced to a more or less organized form. However, both the Anglo-Saxon books and the monks who so patiently listed them were treated in rather shabby fashion. The Norman ecclesiastics despised these books, and many of them were destroyed to make room for manuscripts in Latin. Norman monks had at least one redeeming skill—illumination of manuscripts or books. The art of illumination became so ornate, it cuased some complaints to the effect that writers were not writers, but painters. Even law books were written with beautiful illuminated text in Latin.

In the 14th century, the private distribution of books shows up in the wide circulation of John Wycliffe's completed translation of the Bible. There is also some evidence of private distribution of William Langland's *Piers Plowman.*

The growth of the medieval universities, Oxford and Cambridge, began a new chapter in the history of publishing. The more widespread availability of paper and the increasing demand for books created a new class of book-makers (now they would be considered as bookstores). Some of these were no more than copiers of what others had written, and the rest were wandering peddlars of books, the early commission salesmen or "reps."

With the introduction of printing, the book business took a different turn. In 1476, Caxton set up the first press in the City of Westminister. In his *Legend of Saints,* he said: "I submitted myself to translate it into English (from Latin) and promised to make a reasonable quantity of them for a yearly fee." The number of people able to read was quite small, so not many copies were printed. Literacy is still a problem today. However, the leading booksellers made a point of attending the great book fair in Frankfurt twice a year. It was there that the new books of the world could be seen and, presumably copied elsewhere for a fee — the first evidence of subsidiary rights.

Caxton, though never a publisher by appointment from the Crown, was patronized by Edward IV and Richard III and printed books under their protection. In view of King Richard the III's history, Caxton's career must have been somewhat precarious. Of the 100 or so books printed by his press in Westminister before his death in 1491, he was personnally responsible for the translation of 25, beside editing every one of them.

In 1530, a royal proclamation inveighed against "blasphemous and pestiferous English books printed in other regions and sent into the realm." Worth noting is the fact that in the 14th and 15th centuries the distinction between printers and publishers tended to be blurred. A printer was effectively a publisher. So this proclamation and the Act of 1534 were passed to prevent the import of foreign books considered heretical and to protect English printers from competition. There were, however, a steady stream of such books, including many tracts from the prolific Martin Luther. Tyndale's New Testament was first circulated in 1526 by more or less irregular booksellers willing to become martyrs. Of some 15,000 copies printed, only one or two remain. The rest were burned at St. Paul's Cathedral in London and at Oxford.

After the death of Henry VIII in 1547, the Bible took off. Some 14 editions were printed, but not until after the Privy Council had approved its text as well as that of other books of a religious content. A half-century later, the Crown had the same problem-censorship. Queen Elizabeth I, who died in 1603, was no exception to earlier monarchs. It was at her command that both an author and a printer had their hands cut off for seditious work. Even so, the authorities found it impossible to stop the printing and dissemination of material proscribed by Star Chamber proceedings, i.e., prior restraints. Their real problem was the growth of the Puritan movement under Queen Elizabeth's religious orthodoxy. Elizabethan Puritans simply used secret presses and some mysterious mechanism—clandestine distribution—to disseminate forbidden literature throughout England.

In what most people regard as a golden age of literature, notwithstanding the Star Chamber of religious intolerance, William Shakespeare had Elizabeth I as a patron and protecter. She admired his genius, and Shakespeare was often summoned to her Court to read his narrative poems. Many of his earlier works were printed and distributed by pirate publishers. The distinction between printer and publisher was beginning to disappear. In the 17th century, publishing was effectively a monopoly which flourished with royal assent.

Later in the 17th century under James I, a different phase in bookselling appeared. The number of printers considered necessary was limited by the Crown. In the *Stationer's Register* for 1632, only 109 books were listed, although many more were printed but not registered for various reasons. In the same year, George Wither wrote "Good God, how many dungboats of fruitless works do they yearly foist on his Majesty's subjects; how many hundred reams of foolish, profane, and senseless ballads do they quarterly disperse abroad!"

In the 18th century (1709), the Copyright Act of Queen Anne was passed to end the chaotic state of publishing in England. The pirates were not deterred in the least according to Addison in the *Tatler*. They were, he said, "a set of wretches we authors call pirates who print any book . . . . in a smaller volume, and sell it, as all other thieves do stolen goods, at a cheaper rate." These may have been the first paperback originals but the author was not paid a royalty.

It was not until the late 18th and early 19th centuries that the separation of bookselling and publishing became more or less complete. Few publishing houses had taken advantage of the Companies Act of 1862 which allowed incorporation and limited liability. William Collins & Co. and Macmillan were amongst the first to do so. Macmillan opened a New York office in 1869.

And W.H. Smith & Son, Inc. now the largest book chain in the
U.K., all dated back to the 18th century or earlier. W.H. Smith &
Son was once a book wholesaler, but withdrew from this busi-
ness in the 20th century.

Hit by the Great Depression of the 1930s, bookstores in the
United Kingdom and the United States faced a financially fragile
future. Many went through bankruptcy proceedings, often
because they would not modernize their stores and accept new
display techniques. However, bookstores did begin to accept the
idea of the sale-or-return, or see-safe system of stocking or
ordering books. As early as 1870, the wholesaler of books was an
essential link in their distribution. In the U.K., the leading
wholesaler was Simpkins Marshall & Co. Its founder was Ben-
jamin Crosby who travelled regularly and systematically
throughout the country calling on bookstores everywhere. In
1889, three wholesalers combined to form this company.
Ingrams Book Company and Baker & Taylor, both incorporated
later in the United States, clearly saw the future of book wholesaling as an essential link between publishers and bookstores.

In order to survive in the post-World War II environment,
Simpkins Marshall & Co. had to diversify, or so it thought. It
began to act as a warehouse for books published by the small
presses of the United Kingdom and to fulfill orders for their
books. It also had to promote its own quantity sales by putting
travellers on the road to persuade bookstores to buy in bulk
through the wholesaler instead of the publishers. Simpkins
placed itself in the position of working both for the publishers
by siphoning off the "single copy" sales which were expensive to
process, and against the publishers by soliciting the bulk orders
which Simpkins' salesmen were employed to obtain.

By 1954, it became apparent that Simpkins Marshall Ltd.,
which, by then, had been acquired by Robert Maxwell, was in
financial difficulty. Publishers were simply unwilling to give
Simpkins a discount high enough to allow the wholesaler to
operate profitably. Simpkins was getting books at between 33–1/3
% and 40% and selling to bookstores at 25% or, for large orders,

33–⅓%. The gross margin was completely inadequate, and Simpkins went into receivership.

The immediate effects were alarming. Publishers were inundated with small orders from bookstores, and the cost of fulfilling and processing them caused resentment at both ends of the transaction. The publishers had no one to blame but themselves, since pure Adam Smith economics fixed the discounts without much, if any consideration for the gross profit margins of their best customers, the bookstores. It was at this point that computers entered the book business, often with unpredictable results. Computers of the 1950s were primitive then, and primitive programming led to costly mistakes. By this time, W.H. Smith had completely withdrawn from the book wholesaling business, so it moved into the world of electronic ordering unhampered by any built-in problems of the kind which had caused the demise of Simpkins Marshall Ltd. somewhat earlier.

In a more or less parallel development, the Net Book Agreement was challenged as being contrary to the public interest and allowing the fixing of prices by discounting at fixed percentages of the cover price of a book. During trial before the Restrictive Practices Court, there was evidence suggesting that a successful challenge to the Net Book Agreement would reduce the number of books published and increase the cover price of books that were published. However, in the court's summation the presiding justice noted that net profits of bookstores were modest compared to other branches of commerce and that "in the competitive state of the book trade, publishers have so far been able to resist pressure by booksellers for higher rates of discount."

The effect of this decision by the court was a decidedly mixed blessing. Bookstores began demanding higher discounts and reducing inventory in the interests of higher turnover. Publishers went right on publishing more and more titles, and cover prices reached levels no one had even dreamed of ten years earlier. So much for the conventional wisdom of both publishers and bookstores. Both must learn to live with the computer and telecommunications, i.e., electronic ordering and fulfillment to reduce costs and increase gross margins on each book sold. Publishers in the U.K. have discovered this, as have U.S. chain bookstores and the independents. The 4,500 or so independents in the United States must do the same in order to survive and prosper.

The *Cheney Report* of 1932 and the Book Industry Study Group's 1978 report, both noted the ineffiency of distribution in the book business. From the 16th and 17th centuries to the 20th century, the system we use to get books into the hands of those who will read them for pleasure or information has made no real progress. During the reign of Queen Elizabeth I, seditious books were distributed in a clandestine way by people who would be beheaded if caught. In the 14th century, those who wanted to read books for the same reasons as they do today travelled to university libraries to study scholarly, illuminated texts in Latin. In the 19th century, book travellers literally walked or used trains to get out to the bookstores in both the United Kingdom and the United States. Today, the only real change is in transportation is the jet aircraft. It allows sales reps to get where they want to go faster and at greater expense to the publishers or their distributors.

No other business puts out some 52,000 products on the market every year, each one of them unique, places them in bookstores by the most haphazard means, compels bookstores to sell them without benefit of more than minimal advertising or promotion (there are obvious exceptions, such as Simon & Schuster and some of the other giants who do advertise and support their books), does little if anything to help the book-stores with interior design and display techniques and, in all too many cases, untrained management—and then agrees to accept all the books the bookstore hasn't been able to sell. This is a recipe for disaster, and, with the growth of the big book chains, such as Waldenbooks, Barnes & Noble and Crown Books, publishers may eventually decide not to sell books to the 4,800 or so independent bookstores without some evidence of real economies and more efficiency from a lot of them. Ingrams and Baker & Taylor do a good job as wholesalers, but they can't compel bookstores to invest comparatively modest sums in a computer and telecommunications software to keep track of inventory, re-order books before they're out of stock or otherwise operate with higher gross margins. While anti-competitive pricing of mass market paperbacks is a real threat to the independent bookstores, they did take part in the recent case against some of the mass market publishers. The Northern California Booksellers Association and Cody's in Berkeley seem to have made modest progress in a case brought under the Robinson-Patman Act a year ago. Distribution is still the principal problem, and most publishers, particularly the small presses with limited advertising budgets, seem to have few choices except to be efficient themselves and hope for the best. In the meantime, IBM, Apple Computer, Compaq Computer and literally dozens of software manufacturers are ready willing and able to sell hardware to the bookstores. Software is now being offered at affordable prices, but not by the major manufacturers of hardware. $1,900 for a book inventory management program is affordable, and the computer running this software can also be used to perform other tasks such as electronic ordering of books from either the publishers or the wholesalers. "Desktop publishing" is now an established fact and can only become more sophisticated and less expensive. Computers in the retail bookstore is the next logical step. The "electronic bookstore" is still only a gleam in someone's eye, only partly because of the current high cost of some hardware and software. The light at the end of the tunnel is really the high cost of becoming more efficient, but it's a lot lower than most bookstores seem to realize. Try it and find out! It works well and will clearly increase gross margins.

# Chapter 10
## The Distributors:
## They Don't All Have To Be Inefficient

Enough has been said by now about the inefficiency of distribution of books from publisher or distributor to the retail bookstore. Most writers from Oliver Cheney in 1932 to Leonard Shatzkin in 1982 — that's 50 years — agree that it's hopelessly inefficient. The astonishing part of all this is how little has been done to improve distribution. Without exception, publishers know that there are eager readers for what they publish, and most of them read for pleasure or information. During 1988, about 52,000 new titles will be offered for sale to these readers, most of them through bookstores. Getting these books into the bookstores is not the insoluble problem it may seem. However, it must be remembered that the entire pattern of distribution and the way it grew is a remnant of the past and has to be changed radically in some cases and subtly in others. It must be changed and improved, particularly for the benefit of the approximately 12,000 to 15,000 small presses. They publish an estimated 50% of all new titles offered each year.

Usually, the small presses looking for national distribution of their new titles, enter into two year contracts with a distributor and agree to pay that distributor anywhere from 21% to 25% of net sales — gross sales less returns — with a reserve for returns of about 17½% — as that distributor's fee for acting as such. Twice a year, the distributor has a sales conference, and all its commission salesmen, or reps turn up, usually in New York or Boston, to hear from the publisher's editor all about its new titles. An editor can expect about ten or fifteen minutes to explain the content of from ten to forty titles or more, describe the advertising and promotion plans for each one and whether there have been any sales of subsidiary right made, eg., serial or film rights for one or more titles. Unfortunatly, all too few reps have either the time or inclination to know the books they will be asked to sell to the bookstores. There are simply too many new titles. Unfortunately, all too few of these same reps have either the time or inclination to make the rounds of bookstores in their territories more than once every six months or even to send them the good reviews some of these books get before the publication date of a new title. *Publishers Weekly, Kirkus Reviews* and the *American Library Journal* are the three principal trade journals which do review books. R. R. Bowker now offers a Books in Print on a compact disk-read only memory with reviews. The CR–ROM is updated quarterly, a practice which may make it easier for bookstore buyers to make "buy" decisions from something better than a publisher's catalog. A "reader" for this CD–ROM costs around $900, but it may save money in the long run—fewer returns and the penalty costs of making them. Bookstore buyers like to have their selection vindicated by good reviews, and they tend to look more favorably at the books on the next list from the same publisher. As Arthur Miller once said about Willie Loman in his classic play, *Death of a Salesman,* and this is a paraphrase, He (the book buyer) is a person, and attention must be paid."

The attention most bookstore buyers get is a visit from the distributor's rep twice a year, a selling session which can last from ten minutes to four or more hours. The duration of this session is determined by the number of titles in the distributor's (or the publisher's) catalog and by how much time the book buyer wants to spend discussing each title and hearing about advertising and promotion plans for it. There are always exceptions, of course, but that one visit is usually the last time the book buyer sees that rep until the next of two annual selling seasons. For more than 50 years, there have been two selling seasons. The American Booksellers Association has its annual convention over the Memorial Day weekend in May, and many bookstore buyers attend to see what new titles will be offered on the Fall List, and many of them extend this trip to take a vacation afterwards. The summer months are those in which the reps make their often lonely and difficult rounds to sell their books, so they are not available again until early December for the second annual sales conference for new titles to be offered on the Spring List. Then the sales cycle starts all over again in May, since the reps have to wait until after Christmas to begin their rounds again. Some publishers have added one more selling season in mid-winter.

Commission reps are, of course, an essential part of the entire selling process, particularly for the small presses. They simply can't afford the cost of an in house reps who command a salary of between $40,000 and $60,000 each per year. However, there are a number of distributors that all use commission reps as independent contractors. Their gross income depends on the quantity of books they sell to bookstores or wholesalers. They are paid commissions only on the net sales in their own territory, usually 10% on sale to bookstores and 5% on sales to wholesalers, such as Ingrams or Baker & Taylor.

In the June 10, 1988 issue of *Publishers Weekly,* ran an article on one national distributor, Consortium Book Sales and Distribution, Inc., of St. Paul, Minnesota. Appearing on page 52, the article was entitled "Consortium: A Quality Collective." According to this article, Consortium, a firm started only three years ago, has a dozen "of the most extraordinary small publishers in the country." At the Small Press and Magazine Expo '88 earlier in 1988, Consortium's executive director, Roberta (Bobbi) Rix, Eric Kampmann, president of Kampmann & Co., Inc. and Marilee Talman, president of The Talman Co., Inc., both from New York, all appeared and addressed the same audience. Kampmann was quoted as saying "[Consortium's] group identity could very well translate into better sales to the trade." Kampmann & Co., Inc. represents fifty or more small presses, and The Talman Co. wants to represent two hundred presses. Rix was quoted as saying that "All of our presses show a high regard for content and design, and each has a special identity. Iv'e been lucky enough to bring them all ['the extraordinary small publishers'] together." In addition to the semi-annual sales conferences, each publisher spends time afterward talking to the other publishers to share common problems and work out solutions.

Consortium has 21 commission reps, and, since each one of them has enough volume, their income, while not guaranteed, is worthwhile. These reps know their territory and the trade buyers in most of the bookstores. They also have experience in selling to the trade. These reps are unlikely to push for large advance sales on the theory that such sales make subsidiary rights, i.e., paperback rights, more valuable to the publisher. Large advance sales also have a way of winding up as returns from the bookstores as unsold. It is no accident that Consortium's reserve for returns in its standard contract is 10%, while Kampmann's is 17½ of gross sales. Furthermore, these commission reps know they don't get paid a commission on books that are returned as unsold. The reason for Consortium's policy in this respect is simple. Its small press publishers can't afford to spend a great deal of money on advertising in the trade journals and the print media, while Simon & Schuster or Random House have very large advertising budgets. In any profit and loss statement, operating expenses include advertising. In 1987, Harcourt Brace Jovanovich, Inc. showed selling and editorial expenses of $285.9 million in its consolidated statements of income for the year ending December 31, 1987. An estimated 15% of this amount, or $42.9 million, was spent on space advertising. By way of contrast, Mercury House, a smalll press by Consortium's standards (15 to 20 titles per year) spent $68,000 on space advertising during the same period.

Consortium not only insists that its publishers "share customers [mainly independent bookstores], but also philosophy [a high regard for contents and design]." There are about 4,500 independent bookstores in the United States, so the market for Consortium's small press publishers seems very large. Moreover, these publishers seem pleased with its performance. Allan Kornblum, publisher of Coffee House Press in Minneapolis, was quoted in the *Publishers Weekly* article as saying: "Consortium is pushing us toward an overall professionalism that matches the literary quality and design of our books. It's a lot of work, but for those who aspire to be the next North Points and Black Sparrow., it's definitely the wave of the future."

In her emphasis on good design, Bobbi Rix seems to have the right idea — good design sells books, particularly when her publishers project an image of quality. She also seems intuitively or otherwise, to know that a bookseller will place orders for books that consistently meet her standards of quality. The books with good design will almost always be displayed in good shelf space, and she is very aware of the importance to her publishers of display.

To underscore the importance of *display*, it is useful to quote a short passage from the trial transcript American Booksellers Association v. Commonwealth of Virginia, a case aready discussed in these pages. The witness is Heather G. Florence, Vice-President and General Counsel of Bantam Books. Her testimony was given on direct examination as follows:

> Q. From the point of view of the publisher, what is the importance of display for a paperback book in terms of sales?
> A. Well, it is really critical. More and more these outlets (bookstores) do show all of the books face out, if you notice, in any airport or similar-type rack. Instead of just showing the spines of books, they show the face out. And in the selling process, our key tool that the sales people use is a copy of what we are going to use as the cover for the book. The sales representatives solicit their orders three or four months before we actually ship the books. And what they use as solicitation materials for every book is a copy of what the cover will look like to try and persuade the customer that in fact this will be attractive, it is very likely to create attention at retail displays, and is likely then to sell through."

Bantam Books only recently initiated the publishing of trade or hardcover books. However, it is reasonable to assume that it would find the display of these books just as critical as the display of paperback books. Mercury House believes that the proper display of its books, all of them hardcover, is equally critical and goes to great lengths to design its covers to attract attention in bookstores as well as to call attention to them in trade advertising.

Mercury House does advertise its books in the trade journals already mentioned as well as the the *San Francisco Chronicle-Examiner* (a Sunday combination), the Book Review section of

*The New York Times* (also a Sunday feature) and *The New Yorker* magazine as well as some smaller magazines and trade print media. Advertising, however, is simply not enough, and its cost is too high for a small press. Distribution in an efficient and timely manner has become absolutely essential for the small presses.

Earlier in these pages, the availability of PUBNET became widely known to those in the book business. *Publishers Weekly,* in its issue of March 18, 1988, ran a story on a way of ordering books electronically, i.e., using a computer and modem. From its inception to the present (July, 1988), PUBNET was seen as a way of helping college bookstores order textbooks, getting confirmation almost instantly and delivery in less time. The textbook, of course, must be in print, and a computer search to ascertain its status cost very little—about $0.60. PUBNET is exploring ways of getting its system installed in trade bookstores, and some of their buyers seem to be quite interested in the possibilities. Even today, a book buyer may order trade titles using only the ISBN for that title. Currently, several major publishers, such as Simon & Schuster and Random House are on line with PUBNET.

Mercury House anticipates being on line by the end of 1988, if not sooner. In the meantime, it will use its own program to send good reviews of its books to some 5,700 bookstores which are in its own database. The program prints out mailing labels. On March 24, 1988, for example, a good review of one book, *Eve: Her Story,* arrived at its San Francisco office. The review had run in *The Columbus Dispatch* a week earlier. Within 24 hours, the entire text of this review had been typeset and included in the Mercury House newsletter and sent to 33 bookstores all located in area code 614, since the circulation area of *The Columbus Dispatch* included bookstores outside of Columbus, Ohio. This is a form of electronic marketing, but also a precursor of what better distribution will do for publishers.

Were a distributor to be on line with PUBNET, it might have been able to solicit more orders for the same book. Distributors simply must get into the business of accepting and fullfiling orders electronically. The ability to do so represents a real service to its publisher—clients and the booksellers. Even more than this, it can reduce operating costs by a substantial amount for both. Traditionally, sales reps get orders from bookstore buyers for 5 copies of one title, 12 copies of another and so forth. When there are enough orders to earn a nice commission — the reps have to live — these orders are then *mailed* to the distributor. For about $400, a commission rep can buy a hand held computer weighing about 8 pounds. By keying in orders from bookstores by ISBN and number of copies ordered, he can attach his small computer to an ordinary telephone. A built — in acoustic coupler will send all the data in his computer back to a computer in the distributor's main office. This is only the first step in a network. The distributor must be able to process the orders received by its own PC, store the information and forward some of it to the warehouse. There, it's processed by an IBM 386 with 240MB, enough memory for most small press distributors. Then, an operator at the warehouse with a terminal can process the order and arrange for fulfillment, i.e., shipping the books to the right address identified only by SAN. A nice touch might be to send an electronic mail announcement to the ordering bookstore advising the date and method of shipment, e.g., UPS or book rate.

Instead of computerizes processing and fulfillment, orders are often processed manually — and on non — standard forms. They are (sometimes) entered into a computer as files organized by publisher and its titles showing the discount given on each one. Then, these orders are printed out by publisher and title and *mailed* to a remote warehouse for fulfillment (shipping). In some cases, a disk or magnetic tape is sent to the warehouse and printed out there in the same way. Neither way is at all satisfactory. Errors are possible, and these, when they occur, do the publisher a disservice. Bookstores look to the publisher, not often to the distributor as being responsible for these errors. However, once the orders have been printed out at the warehouse, the books are "picked" by hand, placed in cartons and shipped. It might be noted here that Biblios, Ltd., not far from London, has a robot which has been programmed to "pick" books, load them in cartons and ship them to bookstores with an invoice inside, also printed out by the robot's on board computer and printer.

The distributor's warehouse is the key to efficient distribution. In some cases, orders are processed there. Sometimes they are processed in the distributor's principal office and sent to the warehouse for fulfillment. In either case, orders must be processed by skilled operators using computers. There is a tremendous cost differential in a warehouse where four skilled operators can process 1,200 orders per day and one in which it takes twenty unskilled operators to process the same number of orders. In some cases, a terminal keyboard, if information is keyed in the wrong sequence, will cause some data to be "lost," along with an essential part of the order. This often occurs because of poor software programming.

Software also makes a difference. All bookstores have a unique identifier, a standard address number (SAN), and processing identifies the bookstore placing the order by SAN, the ISBN for each title ordered, the discount in accordance with the distributor's discount schedule, e.g., 40% for from five to twenty four titles, and the quantity of each title ordered to be shipped to the bookstore. The location of each title must appear in the printout, so the person who "picks" them will know the shelf where the book may be found, "picked" and placed in a cart or motorized shelf on wheels. What has been "picked" must also be counted and checked against the actual order, shrink wrapped and placed in a carton for shipment. The address label appears in a window of the carton. Then, subtracting the weight of the carton, a postage meter prints the amount of the postage, and a checker pastes a strip on the carton showing the amount. Small orders are packed in cardboard carton which will hold three or four books, and the ends are stapled together, again to eliminate damage during shipping. A "hurt" book will not sell. It will be returned to the distributor's warehouse along with other books returned as unsold, usually because the bookstore has adopted a policy of returning books unsold after six or eight months. Bookstores may indiscriminately pack different titles in the same carton., so, when they are returned, each title must be counted. Those in good condition are often returned to inventory against the possibility of another order for the same title.

Were distributors to get into the Fourth Wave technology discussed at the Seybold Seminar, they would see the missing factor in traditional distribution, networking. With a file server and workstations, they could cut the time from order to shipment from two weeks to two days and fewer errors. A file server is no more than a computer with 240MB of memory, such as an IBM 386. A workstation is no more than a terminal with a monitor or screen and a keyboard. Using the latter, a relatively unskilled operator may access the file server and give it an order which has been processed as to both publisher, title, discount and buyer. Processing may even mean that orders have been sorted by the number of copies for which the bookstore has placed orders. In most agreements with distributors, the number of books ordered determines the discount. So, instead of manually keying in the details of an order, they are all processed by computer, including the discount to the bookstore, which is automatically calculated and stored in the file server computer. With a distributor doing $1 million a year in net sales, this means that he can operate efficiently with fewer employees needed to process orders. Consortium, for example, uses a mini-mainframe computer and Timeshare software. It operates with a staff of eight people and has its own warehouse in St. Paul. Its sales manager, Stephen Williamson works out of Boston and almost unquestionably uses a computer as part of a network with St. Paul and Consortium, so he can track sales by accessing the distributor's computer. If so, Williamson knows the bookstores ordering books distributed by Consortium, although order processing probably occurs at the warehouse.

Such orders might even be sent in by a sales rep using electronic mail from out in the field. Networks are fast and accurate, and they are commonly referred to as local area networks (LANs) or (wide area networks (WANs). The total cost of a file server and seven workstations is about $35,000, and a LAN will reduce a distributor's operating costs by at least 25%. The location of workstations may be in the distributor's office or at a remote warehouse. Additionally, a publisher may "request" its own orders from the file server using no more than a modem and telecommunications software in its computer. Bookstores ordering its titles may be identified by SAN for simplicity, and the publisher can also send each such bookstore good reviews of the books ordered, either electronically or by ordinary mail. Additionally, a network should have a line printer, perhaps two or three. At times of high demand for printing, the file server computer may control the print queue by establishing priorities with fulfillment having the highest priority, closely followed by invoicing.

Aside from more efficient distribution, there are other ways of selling books, and every member of the small press community needs to go through the drill of submitting its titles for sale to book clubs.In 1987, one of its books, Joseph Cotten's Auto-biography, *Vanity Will Get You Somewhere,* was sold to two small book clubs. Books sold to a book club go to one address, while bookstores, including the chains, have 7,500 addresses. Sales to the chains are most often handled by a representative of the distributor with a visit to the principal buyer for that chain.

With these comments on how the distribution system works, at least for the small presses, another look at the archaic semi-annual selling season becomes necessary. It is currently a fact of life, but it can be changed almost overnight. Distributors must provide their reps with computers, a modem and telecom-munications software — cost about $400. While it may still take them three or four months to make personal visits to all their bookstore accounts, orders may be sent in electronically to the distributor.The same reps can also show bookstore managers and personnel the advantages of having the same hardware and software for an affordable price. Actually, Telzon, in Concord, California manufactures a handheld computer with a wand. All its user has to do is to key in the ISBN and the quantity of each book ordered. The wand is used to "read" the ISBN bar code on books which use this bar code. The cost is about $400. By using this approach to distribution, the time between getting an order and the arrival of the books ordered at the bookstore can be reduced from two to three weeks to about four days. This means that a bookseller may carry a substantially smaller inventory of trade books, because a re — order takes so little time.

Moreover, with a computer and the right software, a publisher can telecommunicate its entire catalog and artwork to the rep. By doing this, a publisher can save the cost of going to semi–annual meetings in May and December to sell all its books in about ten or fifteen minutes. A distributor for twenty or more small presses has about 22 to 25 sales reps who sell books on a commission basis. For each one of these reps to have his own portable computer with interactive software is now about $1,500 or less. A lease would be about $70 per month for three years, and it would be deductible by him as a business expense. With the catalog artwork and copy about each title he is selling on a floppy disk, a sales rep calling on a bookstore buyer can show the catalog to that person, or even copy it into the bookstore's computer and leave it there for leisurely study at a later time. Mercury House can easily put its catalog on a disk at a cost of about $2.00 each. It is the distributor, however, who must decide to make the initial investment in a network plus the hardware and software needed to make it operate. No sales rep will buy even a small handheld computer for $400 unless the distributor has what is needed to handle orders from the field.

In order to sell any books at all, a sales rep must also be familiar enough with each book to describe its content to a bookstore buyer. And he must do this four or five months before publication date for each book. He, too, need not go to those semi — annual meetings of the distributor. He can get all the information he needs as well as a *Crane,* labelled "Uncorrected page proofs" of each book, and read it in the comfort of his own home.

Reps need to know what bookstores will *display* the books they are selling and which ones are in key locations of major market areas. They also need to know which bookstores have done well in the past with books they have sold to buyers in those stores. A distributor must be able to obtain this information from its own records — sales less returns — and deliver this information to its reps either at home or on the road. In publishing, the semi—annual sales conference is designed to get the product (books) into the store in contrast to most other products where the selling job is to move the product (widgets) through the store.

Commission reps all too often tend to concentrate on the big advance sale. This emphasis all too often leads to heavy returns which are never blamed on poor selling practices. They are, however, often blamed on poor buying practices. The sales rep very often thinks he is doing what the distributer, the publisher or both want him to do. If this, in fact, is the case—after all, Admiral Poindexter *assumed* he was acting in a manner consistent with President Reagan's policy of aid to the contras—the distributor has elevated shadow to the level of substance. Advance orders do no more than determine how many books will be in bookstores on publication date for each title sold. Everyone knows that books not in stores on publication date have next to no chance of being sold at all, since advertising and promotion are synchronized with publication dates.

It is impossible to overstate the importance of getting just a few copies of each new title into the bookstores in key locations, and which have good track records because they are displayed in a place where they can be seen as *new* titles. If a distributor gets an advance order of 10,000 copies, it would be amazing if he asked how many stores the orders represented and where they were. It seems obvious or should, that a book with a 10,000 copy advance order from 2,500 stores is much better than an advance order of 10,000 copies from 500 stores.

Thus, the quality of the advance is seldom given much analysis. It is believed by some that Simon & Schuster initially printed 10,000 copies of Allan Bloom's the *The Closing of the American Mind*. Its commission reps may have been told to focus on selling them to bookstores with good track records. As we all know now, this was good policy, and that book became a runaway best seller within two months from its date of publication.

A big advance sale of books seems to have what might be called the mystique of numbers. Distributors tend to become mesmerized and can't wait to call their publisher—clients to report how well their reps have done. The relevant question rarely gets asked — what bookstores have ordered them and can they be displayed well? The point is that, because of location and walk — in traffic, certain bookstores have a high turnover rate — they move books out of the store into the hands of paying customers. Even though distributors may argue that about 90% of the time, the first order may be the only order a particular bookstore may place, this is no longer a rational argument. Re — orders have become simple with the advent of computerized inventory systems. Thus, the big advance is important, argue the distributors. This is a specious raationale. If a book doesn't sell well, the returns will come pouring in after six or so months. *Location* is always the key, but a publisher who is not told which bookstores actually have its books in stock is literally handcuffed.

Its advertising and promotion campaign is geared to publication date. If a publisher doesn't know or isn't told even so much as the cities where the bookstores exist, he can't know which local newspapers or magazines to use for advertising. A publisher simply must know how well its books are selling and where in order to target advertising and promotion such as an author's appearance on local television or radio. A publisher also needs to know whether money in the advertising and promotion budget has been spent wisely or whether more should be spent.

Even the book wholesalers, Ingrams and Baker & Taylor, can track sales by bookstores by the number of orders placed. They use state–of–the–art technology and use it effectively. They also send out monthly publications like *Advance* and *Forecast,* so they have an even greater incentive than distributors to move books *out* of bookstores. It's the distributor who must get them there in the first place. Ingrams and Baker & Taylor both have warehouses in key locations, and they say that if a book is ordered before 10:30 A.M. of a weekday, the book ordered will be delivered to the bookstore within 24 or 36 hours.

However, the system of book distribution in the United States, sometimes referred to as distribution by negotiations between the "rep" and the bookstore, was never planned. Because it was inefficient 55 years ago, the system without any basic changes simply evolved — inefficiency perpetuated.

The entire concept of distribution–by–negotiation is inherently unworkable. About one book in every three sold is returned. Sales are lost because books that should be in bookstores are not available where they should be because of a failure to fulfill orders in an expeditious manner. All of this is dauntingly expensive, particularly for the small presses which do not have deep pockets, only a feeling for books as the repositories for wisdom, humor or knowledge. The cost of well designed catalogs is only the beginning — many reps don't even use these to sell books of an individual publisher. They use only the distributor's catalog, and publishers pay their share of that. Added to this duplication of expenses is the cost of semi–annual sales conferences, the cost of preparing for and attending the American Bookseller Convention in May, editorial time preparing advertising copy and other publicity releases and so on, ad infinitum.

Parenthetically, it should be noted that to the extent a bookstore buys from a wholesaler because of late fulfillment or some other inefficiency — related reason, the penalty to the publisher is substantial. For every $1.00 of business diverted to the wholesaler, the publisher loses about $0.15 because of the discount differential. This means less gross profit for the publisher and less money paid to the author as royalties on his intellectual property.

There can be no doubt that distribution, while not the only problem, is by all odds the most important. We have come a long way from the time when printers had their own bookstore in the 17th century, but we don't seem to have learned very much in over 200 years. While the changes necessary to make it work are not all that revolutionary, there simply must be more people willing to make them. Amongst other things, change requires thinking about how we do things, and this includes bookstore owners and managers who operate on a very slim gross margin now. Current sales for the independent bookstore must be around $200 per square foot of store space. Some bookstores have found that by more efficient operations, they can sell $250 per square foot. By rethinking the way they would like to sell books, they could, by making a wise investment in state–of–the–art technology, increase sales to $300 or more per square foot in the same space.

# Chapter 11
## The Wholesalers-Electronic Ordering of Books Now

Ingram Book Company of Nashville, Tennessee, a wholly owned subsidiary of the Ingram Distribution Group, Inc., and Baker & Taylor, Inc. a wholly owned subsidiary of W. R. Grace & Company, is located in Bridgewater, N.J., They are the two largest and perhaps the major book wholesalers in the United States. There are also others, such as Book People West in Berkeley, California; Pacific Pipeline in Seattle, Washington; and Gordon's in Denver, Colorado. R. R. Bowker lists a total of 952 General Wholesalers and 246 Paperback Wholesalers in the United States. Amongst other things, Ingrams publishes *Advance,* a monthly magazine the purpose of which, as stated inside the cover is ". . . . to provide booksellers and librarians with the information they need to plan and make informed, effective decisions with regard to the purchasing of upcoming hardcover and trade paper titles. Each issue of *'Advance,'* in addition to featuring the services, policies and authoritative information made available by Ingram Book Company, also provides specifics on those titles scheduled to become available during the upcoming month . . . " Any quotations from it and used in this chapter are taken from the June 1987 issue of Advance which was available at the American Booksellers Association Convention in Washington, D.C.

At the ABA Convention, Ingrams announced the availability of a new, free, same-call confirmation electronic ordering program, FlashBack. A bookstore with a computer may now transmit via a toll-free number, and receive immediate information of Ingram stock status, title-by-title . . . . all in a single telephone call. "Electronic ordering," says Ingrams' ad in *Advance,* "is most convenient and beneficial when it is used as a 'by product' of the normal order functions of a computerized inventory management system or a book identification and ordering system. FlashBack electronic ordering is included at no charge as a standard part of IBID, BOOKLOG and LaserSearch."

FlashBack is also available as a "stand alone," an integrated part of some other computer systems. Thus, a bookstore may use FlashBack with an IBM or compatible computer. LaserSearch allows Ingrams to search its database for books in print, but it costs about $250 per month for a bookstore to use this package. Baker & Taylor offers FIRSTcall.

Baker & Taylor publishes a monthly magazine for the trade, *Forecast.* According to a column in the July 1987 issue, *"Forecast* keeps you [the bookstore] ahead of patron demand by providing pre-publication information on each title we've purchased for inventory. Our buyers have recognized the potential appeal that each of the titles included here will have to your library. . . . Titles from 14,000 publishers are available from Baker & Taylor . . . . "

In December, 1986, Baker & Taylor acquired Feffer & Simons, an international marketing firm for over 100 American publishers. "This acquisition," said Baker & Taylor's Preisdent, August Umlauf, "increased the level of service available to overseas customers, enabling them to purchase books and services from one convenient source rather than from a variety of publishers. According to its Form 10-K, "F & S markets English-language books to more than 3,000 library and bookstore accounts in major cities worldwide on behalf of about 200 publishers." B & T also opened a Tokyo sales office, was the major distributor at the first Beijing International Book Fair, and signed agreements to export books to China's university libraries and to the Soviet Union's college and state libraries and book-stores." Feffer & Simons, Inc. is located in New York City.

Baker & Taylor ante-dates 1912 and originally published books. It was also a leading wholesaler or jobber at this time. Doubleday, Page & Co., which began business in 1900, acquired Baker & Taylor's publishing business in 1912. This occurred because Frank Nelson Doubleday who really started what was one of the three largest publishing houses in the world. It was acquired in 1987 by Bertelsmann AG, a West German publisher. Doubleday served his apprenticeship at Charles Scribner as a shipping clerk. He moved into book production, tried advertising, but didn't do too well at this. In 1887, he went to work as editor of Scribners Magazine. In 1892, he was sent to England to arrange for the publication there of this magazine. On the way to London, Doubleday met Sam McClure, the publisher of *McClure's,* also a magazine. The two became friends, and Doubleday, who was not getting along too well with Charles Scribner, did two things. He accepted McClure's offer to join the magazine's staff and proposed to start what became Doubleday Page & Co. in 1900. As an editor of *McClure's* he again went to London and managed to sign up Rudyard Kipling for an advance of £500 to write for *McClure's Magazine*. It sold 100,000 copies of *"The Day's Work,"* not one of Kipling's best.

In late 1899, Doubleday decided to leave McClure's and start his own publishing house. He did this in 1900, having met Walter Page who had left Atlantic Monthly. As Page's biographer, Burton Hendrick, noted, Page saw his job as "an instrument for promoting the social democracy, for advancing primary education, technical training, scientific agriculture, the improvement of country life, sanitation, and for emphasing in the growing mind the dignity of American citizenship." He and Rachel Carson, who wrote *"Silent Spring,"* would have been friends, but this book he missed. It was published in 1957 by Houghton Mifflin & Co. and is still selling almost 30 years later.

In 1908, Doubleday, Page & Co. acquired Sam McClure's book business. The list of authors going with this acquisition was formidable: Joseph Conrad, Booth Tarkington, Conan Doyle, O. Henry and several other distinguished writers. In 1912, Doubleday Page & Co. acquired the publishing division of Baker & Taylor, and the new house was on its way. This transaction probably started Doubleday, Page & Co. on the road to what it had become in 1987, Doubleday Publishing Company, when it was acquired by Bertelsmann AG. It also allowed Baker & Taylor to concentrate on the business it operates today, book wholesaling as a wholly owned subsidiary of W.R. Grace Company.It is probably impossible to say with any assurance that 1912 was an identifiable point in the history of either company, but, for those interested, it seems like a milestone in the history of both.

Baker & Taylor offers IBM-compatible software for electronic ordering, FIRSTcall. Like Flashback, it requires the use of a computer, a modem and telecommunications software. Books are ordered by ISBN and quantity with order confirmation by the next day. Additionally, Baker & Taylor is currently cooperating with the Fort Lauderdale, Florida owners of Books by Wire, another electronic ordering service. Its goal is an effective network of 2,000 bookstores connected nationwide by a computerized telecommunications system that allows not only the transmission of orders, but can perform a variety of functions including inventory control and billing. For example, a Books by Wire member in Boston takes an order either in-store or by phone, then transmits electronically to a fellow member in San Francisco. Same or next day delivery of the book ordered occurs as a gift. FIRSTcall may be used to re-order books from Baker & Taylor before a bookstore runs out of stock.

Ingrams and Baker & Taylor are, of course, competitors, but beween them they can only help move books into and out of bookstores. They can both do more, however, to help get *more books* into bookstores by developing electronic links with the publishers who, after all, make the books available in the first place. This would be at the expense of a publisher's gross margin on books ordered this way, but by an estimated $0.15 per book. No matter how it's done, the goal is to get more books into the hands of those who will read and enjoy them. A second goal is to reduce the number of books returned by bookstores. Books by Wire tends to move in this direction. A book ordered and delivered as a gift, whether it's fiction or a cookbook is less likely to be returned than one in stock by a bookstore.

Book wholesaling in the United States is widely misunderstood. Publishers in this country tend to be envious of European retail networks. However, neither the Dutch nor German system would work well here because of antitrust laws — the

Sherman Act and state laws, such as in the Cartwright Act in California. The system in the United Kingdom could easily be adapted to conditions in the United States. It is interesting to note how distribution evolved in this country as noted in the Publishers Weekly of November 27, 1972.

"Prior to the War and Depression, many booksellers served their local public and educational libraries, thus enlarging their income and increasing their value to the communities. When the wholesalers absorbed this function, they in fact competed with these retailers and, we might add, in a most remarkable way. They persuaded the publishers to continue to extend, or even to increase, the discount they had received when they were still purchasing books for resale to retailers, and they in turn offered to libraries (on a contract basis) an up-to-then unprecedented discount roughly equivalent to that which they might have given to the retailers they were abandonning."

Accordingly, the wholesalers have shifted a substantial part of the library business from the retailers to the wholesalers. Unfortunately, there was little or nothing the retailers could do except gnash their teeth. In fact, this shift, which was quite substantial, tended to weaken the retailer by removing entirely a reliable portion of his business and along with it a stable source of income. It also weakened the value of the book wholesaling service to bookstores, since many of them were understandably reluctant to continue carrying an inventory for which there was no library market any longer.

As recently as five years ago, Baker & Taylor as well as Ingrams Book Company probably sold an estimated 85% of their books to libraries and about 15% to bookstores. While the reason for the new emphasis on sales to bookstores by wholesalers is only speculative, libraries in many cities tend to suffer from municipal budget cutting since other municipal services have demanded and often gotten a higher share of public funds.

Publishers, at least the giants, seemed indifferent to this shift in business from the retailer to the wholesaler selling to markets once served by the bookstores. The shift may have cost them money because of the higher discounts offered to wholesalers.

For the giant publishers, the system passed the crucial test: it worked. However, the small presses cannot afford to be indifferent. Most of them have little or no access to the library market. Their only market is the independent bookstore and, if they're lucky, the chains, such as Waldenbooks. If the small presses use a distributor, the commission salesmen can sell to either the wholesaler (a 5% commission, but the orders are apt to be larger) or to the retailer (10%). Then, the same salesman may and probably will sell to the wholesaler's customers, the bookstores, often offering slightly higher discounts to make at least the initial order one from the publisher

The wholesalers offer bookstores a maximum discount of about 43% from the cover price, and a publisher's commission salesman who, after all makes his living this way, may offer a discount of from 45% to 48% even for a small order for six copies of a book. He or she may make less by way of commissions, but by discounting the inventory of other publisher-clients, the orders tend to be larger. A sale of 5 to 25 copies calls for a discount of 40%, not 48%. Multiply this discount differential ($1.26 per copy for a book with a cover price of $17.95) by the number of books sold by small press commission salesmen each year, and the loss to the small pressses is staggering, especially when one considers the fact that the small presses publish an estimated 50% of all books published.

Buying from the publisher has two attractive features for the retail bookstore — a higher discount and an advertising allowance plus things like a freight pass through (FPT) price. A publisher may, for example, sell ten copies of a book with a cover price of $17.95 at a 40% discount. This means that the price of one such copy to the bookstore will be $10.77, and ten copies will, without an FPT price, will be $107.70. The FPT price might be lower by about $2.50, or $105.20. Alternatively, the publisher's invoice price may reflect a 40% discount against $17.45 instead of $17.95. Thus, the publisher's invoice price for one copy will be $10.47, so ten copies will be invoiced to the bookstore at $104.70. There are many variations on this, but the principle is the same — the bookstore gets the benefit of part of the cost of shipping books ordered from the publisher instead of a wholesaler. A wholesaler usually identifies books as to which the publisher has offered an FPT price, and this appears in lists sent to bookstores monthly by the wholesalers. The publisher's advertising allowance works in essentially the same way—for the same ten copies first mentioned, its invoice cost to the bookstore will be less by a modest amount for these ten books, eg., $2.00. The point is that the bookstore's *effective* discount is more than 40%, and may be as high as 44% , $10.05 for one copy of a book with a cover price of $17.95. A wholesaler's maximum discount is almost always $43% on sales to a bookstore which normally absorbs the cost of shipping these books, thereby reducing its gross margin when they are sold at the cover price. No one seems to have thought of telling the bookstore that, by using a computer, modem and available software, he can do *comparison shopping* and ordering, all electronically. He can determine quickly whether he will get a better price, i.e., a higher discount and other fringe benefits from the wholesaler or the publisher. In a bookstore which operates on a slim gross margin, a discount differential of 1% for these ten books represents $1.80, a slightly higher gross margin, but enough to make a big difference, if 800 books are all getting the same favorable discount–$1440–enough to pay for the software to do comparison shopping within one selling season.

R.R. Bowker's Books in Print With Reviews Plus has a CD–ROM database with about 750,000 titles. The Format menu offers several options, and one of them is electronic ordering. A bookstore may order a title, if it's in print, from Baker & Taylor, Blackwell, Brodart, Ingrams, PBD–Europe, IBID, Wordstock or Other. The same book may be ordered from its publisher, but only if that publisher has the software to receive and record incoming electronic orders. No publisher or distributor should be without it.

On top of all this, the book business is so completely different from any other business, customer demand is a major factor in selling books. If a bookstore does not stock a title a customer wants, the bookstore can search his microfiche to see what wholesaler not only carries it but also to find out if delivery can be made soon enough to satisfy the customer. If the answer is unsatisfactory, the sale is lost to the wholesaler, the bookstore and the author.

A wholesaler may have an inventory of 400,000 books but it makes no difference if the one the customer wants is not included. The order is automatically cancelled. The wholesaler wants the minimum profitable inventory, and what it does have will include backlist and some, but not all frontlist titles. A wholesaler has a pretty good idea of the titles he can sell to the bookstore and gets it by watching which publishers advertise in the trade journals and other print media. The wholesaler can also make an educated guess that a publisher who spends money on this type of advertising will also use a distributor. He also knows that the distributor's commission salesmen will sell these books to some but not all bookstores. So what does he do? He makes an educated guess that he can sell these advertised books and buys them from the publisher in quantities sufficient to meet anticipated demand, at least for re-orders.

In 1932, when the *Cheney Report* was released, there were no computers. IBM and Burroughs offered nothing more complex than adding machines. It was not until after World War II that the first real computer, Univac, made its appearance. Instead of semiconductors and other hardware such as transistors which are commonplace today, Univac used vaccuum tubes which had a way of failing or burning out at awkward moments. It was not until 1982 that IBM and Apple Computer offered the first personal computer, although the mainframe was in widespread use in the United States and Great Britain. Since 1982, however, the PC rapidly became more sophisticated and less expensive. One of the country's leading developers of software, Microsoft, Inc., developed the disk operating system (DOS) in 1981, and the revolution in personal computers was beginning. Almost overnight, dozens of companies were formed to exploit this market, and now there are an estimated 1,200 companies offering software alone. Lotus Development Inc. and Digital Communications Inc. (Microstuf, Inc. was acquired by it in 1986) were only two of the early entrants into this field, and, with Ashton-Tate

Company, word-processing software became quite commonplace. There are now about 40 companies in this field alone. In 1983, one of the other companies to enter the telecommunications field offered the modem, Hayes Microcomputer Products, Inc. The modem was an essential component allowing data transfer from one computer to another in a remote location and did so over telephone lines. At various times before, during and after World War II, other companies emerged and became leaders in the field. They included Hewlett Packard, Digital Equipment, Inc., Texas Instruments and Compaq Computer, to name only some of these industry giants.

The appearance on the scene of so much computing power, reasonably priced, modems and truly sophisticated software began to change how most businesses operated. There was considerable reluctance on the part of publishers to change the way they operated. Some authors, however, almost forced a few publishers to at least accept manuscripts typed using word-processing software. Even the use of applications software in-house by publishers for purely business data processing was very slow in coming. The most important of all functions in all publishing houses, the editorial function, was the last to be given any attention at all. It was not until 1983 that typesetting software made an appearance on the scene, and it has rapidly become far more sophisticated. While there are many printers now on the market to print editorial output, Hewlett Packard was the first to introduce the laser printer. It used the Canon engine to print text at 300 dots per inch, not high enough to produce book quality copy. Then Tegra, Inc. introduced its Genesis printer with a resolution of 1,000 dots per inch. The Linotronic 300 was a very expensive printer used by many commercial printers to print camera ready copy with a resolution of about 1,800 dots per inch, but its cost was too high for the small presses who published too few books to recover this cost in the form of savings plus depreciation. Belatedly, software developers discovered they had a huge market in the publishing and bookselling business, particularly the small presses.

Deliverance Systems, in San Rafael, California developed a modular software system specifically designed for the small presses. The basic module, which has a retail price of $2,295, handles orders, returns and payment entry, along with integrated accounts receivable and inventory tracking. Various add-on modules handle sales and promotion analysis, backorders, fulfillment, consignment tracking and reporting, custom mailing list generation and royalty tracking and reporting. Unfortunately, it tends to treat all small presses as though they operated without a national or regional distributor and fulfilled orders from their own warehouse. Some do, but most small presses use distributors. Bookmaster, offered by an Atherton, California firm seems to move in the right direction. At a price of $4,950, Bookmaster software is designed for both publishers and wholesalers. It calculates discounts, royalties and commissions. Additionally, it will handle payment processing, credit control and schedules of accounts receivable along with inventory management. For reasons difficult to understand, however, software for bookstores, including inventory management and electronic ordering, have not been widely used where it would be most useful, the bookstores themselves, many of which do not even use computers at all. IBID and Booklog are two such systems, but expensive. Wordstock is another. Even the most fundamental need of a bookstore, general ledger accounting, has received little attention. In the meantime, too many independent bookstores use outside accountants at a substantial annual cost to prepare a balance sheet and a profit and loss analysis. Taproot Accounting System, expects to deal with this problem with its software scheduled for release in March, 1988. Mercury House installed this system in early 1988. It is unique in the sense that the system which can start on a single computer and grow with the company into a multi-computer network without the need for additional programming or more expensive modules. Its developers expect to offer their system at a price even the samll press and the independent bookstore will find affordable, about $2,400, somewhat less than the amount a bookstore pays an accountant each year. Small presses want to be able to move their books into bookstores, and do so at less cost than the current ineffiency of the distribution systen permits. A bookstore without a business plan can't be expected to know what its real objectives should be other than selling books at a net profit which is enough to allow its owners to enjoy a good life in a world they all love, the world of books. By itself, this is simply not enough. Bookstores need to know whether the money they spend is spent wisely and in places which increase the net profit they currently enjoy. The wholesalers and the small presses both see this, and use state-of-the-art technology to move books into bookstores. It is up to the bookstores to move them out and into the hands of the consumer, and to do so at a higher gross margin and a higher net profit. This includes textbooks which all to too few people consider as "books." Bookstores have sold them for many decades to people interested in art, history, science and literature as well as technology and computer languages. The existence of databases with massive amounts of information, many of them barely known except to those with computers to access them, retrieve the information they contain and edit the result as books, including textbooks. This has become possible only in the last two or three years.

# Chapter 12
# A Rising Tide of Mediocrity in Our Schools

The United States is the largest and richest market in the world for books in the English language. However, publishers not showing more interest in ending illiteracy at all age levels may be missing an opportunity to enlarge that market by an estimated 40 million potential book buyers. The stakes in money alone are enormous, since the American market includes publishers of textbooks written for all age levels from kindergarten through college and post graduate education. For the July-September 1988 period, for example, the *Dessauer Report* showed estimated net book sales of Adult Hardcover trade books at $532.4 million, an increase of 14.3% over the same period for 1987. Hardcover Elhi textbooks showed estimated net sales of $611.1 million for the same period during 1988, an increase of 5% over the same period during 1987. What follows is an analysis by this writer of that market, beginning with reading and how it might be taught in a way that expands the market for *all* books. Educational reform and a good working knowledge of American history go to the very heart of the problem.

There are, it is estimated, about 23,000,000 illiterate people in this country — they can't read. There is also a growing underclass of children who move through school, beginning with kindergarten and ending with high school, who cannot read. Without actual figures from some 14,000 school districts in the United States, it is literally impossible to do anything more than estimate the number of young students who have already dropped out of school entirely. It is also impossible to estimate the number of students who may, for whatever reason, decide to leave school at a point where the most they can expect is a job paying a minimum wage, perhaps a little more with vocational training. The estimated loss of productivity may well be measured in the billions of dollars.

The test scores of 1988 high school graduates paint a bleak picture of education in the United States, a nation still "at risk." Average Scholastic Aptitude Test (SAT) scores declined for the first time in eight years. The verbal SAT test section, for example, measures skills, such as reading, history and social studies, and a perfect score is 800. In California, a state that spends less on education than 25 other states, the average score on the verbal section was 424, the same as it was in 1987. Only 44% of the 1988 graduates took the test at all.

In Texas, the average score was 417, and in Indiana the average score was 412, 5 points lower than Texas. In Massachusetts, the average score on the verbal section was 432, but 73% of the 1988 high school graduates took the test. Those taking the SAT tend to be academically stronger than those not taking it at all. In Georgia, the average score was 404, in South Carolina it was 400 and in North Carolina, it was 401. Financing the education of an entirely new generation in the skills needed to function in an increasingly competitive and technological world has, very simply, been both neglected and under-financed during the last eight years, even such a basic skill such as reading.

In the election of November 8, 1988 the Bush-Quayle ticket carried the once solid south, traditionally a Democratic bastion. Virginia, North and South Carolina, Georgia, Florida, Alabama, Louisiana, Mississippi, Tennessee, Arkansas, Oklahoma and Kentucky all voted overwhelmingly for this Republican ticket. Amongst other things, this means that minorities, most of them black and Hispanic, stand to lose many of the gains of the civil rights laws of the 1960s. Racial harrassment at all educational levels is very likely to increase, and it will come from white students who seem to feel threatened by gains made by minorities over the last 20 or so years. Ugly incidents at some universities outside the south have become almost daily occurrences, particularly at those institutions of higher learning with minority students comprising some 40% to 50% of the total student population. As a result, many minority students live in an atmosphere of intolerance, bigotry and fear. Hardly any university or college is free of bigotry. High school graduates now starting college do not seem to have had any knowledge of the civil rights laws passed in the 1960s and tend to see minorities as somehow threatening to them on the basis of color or ethnic origin. The University of California at Berkeley, Stanford, Yale University, Dartmouth and many others must somehow deal with a rising tide of intolerance and racial harrassment.

Section 501 (3)(c) of the Internal Revenue Code (Title 26) exempts these universities from payment of income tax, and contributions made to them may be taken as deductions on the income tax returns of those making such contributions. However, there are civil rights laws making denial of rights "under color of law" a criminal offense. 18 U.S.C. 242 provides in part that "Whoever, under color of any law . . . willfully subjects [any person] to the deprivation of any rights . . . secured or protected by the Constitution or laws of the United States . . . by reason of his color or race . . . shall be fined not more than $1,000 or imprisoned not more than one year, or both . . ."

Universities, whether public or private, enjoy tax exempt status. In addition, they must provide a safe place in which students may work, i.e., learn after having been admitted for that purpose. However, only the Department of Justice may initiate an action alleging a violation of 18 U.S.C. 242, since there is no private cause of action allowed under this section. A private cause of action may be initiated alleging a violation of 42 U.S.C. 1983 which provides that "Every person who, under color of state law, . . . " deprives a student, for example, of these civil rights "shall be liable to the party injured." The phrase "under color of law" means the same thing under both of the above sections. See Canty v. City of Richmond, Virginia Police Department, 343 F. Supp. 1396, affirmed at 526 F.2d 587 (1975), cert denied at 423 U.S. 1062.

There is, indeed, a rising tide of mediocrity in our educational system, and black students from kindergarten through college are its real victims because of discrimination and racial harrassment from other students, all white. They are not without a remedy which may be pursued through the courts using 42 U.S.C. 1983 and Rule 23, Federal Rules of Civil Procedure. Rule 23 provides that one or more members of a class may sue on behalf of the entire class. In the case of universities which take little, or no effective action against bigotry and racial harrassment, a Rule 23 class action may name the Commissioner of Internal Revenue as defendant. Having granted tax exempt status in the first place, the Commissioner may terminate that status upon a finding that the universities allow the deprivation of some students' civil rights by not providing a safe environment to learn, are no longer engaged in solely educational activities. In Scripture Press Foundation v. U.S., 285 F.2d 800 (1961), cert denied 368 U.S. 985, it was held that the Commissioner might revoke the tax exempt status of church upon a finding that it was no longer engaged in solely religious activities.

There are other reasons for actions making universities and high schools initiate so-called "black studies" programs as part of the total curriculum. No white student may graduate without taking this course, and it should require a history of black contributions to American history and culture, including the history of civil rights under the 13th and 14th Amendments and the school desegregation cases going back to 1954. In Brown v. Board of Education of Topeka, Kansas, 349 U.S. 294 Chief Justice Warren, writing for a unanimous court, held that "racial discrimination in public education is unconstititional." Such a history book for different age groups should show Martin Luther King, the brutality of Selma, Alabama and the Governor of Alabama standing at a school house door symbolically barring the door so a courageous black girl could not enter its learning environment reserved for whites only. The civil rights laws of the 1960s soon followed these acts of defiance of the Supreme Court's mandate. All of this could easily be included in textbooks for use in elementary, secondary and high schools as well as university levels. At all of these levels of education, the course should be required as a condition of promotion and graduation.

In the *San Francisco Chronicle* dated October 31, 1988 a headline read **"The Burgeoning Crisis in California's Schools."** Noting that some schools have made "dramatic adjustments," Angie Cannon, Staff Writer for the Chronicle, went on to report that most schools have done little to cope with the special needs of immigrant students. The story also reported that "California's public school system is . . . on the front line of a demographic and cultural revolution." In the figures from the California Department of Education, the ten counties with the greatest number of English-deficient students were listed. Alameda, Santa Clara and San Francisco showed a total of 65,937 such students, Fresno County reported 16,050, Los Angeles County had 282,500 English-deficient students, and the combined total of San Bernardino, Orange, Riverside and San Diego accounted for 128,257 more. The total number of English-deficient students in all ten counties for 1987 added up to 492,744 of which 72% were Spanish speaking students, or 354,775. In 1988, however, there was an increase in one year to 475,775, an increase of 33.9% over 1987. To make the problem more difficult, California voters approved by initiative-Article III, Section 6-adding a "common language" requirement to the state Constitution. The common language was English, and Section 6 (d) allows any person "to enforce this section" in the courts. Unfortunately, the voters did not understand the nature of the cultural and demographic revolution that was occurring, and the results of this failure to see what was happening have now appeared in *The San Francisco Chronicle*. On November 8, 1988 Florida's voters approved a "common language," English, amendment to the state constitution. In the near future, the Florida school system will have to come to grips with the same problem as that found in California.

These initiative measures almost unquestionably had their origin in latent nationalism or xenophobia, a fear and hatred of foreigners. Moreover, there are very few credentialled teachers fluent in Spanish, let alone Chinese, Vietnamese or Thai. Large employers did nothing to discourage this nationalism for the very simple reason that it would cost money to train employees to read even basic safety instructions as well as training manuals for office machines, such as computers.

Some teachers argue that these students made a choice to live in America and must learn English. Actually, their parents made the choice, and their children were the innocent victims of an inadequate, hopelessly inefficient approach to bilingual education. The first point to be made is that many students are illiterate in their own language, having come from Mexico and Central America. Their parents were poor, and the children got little formal education in the country of origin.

This worsening situation seems soluble, but only if teachers will learn to use computers in the classroom and paid for by the state. Spanish-speaking children can learn English in less than a year, if they begin in kindergarten at age 4 or 5. The key to doing this is what may be described as "bilingual software" and a voice synthesizer that pronounces letters and words in English-explicit phonics.

This approach is not unlike what is described as "whole language," a somewhat controversial topic. Whole language is thought to encourage literacy by combining reading, writing, speaking and listening into a unified whole. This approach has its critics. They argue that it ignores basic skills, and that children simply memorize specific words rather than learning to read.

Many educators believe that the ability to soak up words is phenomenal. A four-year old may know as many as 3,000 words. However, the speed at which they learn new, unfamiliar words seems to decrease when they actually enter kindergarten. Other educators argue that "Yes, phonics is important, but one shouldn't get the whole class being drilled on the letter P or a word like pet." A dog is a pet, so conceptual clarification is easy for a child.

Louis (Bill) Honig, California's Superintendent of Public Instruction is ambivalent, arguing that phonics must still be taught in the earliest grades. Honig recognizes that the whole language people want children to read for meaning from the start. "But," he seems to argue, "children don't know the meaning of all the words." Of course they don't! They are told to look the word up in a dictionary. So, instead of getting an instant definition by using a computer with wordprocessing software, the child has been made to stand in line to get at a dictionary. No teacher can possibly find enough classroom time to handle definitions for 20 or 30 students, all with different learning curves. With a computer and wordprocessing software plus a voice synthesizer, a child will require less individual attention from the teacher, especially if the word retrieved from the software is used within the context of a simple sentence, eg., "My dog is a pet." Memorization is not necessary at all, only conceptualization of an image already familiar to him or her, such as a friendly cocker spaniel.

Most wordprocessing software programs have a dictionary or thesaurus feature. Multimate Advantage (Ashton Tate) and WordPerfect (WordPerfect Corporation) both have this feature, and just about anyone can retrieve the definition of an unfamiliar word with a single keystroke on the computer keyboard-Alt t. Any definition may be retrieved in about 1 second. With five choices, all numbered, a user simply keys in the numbered synonym, and the word used is replaced on the computer's monitor in less than a second, eg., instant, (1) amongst the 8 alternatives to the word "second."

With a few refinements, Spanish may be learned in the same way using any good Spanish-English, English-Spanish dictionary or thesaurus feature in a wordprocessing program. Appleton's New Cuyás Dictionary was used for the examples in this text. This "bilingual software" needs to be written as a program, however, and one that a five-year old child can use. The Hennigan School in Boston uses computers to teach children to read and do simple math, but in English. Aside from a voice synthesizer, a "mouse" represents another refinement. A "mouse" is simply a device which can roll on a flat surface, and it moves the cursor on the computer monitor or screen. When the cursor locates the word to be defined, a user simply "clicks" the hand-held "mouse," and a definition is seen on the monitor, and the synthesizer pronounces the word. In English, for example, the word "cat" appears as, let's say, a feline animal, ie., catlike. In

Spanish, the word for cat is "gato" or "gata." So a child learning English will see a familiar word, use the "mouse" to find its English equivalent. "Nosotros tenemos el gato en casa." By using the cursor, the child can get a familiar word, cat, within the context of that sentence and also "We have a cat at home." Then, a phrase "Que la pasa?" will be found to translate as "What's wrong with her?" and so on with many examples available.

The point is not complicated. A 5-year old Spanish-speaking child can learn to read English, even to pronounce most words commonly used at that age level, in less than a year, but only if there are computers in the clssroom. Its "bilingual software" will have an Spanish-English thesaurus and a voice synthesizer. Each classroom needs a sympathetic teacher who is reasonably computer-literate. This means only that the teacher must know the sequence of keystrokes necessary to cause the desired result.

The Hennigan School in Boston is a public school with 220 students and about 100 computers. This school has students from kindergarten through 6th grade. On a visit to this school on October 15, 1988 this writer spent several hours with a few of the children, and they took real pride in showing what they had learned-reading and simple math. One was six and the other was barely eight. The computers used were IBM PCJrs. They had monochrome monitors and a line printer. They used this to print out simple graphics and a box divided into the dissimilar fractions they had learned. International Business Machines is now marketing what it calls the IBM Personal Computer Classroom LAN (Local Area Network) Administration System. It runs on a classroom server, essentially a microcomputer with some 80MB of memory, and students may access this server for every classroom function including lesson assignments for individual students and assigned by the teacher. IBM also offers Writing to Read, software for use in the classroom by kindergarten students. This program has been tested by the Educational Testing Service (ETS) in Princeton, New Jersey, beginning in 1982, and it works. ETS found that children could handle the technology and the movement from one workstation to another. Writing to Read was designed to help teach kindegartners and first graders how to write anything they can say and read anything they can write. Over 1,300 schools with more than 90,000 children are currently learning to read and write using the IBM system just described. The total cost of installing about 45 PS/2 Model 25 computers, a classroom server, network hardware and the software is about $50,000. This setup is about right for a school with 90 students. These students, many of them from diverse racial and socioeconomic backgrounds with different pre-school reading and writing experiences, represent an enormous future market for books from all publishers. These students will be both literate and find reading to be a pleasure.

Small presses may want to consider moving into this educational market to help both themselves and those who need help in learning to read. Aside from the sheer altruism of helping others to help themselves by reducing the current school drop out rate, the small presses would create an entirely new and enormous market for their own books. One way of approaching the problem of illiteracy is to publish textbooks for use by all from 4 to 5 and 50-plus years of age. Hardly any publisher's director of marketing and sales would overlook the potential market for *all* books, even into the next generation by helping so many people to learn and enjoy reading. This includes millions more students just beginning to learn how to read. The textbooks *they* use represent an enormous market. Why not get into it as a small press? Notwithstanding recent statements from the Secretary of Education, William Bennett, that educational reform has made some public school students' score higher on tests, we are still, he said, "a nation at risk." There will never be a better time to publish better textbooks in the areas of history, mathematics, science and social studies.

In 1983, the National Commission on Excellence in Education issued its report, *A Nation at Risk*. It found that "a rising tide of mediocrity" was engulfing our schools and "threatening our very future as a Nation and as a people." Five years later, the Secretary of Education, William Bennett, reported to President Reagan. He told the President: "We're doing better. But we're not where we should be . . . . We are still at risk."

The claim that we are doing better rests in part on the national mania for subjecting students to batteries of tests ranging from the Stanford Achievement Test (SAT) to the California Achievement Test (CAT). Many school administrators have begun using "student" test scores on the CAT as one way of evaluating "teachers" for salary increases or even to continuing to hold their jobs. Unless teachers could "teach the tests" and the students did not test well, they were presumed incompetent. Many of these same administrators have hired outside consultants to help align curriculum content, including textbooks used in the classroom, with the requirements of the CAT and other tests such as the SAT. There are about four major publishers who churn out these standardized tests. They include CTB/McGraw Hill, Science Research Association, The Psychological Corporation and The Riverside Publishing Company. *The Literary Market Place* (LMP) lists The Riverside Publishing Company as a subsidiary of Houghton Mifflin Co., a publisher of textbooks and "test publications." CTB/McGraw-Hill is listed as a division of McGraw-Hill, Inc., also a publisher of textbooks and "standardized tests." The LMP for 1988 does not list Science Research Associates. The Psychological Corporation is listed as a subsidiary of Harcourt Brace Jovanovich, a major textbook publisher, and this subsidiary markets the SAT. British Printing Corp. PLC, owned by Robert Maxwell of London, has just succeeded in buying Macmillan, Inc. for $2.4 billion, and this major U.S. corporation publishes textbooks on a very large scale.

It seems clear that control of curriculum content, including what textbooks are used in the classrooms, has been slowly transferred from the local school districts to the publishers of textbooks. "Buy our textbooks," they say, "and your students will do better on test scores." The other side of this coin is also clear. School administrators buy and administer these tests designed to make it seem that they are doing a superior job of teaching or, as the Secretary of Education said, ". . . . to make progress" out of "the nation at risk" stigma.

Some of the major publishers of standardized tests continue to publish textbooks that were the subject of harsh criticism in a study issued by the Teachers College at Columbia University in late 1987. Amongst other thing, this Report noted that publishers are increasingly in the business of appeasing willful interest groups. In the case of standardized test publishers, the "willful interest groups" can be seen as school administrators who want to satisfy their constituents, the parents of school — age children and the taxpayers.

Many states where tests are given on a statewide basis all claim to testing above the national average. However, standard criteria for measuring educational performance, such as per capita income, graduation rates, performance on college entrance exams, statewide literacy rates and the amount spent for public schools per student all show that some of these states rank below the national average. They include such states as Alabama, Georgia, South Carolina, North Carolina, West Virginia, Tennesse, Kentucky, Arkansas, Oklahoma and Texas. With the single exception of West Virginia, the Bush-Quayle ticket carried all these states in the election of November 8, 1988. Even inner city school districts, often thought to be below the national norm, reported test results *above* the national average.

Curriculum content, including textbooks, very often determines how students learn, as well as what they learn. It was not until 1979 that Frances FitzGerald wrote *America Revised: History Schoolbooks in the Twentieth Century,* a book which illuminated areas of both education and textbook publishing that had been given little or no public attention. In the 1950s, history textbooks preached a blatant chauvinism and a mindless materialism. In 1957, for example, the Soviet *Sputnik* sparked a demand for a better science curriculum. We could not allow ourselves to fall behind the Russians. In the 1960s, however, with the war in Vietnam and the civil rights revolution, many Americans were compelled to re-examine themselves, their nation and the world. In some areas, there was an infusion of modern scholarship which tried to improve the textbooks our public schools were using. All too often, however, these efforts by scholars ran into the textbook selection process used by many states. The competing interests of religion and social responsibility combined to reject scholarship and produce mediocrity and even censorship in textbooks. One of the major arguments in education centered on the question of basic skills, such as reading and writing. Thus, in the 1980s, the nature and use of textbooks was beginning to get serious attention. Unfortunately, the textbook and educational field continued to be dominated by a very few large publishers, and the small presses tended to remain on the sidelines.

Few people think of textbooks as "books" sold in bookstores. They are clearly present in bookstores, and most if not all of them reach the retailer from either the publishers or the wholesalers. If a student is interested in almost any conceivable subject, he or she can browse in a bookstore and buy books on that subject. A student could do a lot worse than reading Burdett Loomis' *The New American Politician: Ambition, Entreprenurship and the Changing Face of Political Life.* Published by Basic Books, Inc., a subsidiary of Harper & Row, Publishers, Inc., this book was reviewed in the Book Section of *The New York Times* for November 13, 1988 and discussed the role money plays in American politics today. If, on the other hand, the subject of interest is 17th century Russia, the student might want to read *Peter The Great,* by Henri Troyat, translated from the French by Joan Pinkham and published by E.P. Dutton. Arguably, Peter the Great, whose reign began in 1682 and ended in 1725, moved Russia into the Western world from which it has never departed. Troyat described the innovative side to this Tsar's murderous rule and the terrible toll in lives he exacted. Peter the Great was no better or worse than Ivan the Terrible or Joseph Stalin. If, on the other hand, a student's interest lies in the history of espionage, he or she might want to read Phillip Knightly's *The Second Oldest Profession.* Of this book, John le Carré said: "If Reagan, Gorbachev, Thatcher and Mitterand only manage one book a year, they could do a lot worse than pick up Phillip Knightley's and discover what imbecilities are committed in the hallowed name of intelligence." Others include William Greider's *Secrets of the Temple,* an excellent book about the origins of the Federal Reserve System and the power of its Federal Open

Market Committee which can raise or lower the interest rates people pay for just about everything. Its deliberations occur in secrecy, hence the title. There are many others, such as *Redeeming the Time: A People's History of the 1920s and the New Deal*, Joseph Cotten's autobiography, *Vanity Will Get You Somewhere*, *Mayday: Eisenhower, Khrushchev and the U-2 Affair, Portraits of the Fifties, Portraits of Paris, The Day Nothing Happened* and *1949: The First Israelis.* The best seller lists are full of others, all of which, including cookbooks, must be treated as textbooks.

Students learn because they are curious, and the many good teachers know this. Learning, at least from textbooks and teachers, can be an exciting experience, and it begins with the first day in school, kindergarten through grades 1 to 8 and never really ends. A student's access to knowledge currently lies in textbooks used in the classroom. Wisdom is something else, the compassionate and ethical application of knowledge to one's own environment.

In his book, *Understanding Media,* published in 1957, Marshall McLuhan said we were suffering from information overload. Thirty years later, the evidence of this information "explosion" may be found in databases around the United States and Western Europe. Lexis and Nexis, from Mead Data is in widespread use by lawyers. Newsnet offers more than 300 on-line services covering 35 industry areas including *The Seybold Report on Publishing Systems, Wiley Book News, Editors Only, Japan High Tech Review, German Business Scope* and *Latin American Debt Chronicle,* to name only a very few. The Securities and Exchange Commission's Electronic Data Gathering, Analysis and Retrieval system, known as *EDGAR,* in a report dated December 31, 1986, noted that electronic filings of corporate America increased from 6,900 to over 11,900 in the six months ending on that date. Students interested in what corporations in the United States have done to finance acquisitions and mergers can easily access this information.

Other databases include Dialog, with its Books in Print and other information, all on-line, *The New York Times* and *Dow-Jones, Inc.,* with more than just daily closing prices on the various exchanges in the United States. The Library of Congress has listed all of its books on a computerized system by title, author and subject matter. So have many public libraries. University libraries, the repositories of knowledge for centuries, have done the same. Indeed, much of the research for this book was pursued in the library of the University of California at Santa Barbara, using computerized search technology. In addition to a treasure of books, this library had issues of *Publishers Weekly* going back to before 1920. Why not use all this information to write textbooks for use in the classrooms of California and other states? Dialog, a California database, offers an electronic American history course which can be printed out for the benefit of students. Teachers will need to learn its search methods, and Dialog offers frequent classes for those willing to spend a day learning them.

Textbooks can be written by students in grades 1 through 8, even kindergarten, with some help from teachers and older students willing to show their younger counterparts how to operate computers and access all these databases, such as Newsnet's *Social Sciences* and *Environmental Compliance Update*. M.I.T.'s Media Laboratory in Massachusetts is where student-designed textbooks might begin. There, for example, Seymour Papert, the inventor of LOGO, a computer language for children, is currently directing a pilot project in which elementary school students are encouraged to explore new uses for computers. The Media Laboratory has a promising demonstration model now, but it's a "personalized newspaper," not yet a textbook. LOGO, however, is primarily graphics-oriented, but it can and has been used in kindergarten in a way which allows children to "tell" a computer to show a tree, a dog or even an elephant on the monitor used with the computer, sometimes in at least 16 color combinations or more.

The school used to create this unique learning environment is located in the Jamaica Plains area of Boston, the Hennigan School. It is a public school in a racially mixed neighborhood and has classes running from kindergarten through 6th grade. For about 220 students, there are 100 computers. Children of four have begun to learn basic skills, such as reading and simple math. Using Logo, some children can and have used a line printer do print out graphics and ways of showing dissimilar fractions in graphical form. They seem to love what they are doing, and two of them took great pride in showing this writer how a computer works amd what it will do for them.

Why not let students write their own simple programs with help and print their own kindergarten graphics, ie., pictures, maps and drawings of toys? Text would appear later, probably in 2nd or 3rd grade, and become more detailed as the learning curve improves. A geography texbook and how it might be done in the classroom may make the point. Unlike a history textbook, with either the reference to religion or its complete omission, geography is non-controversial. Hardly anyone still thinks the world is flat, even the religious fundamentalists or the "secular humanists" or "creationists."

Today, there are satellites orbiting the globe in either geo-synchronous or earth orbit. Some of them have been placed there by private, commercial firms and routinely gather and transmit data to these firms. Computers are used to translate digital signals into fairly high-resolution pictures, which may then be sold to others. The range of data used in this manner is expanding by an exponential factor. The location of earth resources can be mapped with great precision as can the location of cities, their buildings and parks and their street grid designs. Today, the resolution of satellite photographs can resolve objects as small as ten meters, or about 39 feet. Within a few years, the resolution of earth objects is expected to be one meter, 3.9 feet, or even better. For students in New York City, Chicago, Dallas, Los Angeles or San Francisco, mapping another city, such as London, Paris, Rome, Cairo, Moscow, Teheran, Beijing or Rio de Janeiro, which many of them may never visit in their lifetimes, would be an enormously exciting and stimulating experience. In the long run, a geography textbook using these with explanatory text by teachers would cost publishers less money than the long, expensive adoption process followed in 22 states now. Color transparencies of agriculture in Algeria and the destruction of Brazil's rain forest are absolutely breathtaking.

Opposition to civilian use of such privately-obtained data has been slow to surface, but, as resolution increases, the Department of Defense has become increasingly concerned, almost in a direct ratio to the increase in resolution. National security may be compromised by the widespread availability of photographs of U.S. troops, weapons and missiles. However, this argument works both ways. Recently, the Department of Defense published a satellite-obtained photograph of a Russian radar installation under construction in Pechora, near the Kara Sea and may use this to ask Congress to appropriate more funds for its own program. The photograph was made using data from a privately owned satellite. In the meantime, Soviet satellites are busy mapping the United States and some of its military installations. The legal challenge to the public sale of privately obtained satellite photographs may well be made by the press under the First Amendment's guarantee of freedom of speech and of the press.

The Soviet Union, regardless of the outcome, will continue to use satellite photography smiling all the way to the Kremlin or the KGB in Dzerzchinsky Square carrying pictures with a resolution of one centimeter, 0.39 inches. While geography as a subject studied in the classroom may not be controversial, one way of making it more understandable and stimulating to 5-year old students seems certain to generate much heat and very little light, namely, a Department of Defense classification of Top Secret. This means only that its satellite photographs will not be available to students who want to study geography by looking at high resoluton pictures of Cairo, Caracas and Moscow or Beijing in their textbooks with street grids, historical sites such as the Colosseum in Rome or St. Mark's Square in Venice. Even so, ways of learning from student-designed textbooks in California and elsewhere must continue. Since 1983, IBM has spent $100 million to support 3,000 research projects dealing with ways of integrating computer technology with education. Apple Computer is moving in the same direction, namely, developing ways to make the computer more effective as part of the learning process in the schools. Very soon, both teachers and students will probably find out that textbooks designed by both may be the answer. Small presses have a sound reason for wanting the computer to become part of the learning process. With about 23,000,000 people illiterate in the United States today, helping the next generation to learn to read will greatly expand the market for books of all kinds, including theirs.

How children learn words and how to read was the subject of an article in the September, 1987 issue of *Scientific American*. It was written by George A. Miller and Patricia M. Gildea. "The key," they said, "is to see words in intelligible contexts. A dictionary is often misunderstood, but an interactive video (a computer's monitor) can mobilize the natural ability of a child to learn from context." According to the authors, most schools tell the 4th grader to use the dictionary to define an unfamiliar word and use its meaning in a sentence. Most children seem to dislike dictionaries, since they are told to use these word definitions in a way which interrupts and slows down the learning process. For example, a child may be given a sentence with an unfamiliar word–one with two or more senses–and told to look it up in the dictionary and decide for themselves which sense the author had in mind. Results were often unpredictable. A favorite example quoted by the authors of the article came from a 5th grader who had to look up the word *erode*. He found that it meant *eat out* or, alternatively, *eat away* and came up with the sentence: "Our family erodes a lot." Another example required the use of *correlate*, defined as "1. be related to one another, and 2. put into relation. The child will usually recognize the concept–be related–and compose a sentence: "Me and my parents correlate, because without them I wouldn't be here."

In the article, the authors suggest a better way to learn is by, amongst other things, recognizing the motivation to discover meaning in "linguistic messages." Dictionaries are too slow, and their use in elementary schools is "likely to compound interruption with misunderstanding." A human tutor would be much better.

According to the authors of the article, the reading vocabulary of the average 17-year old high school graduate is about 80,000 words, including names, places, friends and so forth. This means he or she has learned an average of 4,705 words a year for 17 years, or 12.9 words a day. "Children," said the authors. " must have a special talent for this kind of learning." The ability of preschoolers to soak up words is phenomenal. However, the speed at which they learn new, unfamiliar words seems to decrease when they actually enter nursery school or kindergarten. In learning a new, unfamiliar word there, conceptual clarification and phonological drill (pertaining to the science of speech sounds), there is simply not enough classroom time to teach more than 100 to 200 new words a *year* in this way. What the authors seem to emphasize is the very real importance of providing the information while the child still wants it, not from a dictionary at home or even in the classroom. Too slow and inefficient. The only realistic alternative is the computer which provides *instant* information.

Oxford University Press offers a paperback *Advanced Learner's Dictionary of Current English.* It costs about $9.00 per copy, and there should be two or three of them in every elementary school classroom. It not only offers definitions of words, but also uses simple sentences using the word defined in context. The word, erode, for example, is defined as "wear away; eat into:" The sentence using this word reads: "Metals are eroded by acids." and another sentence might read: "Wind and rain cause soil erosion." In Appleton's New Cuyá's Dictionary (Spanish-English and English-Spanish), the word "erode" is defined as *corroer, roer and comer* as well as *corrosivo.* In many cases, a word is used as part of a phrase, but rarely in a simple sentence.

Bilingual education could easily be the beneficiary of computer technology with the use of "split screen" monitors. It is comparatively simple to "see" A History of the United States and Una Historia de los Estados Unidos on the same monitor, side—by—side and read simultaneously. So could use of common expressions like *pasar por los armas* (to take a penalty shot as in basketball). *La capacitión bilingüe es muy importante.* Another way of doing the same thing is to program a computer to show a new word, such as "to erode" in Spanish and using a simple Spanish sentence with its use in reverse video — highlighted. The child learning English can then move the cursor with his or her "mouse" to the highlighted word and "click" the "mouse." Instantly, the computer's monitor will show two or three more simple sentences using the word, *erode,* in its different senses, ie., *eat out* and *eat away.* With the phrase *¿Que le pasa,* the word *le,* would be "clicked" by the "mouse," and the English word, *him,* would appear in its place on the monitor. Xerox manufactures hardware which uses a split screen monitor which would make it easier for a student to type a paragraph, or even more, in English, translating from any one of 40 basic languages on the other side of the monitor. Or a Spanish child in elementery school might type a translation from Spanish into English as homework. The basic system costs about $7,000.

The transition from published textbooks to classroom—designed texts would be simple, and California might be amongst the first of the 50 states to underwrite a state-wide project to do this. Assembly Bill 1820 calls for the formation of a Human Corps within public and private schools with post-secondary students providing at least 30 hours of community service in each academic year. A.B. 1820 has amended California's Education Code to add Section 99100 to this code. The Legislative intent, as stated in Section 99100(a)(7) states "Our state faces enormous unmet human needs and social challenges including undereducated children, especially minorities, increasing illiteracy and teenage pregnancy, environmental con-tamination, homelessness, school drop-outs, and growing needs for elder care." Why not define community service as giving elementary students and their teachers help in writing textbooks which will help solve some of these "unmet human needs?" A growing number of high school, undergraduate and graduate students are finding time to do local volunteer work. There is a real personal commitment involved in tutoring children who live in an inner city ghetto neighborhood or have parents who live on incomes below the poverty line. A volunteer who is able to get closer to those he or she tutors learns a great deal about the student—the story of their past, what's troubling them, what they want, what scares them to death and the economics of their neighborhood. These volunteers are expected to see the Human Corps as a way of connecting their personal commitment with the life of the mind by helping students write their own text books with some guidance from teachers on the classroom firing line.

In 1985, California's Legislature also amended the Education Code to add Section 60200.5. This amendment states: "(Textbooks) adopted under this chapter shall, where appropriate, be designed to impress upon the minds of pupils the principles of morality, truth, justice, patriotism, and a true comprehension of the rights, duties and dignity of American citizenship, and to instruct them in manners and morals and the principles of a free government . . . . "

What the Legislature intended by this 1985 amendment is not entirely free of ambiguity. However, the language of the amendment is unambiguous. Textbook publishers need no longer perform their role as Ministries of Truth for children, at least in those textbooks dealing with "the principles of a free government." Presumably, this means a working knowledge of the Constitution and its history on the part of publishers' editors. They can now respond to localized criticism from special interest groups that truth is now mandated by law. Will truth also require textbook publishers to say something about the role of religion in the history of the United States and not run afoul of the Establishment Clause of the First Amendment by a statutory requirement that "secular humanism" and "creationism" be included in history textbooks? The Establishment Clause requires judicial neutrality and should not perpetuate the tyranny of the fundamentalist minority by upholding such a statute. To do so would deny centuries of history where the Bible was a source of inspiration for many people, but not the only such source, since scientists from Newton to Einstein, Edward Teller and Pasteur found their inspiration from many areas of intellectual activity. To now intensify the fury of this battle by demanding that "secular humanism" and "creationism," which call for a literal interpretation of the Bible, is no more than a contemporary version of *Newspeak* and denies centuries of intellectual activity.

To any one who has read George Orwell's *1984,* the Ministry of Truth was an enormous pyramidal structure where one could see a sign with the three slogans of the Party:

WAR IS PEACE

FREEDOM IS SLAVERY

IGNORANCE IS STRENGTH

This was *Newspeak,* the official language of Oceania, and it was designed to meet the ideological needs of *Ingsoc,* or English Socialism. The purpose of *Newspeak,* as suggested by the Party's three slogans, was not only to provide a medium of expression for the world view and mental habits appropriate to *Ingsoc,* but to make all other modes of thought impossible. A 20th century version of *Newspeak* in this country was a textbook which began as one with an internationalist perspective and 30 years later, after many revisions, became a strident, anti-Communist tract, another of President Reagan's "evil empire" textbooks. Most objective observers would agree that Communism or Marxist-Leninist dogma in the Soviet Union has produced a totalitarian state which is an economic, political and moral failure. Most of these same observers might also agree that, ever since Peter the Great, the people of that country had neither the cultural nor philosophical history necessary to support or even understand a free government, such as the one in the United States. Discrimination in speech by any president describing another government should be diplomatic at a very minimum, if only for the benefit of children who don't know what an "evil empire" is and get no help from textbooks.

For years, children have had to read textbooks, usually all of each of them. They have never been asked to criticize them for style or content, even though most if not all of them have heard their parents say things that would cause them to question content. Now, however, textbook publishers may use legislatively mandated standards which call at an absolute minimum, for truth in impressing "upon the minds of pupils the principles of truth and justice."

Will a history textbook begin about where it should, with the events, including the Revolutionary War, leading up to the ratification of the first ten amendments of the Constitution in 1791? The Bill of Rights seem quite basic. It includes such fundamentals as freedom of speech and the press, the establishment of religion clause, freedom from unreasonable search and seizure and the right to trial by jury. Will textbook publishers and their editors give students an adequate analysis of the events, including the Civil War, leading up to ratification of the 14th Amendment—due process of law and equal protection of the laws? What will these textbooks have to say about the 16th Amendment which allowed Congress to impose a tax on income, the 18th Amendment prohibiting the manufacture, sale or transportation of intoxicating liquors and the 21st Amendment which repealed the 18th as an abysmal failure?

Passage of the Wagner Labor Relations Act in 1936 was a milestone in the history of unions. So was passage of the Taft-Hartley Act in 1947, its veto by President Truman and its adoption by Congress over that veto. Will the history of labor relations as it appears in textbooks also name the companies which used security guards as strike breakers amidst bloody violence? These are all unanswered questions, but it's reasonable to ask whether the new emphasis on textbooks will impress upon students the importance of "truth and justice."

In California, the Superintendent of Public Instruction is an elective office. Its present incumbent is Louis (Bill) Honig who recently charged that "Textbooks are like television. They aim at the lowest common denominator. The marketing people, not educators, are running the show." What he didn't say was that state school boards in California and other states "adopted" these textbooks which had been "dumbed down" for decades by "educators" who seem to have forgotten how they themselves learned in an earlier school, or, in fact, whether they enjoyed the learning process at all. If, by "educators," Honig meant the members of the State Board of Education, it should be noted that all, if not most of them were appointed by a conservative Republican Governor with a conservative agenda for education and a few other areas, such as environmental protection.

On August 2, 1987, The New York Times published a special section entitled "Education Life." In this section Edward B. Fiske had a few things to say about textbooks. "Critics' complaints about textbooks," he said, "are essentially threefold: First, they have been 'dumbed down' to accommodate the lower academic standards that prevailed during the 1960's and 1970's, prompting the current school-reform movement . . . Specific targets of reform are the 'readability' formulas." These procedures, developed after World War I, rate the difficulty of passages by measuring sentence length and checking vocabulary against established lists of words children are likely to recognize at various ages. Critics say the formulas encourage choppy writing that will eventually will discourage students from reading . . ." Fiske went on to describe the third target, the second having been the absence of religion and other controversial subjects from textbooks. "Third," he said, " academic skills have taken precedence over meaning and content in textbooks. Instead of delving into solid children's literature, elementary school' students read specially fabricated bite-size passages and then fill-in-the-blanks exercises to demonstrate they have picked up some detail and can locate a main idea." These exercises are known as "skill drills," and they bear no reasonable or rational relationship to reading, once again the banality of mediocrity. Textbooks, it seems, are designed by a committee, written by a committee and selected by a committee to please all and offend none, according to one educational consultant from Manchester, Conneticut, Connie Muther. Why not leave the writing of textbooks to the dedicated teachers on the classroom firing line and the students who should be the principal beneficiaries of content? The overworked teachers should welcome help from college — level students as proposed in A.B. 1820. It passed the Senate in Sacramento on September 3, 1987 and has been signed into law by the Governor. Unfortunately, Governor Deukmajian, a conservative Republican, used his line item veto to nullify the modest appropriation of money needed to start the Human Corps on its way.

Some textbook publishers are beginning to fight back. Herbert Adams, the former president of Laidlaw Educational Publishers, was quoted in the Times article as saying: "The implication is that the industry is made up of charlatans and that all textbooks are lousy. It's just not so. There are some good textbooks out there, but they are not necessarily the ones that sell. If there were profits in good books, you'd have good books." Moreover, said Albert Bursma, Jr., president of the school division of D.C. Heath & Company, it's easier to to produce textbooks with high reading levels than to turn out their "dumbed down" counterparts. "The writers are all Ph. D's. You have to work hard to get them to simplify anything." The bottom line must, of course, be profit for the publishers, because it takes as much as five years and an estimated $4 million to write a textbook and get it adopted by the 22 adoption states, including California.

If Louis (Bill) Honig is really serious about persuading the State Board Of Education to "adopt" better history textbooks, he could do a lot worse than reading Columbia University's Report by its *Educational Excellence Network*.

*American History,* published by Harcourt Brace Jovanovich, came in as one of the better history textbooks. According to the its reviewers in the Report, it was "the most successful in creating an engaging narrative of the national past." This text was written as a junior high school textbook. At the high school level, Ginn & Co.'s *A History of the United States* was treated as "the most literate and effective narrative of the eleventh-grade books surveyed." The Report again asks Why? The answer seems to have been that the authors themselves, Boorstein and Kelley, "maintained an active and executive position in its creation, reportedly much to the consternation of the publisher." It was not written or designed by a committee, as too many textbooks have been in the past. The lesson from all this is that education is too important to be left in the hands of publishers and local adoption systems without any participation of teachers on the firing line and students themselves with help from college-level students who have been the most recent beneficiaries or even victims of poor history textbooks.

All of this seems to suggest that the small presses, in combination with the Human Corps, at least in California can and perhaps should review the entire question of how history textbooks are written and either adopted or selected for use in the schools. Notwithstanding some exceptions such as Random House, one textbook from Ginn & Co. and another from Harcourt Brace Jovanovich, publishers seem to fall far short of treating history as an engaging part of our national heritage.

Harcourt Brace Jovanovich, Inc. was incorporated in New York in 1919 and is one of the world's notable companies. It is also one of this country's largest textbook publishers. The other very large textbook publishers in the United States include Simon & Schuster, a wholly owned subsidiary of Gulf & Western, Inc., McGraw Hill, Inc., Macmillan Publishing Company and Random House Inc. which has a school division. There are many others, all of whom publish textbooks in a very competitive market, particularly for textbook sales to the three largest states, Texas, California and New York where these states have traditionally spent enormous sums on textbooks, many of which, at least in California, may have to be completely rewritten as a result of the textbook reform movement and amendments to its Education Code.

Encouraging students, with the help of teachers and college-level students, to write their own textbooks will save all of the textbook publishers millions of dollars in the long run. Elementary schools are quite likely to provide a much better learning environment, and students in grade levels 1 through 8 will enjoy the learning experience far more than they have in the past.

Textbook publishers continue to find themselves stymied by judicial interference. On August 24, 1987, the U.S. Court of Appeals for the Sixth Circuit, in Mozert v. Hawkins County School Board, reversed a lower court in Tennessee. There, the U.S. District Court held that a Tennessee statute requiring all students attend to attend "reading classes" using Holt, Rinehart

& Winston textbooks was inconsistent with plaintiffs' sincerely held religious beliefs and, accordingly, a burden on their "free exercise of religion" rights in a constitutional sense. It was this ruling which the U.S. Court of Appeals reversed and sent back to the lower court with instructions to dismiss the complaint. In a separate, concurring opinion, Judge Boggs said: This is not a case about fundamentalist Christians or any particular set of beliefs. It is about the constitutional limits on the power of school boards to prescribe a curriculum." All that plaintiffs asked for was an accomodation from the school board — excuse complaining students from reading the textbooks which were offensive or provide alternative textbooks. They didn't get this accommodation, so this *textbook* case will probably be heard and decided by the United States Supreme Court.

If so, teachers may be the losers, as they were in Bethel School District v. Fraser decided in 1986. There, the Court upheld the power of a school district to impose sanctions on a student for use of sexual innuendo in a commencement ceremony at a high school against a claim of the First Amendment guarantee of free speech. Having said that public schools serve the purpose of teaching fundamental values "essential to a democratic society," Chief Justice Warren Burger proceeded to deny one of those very values — free speech. As the dissent noted, however, three teachers had reviewed Fraser's speech in advance and did not give him any notice of the likelihood of discipline. The school, however, took the position that Fraser had violated its rule which provided for sanctions for "acts which disrupt and interfere with the educational process." And as the U.S. Court of Appeals for the Ninth Circuit noted: "The record now before us yields no evidence that Fraser's use of a sexual innuendo in his speech materially interfered with activities at Bethel High School." Moreover, "Fraser," said Justice Stevens, "was an outstanding young man with a fine academic record. The fact that he was chosen by the student body demonstrates that he was respected by his peers." It seems clear that Fraser was in a better position to decide whether the use of sexual innuendo would offend 600 of his contemporaries in a non-classroom setting than "judges who are at least two generation and 3,000 miles away from the scene of the crime," as Justice Stevens noted. A school regulation which defines "disruptive conduct" with so little precision seems to be a prior restraint on what students might say outside "the educational process" and requires advance approval of what *is* said.

The "civics" lesson taught in Fraser by the Supreme Court is at the same judicial level as that taught in Hazelwood School District by the same Court. In that case, a majority of the Court (5–3) held that a school principal could excise articles in a high school newspaper if he considered them "unsuitable, or inappropriate" for perusal by the student editors' contemporaries. For First Amendment purposes, high school students seem to enjoy second class citizenship on the wholly specious rationale that they must be protected from themselves by being treated as "wards" of the state.

If students are made to feel that such speeches or newspaper articles require advance approval, teachers will have to carry the same burden as the owners of bookstores were required to bear by a Virginia statute in American Booksellers Association v. Commonwealth of Virginia, a case already mentioned in these pages. With the present balance between moderate and conservative justices, there may be a case before the Supreme Court measuring a textbook for constitutionally offensive content before using it in the classroom. In such a case, there would be an impermissible burden on both teachers and state boards adopting textbooks which would clearly interfere with the educational process. Students will be the real losers, all due to judicial interference with the learning process at an early age, just when they are so eager to learn.

School boards who "adopt" textbooks are the principal offenders in this whole sorry story. Textbook publishers who try to satisfy every possible interest in a pluralistic, bicultural society with ethnic diversity wind up making just about everybody dissatisfied.

# Chapter 13
## The Bookstores Revisited-1992

Notwithstanding the pace of change within the last ten years, not all publishers or booksellers seem ready to accept or use modern technology, such as the computer. Harper & Row only recently discovered it could produce its catalogs in a few days, instead of eight weeks at an annual saving of more than $200,000. At Simon & Schuster, computer technology has finally "being seen as a tremendous asset," according to its vice-president of office technology. Booksellers, however, seem slow to move into computers, probably because of the intimidating costs of hardware and software. A complete system with inventory and control features, general accounting and invoicing together with a Books in Print compact disk and electronic ordering costs about $14,000 or may be leased for around $250 per month. For 1988, the number of booksellers with computers represents an estimated 25% of the total of about 6,500 trage or general bookstores. The bookstore of 1992 may well be quite different from those opened or operated in 1988.

On or before December 31, 1992, Europe will become a single market with 12 countries having a combined population of some 325,000,000 people. This is the European Economic Community (EC) or the Common Market with its own Supreme Court, now known as the European Court of Justice in Luxembourg. This court has already decided cases affecting publishing and bookselling within the EC and is certain to change even more industry practices within the next 2³/₄ years. At least one change certain to occur is the far more widespread use of the computer in both publishing and bookselling. Electronic book-ordering software, such as BookBase and Pubnet is bound to proliferate, even though a U.K. system, Teleordering, has had a headstart on both. Essentially, all three allow a bookseller to place orders for books by using a computer with a 2,200 bps modem, have the orders processed overnight, sorted by publisher which confirms the orders and fulfills them by shipment, usually within two days from the date of receiving them. As a result, booksellers will be able to carry less inventory than they do now. Re-orders of books selling well can be processed and shipped quite rapidly.

In a 1989 bookstore, the median selling space for shelves and display of books, passageways and a counter to record transactions is is 1,200 square feet. A small, private office for the manager or owner is not included. The new bookstore of 1992, assuming the same selling area of 1,200 square feet, will still have a very large additional cost—book inventory. While it won't happen overnight, the title inventory is quite likely to have an international flavor not currently available in some general bookstores. Bertelsmann A.G. of West Germany owns Bantam Doubleday Dell, and Macmillan, Inc. is now owned by Robert Maxwell's British Communications PLC. Books published initially by Bertelsmann in West Germany or in Spain by one of its subsidiaries may turn up in English, of course, in Doubleday Book Shops.

For a bookstore of 1,200 square feet, the probable cost of an inventory of 12,000 to 15,000 books is about $85,000 at the discounted cost of the books to the bookstore. The number of titles stocked will vary, but the number of titles will clearly be less than the actual number of books in inventory. A ratio of titles to inventory may be about 2.5. This means that, if the owner stocks 6,000 titles, there is an inventory of 15,000 books. It also means that, except for bestsellers, new books and stock that hasn't been sold, there is very little *display* space for books where a potential customer may *see* the artwork on the dustcover. The proprietor will not want to run out of best sellers and books the buyer thinks will sell well and which he or she has ordered on the basis of publishers' catalogs. The proprietor knows that a bookstore of this size must earn at least $180 per square foot annually from the sale of books, hardcover, trade paperback or mass market paperbacks, to enjoy a reasonable income before taxes. He or she also knows that there will be other costs of operations, such as full and part-time personnel and local advertising as well as extra mailings to alert customers to new titles just out. If these aren't sold within a relatively fixed time, they can be returned.

The recurring problem of returns haunts both booksellers and publishers. Jan Wiesenfeld, a returns expert after 13 years in a bookstore, wrote an article in the January, 1989 issue of *American Bookseller*. In it, she was critical of publishers' returns policies and the difficulty of getting credit confirmations for books returned. These are always sent to a warehouse separated by light years from the credit departments of most publishers. Here, again, is an opportunity to reduce time and costs by using computer technology and wide area networks. Some publishers insist on invoice information, while others will accept returns without this paperwork. "In addition to returns terms," she wrote, "an incredible waste of time and money occurs on a daily basis in the processing of credits."       However, in the *American Bookseller* for September, 1987 there is a study by Betty Fleming, herself a bookstore owner. She suggests that there are definite limits on returns. The larger the returns the smaller the profit to the bookstore. "Vital net profit, she says, "begins to be devoured when returns reach the range of 15% to 20%. Above 25%, red ink prevails."

Long before 1992, bookstores will have made another startling discovery, and some of them have already seen the future. Only the publishers make any profit from returns. The giants simply saturate the marketplace with their books, knowing that returns are inevitable. A predictable returns percentage has been built into the price structure of the books ordered by bookstores and actually sold to customers. Some publishers, including Mercury House, are willing to offer higher non-returnable discounts to bookstores. When these decide to give the books they *do* order better *shelf space for display,* they are likely to see a dramatic rise in gross margins. They will also see better sales figures. Some bookstores, pressured by escalating costs, have already become financial vigilantes. They could also take another look at what the computer and electronic ordering of books can do to control costs. The future is really here, but it's going to look a lot better in 1992.

The bookstore of 1992 will look very much like a well designed bookstore of 1989, but there will be some crucial differences. The total sales or display area will be no more than about 1000 square feet, and *most* books will be displayed face out. For books not actually displayed this way, there is a new technique for the assembly of images and their immediate display. In the week ending October 16,1987, Patent No. 4,700,181 was patented for Computer Graphics Laboratories, Inc. of New York City. The assembly of images and their immediate display has a use of considerable importance to bookstores. The technique can free bookstore personnel to sell books, and it also means that the bookstore itself will not need an inventory of all the books it wants to sell. A customer can select some books — backlist, for example — from a television screen where the artwork and flap copy may be seen in full color.

In this way, buyers or browsers will see what an artist has done to attract their attention to each title. All books will continue to be displayed by subject matter, i.e., new fiction, non-fiction and textbooks all by familiar categories, such as history, economics, philosophy, biographies and so forth. One of the crucial differences will be, at least with new bookstores, that they will be "electronic bookstores within a store," a concept pioneered by ARA Services, Inc., the largest distributor of magazines and mass market paperbacks in the United States.

About six years ago, ARA set up a complete bookstore within a giant supermarket — a shopping mall with more variety would be better in 1992. The bookstore within a mall will carry in its inventory hardcover books, trade paperbacks and mass market paperbacks. The number of titles stocked will be small — no more than 1,100 titles — probably much less. The reason, "publishing on demand" allows a smaller inventory (probably about 1.2 books in inventory for each title stocked), because, by printing and binding only the titles the manager, buyer and owner thinks it can sell, he or she can quickly replace copies sold by printing and binding more of them, in full view of the buyer or browser.

A growing number of shoppers, in this case, potential book buyers who read for pleasure or information, are not the usual mall shopper. They visit the mall for a variety of purchases including books. In the bookstore of 1992, they will be able to browse and buy in a comfortable environment, one in which they know the bookstore has complete control of inventory. If a title is temporarily out of stock, they will be able to see a new copy printed and bound while they wait, no more than ten minutes or so. Prices *will* be lower.

Unlike the ARA Services concept, the "electronic bookstore" within a mall will not sell remainders. Remaindering will disappear, as it should, and the bookstore will be able to keep its display of books fresh. The publisher will have all his frontlist and backlist titles stored in a computer on a compact disk-read only memory (CD-ROM), which, by 1992, will store the equivalent of 450,000 pages of many different books. Alternatively, the bookstore managers will select titles from the publishers' catalogs which, complete with artwork in color and text describing each title will be sent to the bookstore on a disk in order to allow printing no more than two or three — perhaps more — copies of each one. The limit can and very likely will be the subject of negotiation with the publisher whose disk will not allow printing more than the negotiated number of copies — it will then self-destruct. Thereafter, the bookstore will have to buy the right to print more copies by accessing the publishers' mainframe or CD-ROM using high speed telecommunications software, and a modem capable of sending text at a rate of at least 9,600 baud (bits per second) or about 1,100 characters per second. This means that one average page of a book will be sent in 3½ seconds and be printed as it is received. With fiber optics and about 3,000 characters per second by 1992, an average book page will be received in *one* second, and a 300 page book can be printed almost simultaneously in less than ten minutes. The hardware used by the bookstore will be able to print this text, using both sides of the paper — book quality — as it is received from the publisher. By 1992, most, if not all telephone lines will be made from optical fiber, so there will be no text distortion. To prevent "pirating" of books by people who seem to enjoy tinkering with the files in other computers, all text will be encrypted, and a publisher will know exactly how many copies of each of its titles the bookstore has printed.

One assumption has been made which may not be valid until years later, if at all. Some computers will be able to use superconductive materials now not even in the development stage, so there will be no loss of efficiency or energy. With computers made this way, the speed of operation, whether in 1992 or later, will be at a level not even imaginable in 1988. Currently, a Cray Research computer will perform calculations at a rate of about 100,000,000 per second (100 MIPS). The computer of 1992 will not perform at this speed and need not do so. It is the telecommunication technology, which now — 1987 — sends 1,100 characters per second. In sending text from one such computer to another one of the same design, the text of an entire book can be sent, received and printed in unbound form in a very few minutes. New printers will be able to spew out text, printed on both sides of the paper, at a rate in excess of 60 pages a minute, all typeset with high resolution. By eliminating the photographic process used in making plates in the past — they will no longer be needed — the printed paper with text resolution of over 1,800 dots per inch (dpi), the pages will immediately be perfect bound, either in cloth for a hardcover, or as a trade paperback, or a mass market paperback.

The Sulby Mark II perfect binder can produce up to 60 copies of a book in one hour, and it costs about $12,500 for a new unit. It is about 4 feet high, 10 feet long and 3 feet deep — in a word, bulky — and not suitable for use in a bookstore. However, it has a major drawback. It takes at least one trained technician to operate the unit and keep it supplied with, of all things, glue. The perfect binding equipment or unit, will occupy no more than 50 cubic feet, and it will blend into the bookstore's interior design; it will be driven by software in the bookstore's computer. The latter will also automatically alert untrained sales personnel to the need for more glue or electronically refill the container with either more glue or a new adhesive material better than glue. All pages in a hardcover, trade papeback or mass market paperback will be of uniform size, 5½ by 8½ inches, and since the photographic process has been eliminated, no crop marks need appear on the pages, all of which will be numbered with headers and footers as well as chapter headings and numbers with subtitles in the text where appropriate. One commercial printer, R. R. Donnelly & Sons, Inc. is reported to be experimenting with a small, attractively designed perfect binder which will be able to bind books very rapidly, perhaps as many as 50 or 60 books an hour, and do this with many different titles.

So-called "coffee table books" (photo-engraved art with text) will also be available in the bookstore of 1992 and in color. An image controller developed in 1987 can generate an image of text and graphics and send both to an imagesetter for output on both plain paper or photographic paper. Output of the imagesetting printer was about 20 pages a minute of both text and graphics in 1987. By 1992, the output will be over 60 pages per minute with computer architecture which provides a high speed stream of data to the imagesetter. The front-end computer may be an IBM or IBM-compatible, and "bitmapping" will reach a speed unheard of in 1987. For the bookstore of 1992, the cost of the hardware and software to do all this is expected to be less than the opening store inventory costs of 1987, about $65,000. That amount paid only part of the opening inventory cost in 1987.

For the bookstore of 1992, it will also be possible to print in-store books from all English-language publishers via satellite transmission of data. In 1987, for example, Mercury House acquired the U.S. rights for a novel written by Jennifer Potter, *The Taking of Agnès.* Had all this technology been available in 1985, when it was first published in Great Britain, the entire text would have been on a floppy disk from which it could have been sent via telecommunications software to Mercury House and captured to a disk for typesetting in-house. Another novel published by Mercury House in 1987 was *Diamante,* by Enzo Siciliano. It was translated from the Italian by Patrick Diehl in

Berkeley, California. Another novel, *Rumor of an Elephant,* was translated from French, and a third, *Martyr,* was translated from German. All of these books, by 1992, could have been translated into English in Milan, Paris and Hamburg, respectively, and sent to San Francisco via satellite, or to the bookstore of 1992.

Indeed, while translation software is not yet available, Xerox offers a computer plus software which makes possible the translation of a book in one language into English and *vice versa,* using a translator fluent in both. The characters in Russian and Arabic are quite different in shape. So are those in Farsi and Chinese. The shape of these characters or ideographs is *recognized* by the software in essentially the same way different fonts or typefaces are recognized by typeseetting software now. Thus, it is possibe to write software which generates text in one column of a computer's monitor, eg., Arabic, while the translator uses the other half of the same monitor's screen to type in the English translation. Then he or she simply transfers text to a disk in ASCII which is then copied into another computer's word processing software for editing, typesetting, printing and binding as a book. The entire process should not take more than ten days. In its computer, Xerox has stored *all* the Western European languages as well as Chinese (Mandarin and Cantonese), Japanese, Arabic, Farsi, Greek, Russian, Indonesian, Malaysian and Swahili. Think of it! All the literature in our global village will available in English, and books in English will be available to people who want to read them in their own languages. All of this tends to make the bookstores of the future the repositories of knowledge the libraries of the 13th and 14th centuries were along with the libraries of today. These bookstores will be able to publish such books on demand in the same way they publish and sell books by American authors. Cover prices are apt to be lower than they are today for a number of reasons, ie., less inventory.

Not to be overlooked in what may seem to be a somewhat futuristic concept, is both the feasibility of selling books this way and the enormous savings from having such a small inventory. The technology capable of doing all this is available today — 1989 — it just hasn't been adapted for use in bookstores. Books need no longer be ordered on consignment. A bookstore will print and bind only those it thinks it can sell. Alternatively, books may be printed and bound by a computer center serving all bookstores within its service area. Inventory management and general ledger or accounting software is available today at fairly reasonable cost as is typesetting and telecommunications software, the fundamentals. Computer technology has become so sophisticated and less expensive with the passage of time, it's not out of the question to visualize all of this happening before 1992.

For those bookstore proprietors somewhat fearful of using computers and software, affordability and simplicity of operation will be the key. Even today, in 1989, most software is menu-driven. In a bookstore, the menu will consist of a limited number of options. Each one will deal with different operations of the business, such as inventory, invoicing and sales. Another choice on the menu might be communications which would allow electronic ordering from a publisher or its distributor and almost next-day confirmation and fulfillment. A bookseller may order books electronically in 1989 in the case of Mercury House, using either BookBase or Pubnet. By 1992 or earlier, publishers in London, Paris, Milan or Munich may request a catalog from Mercury House, receive and print out the text and graphics by software comparable to facsimile transmission.

Finally, consider the alternatives, operating without this technology and wasting valuable time in obsolete tasks. For 1989, a small, independent bookstore with 1,000 square feet must earn at about $200 per square foot of selling space. The real alternative lies in the future — now in a limited way — earning over $350 per square foot. Publishing on demand and electronic ordering are just around the corner. For an investment of less than the cost of an opening store's inventory, a bookstore can do publishing on demand for significantly less investment than the cost of an opening inventory. For less than $2,500, a bookseller may place most orders by using BookBase or Pubnet. Think about it!

# Chapter 14
## Some Thoughts on All Books, The Arts, Education and the Law

In a more perfect world—the global village—small presses would publish more books, whether frontlist or backlist. They would also be more profitable, and their publishers would be more secure in the knowledge that they had made a genuine contribution to public enlightenment and the pleasure of those who enjoy reading books. Some observers say the small presses are doing this now, albeit slowly and on a modest scale. Some of the small press books include *The Birth Dearth,* which warns that our declining birth rate may threaten the West. It was published by Pharos Books. *Diplomatic Crime,* published by Acropolis Books is another. It discusses the many abuses of diplomatic immunity from just about anything except being declared *persona non grata* and sent home by our State Department. A major beneficiary of all this small press activity is the bookstore. People are beginning to discover that the publishing giants don't have a complete monopoly of the market for quality books.

According to one literary critic, UIlrich Greiner, West German publishers seem to suffer from the same problem–not enough quality books. In its issue of October 9, 1987, *Die Zeit,* a distinguished weekly newspaper, ran an interesting article. Its headline read: **Büchermesse und Büchermasse,** a nice play on words. Freely translated, it means Fair of Books and Masses of Books, and then its author, Ulrich Greiner, asked: Was ist los mit der Literatur? What's wrong with the literature? "Every third year," he wrote, "a new top-class car model, every year a new *Zeitgeist* and every season, a new hem line. With routinelike uneasiness, we are informed that the just opened Frankfurt Book Fair is the biggest that ever was! Almost 100,000 new editions. Who is going to buy them, who is going to read them? And if we can't read everything, at least we want to know: where is the hare running? What is the new literary trend? Which is the big novel of the season? . . . There is none. Trends are killing each other . . . In Frankfurt, the book is reduced to the lowest common denominator." One may wonder if Allan Bloom has sold the German rights to his book, *The Closing of the American Mind.*

And in that same more perfect world — not yet thought of as a global village — students from kindergarten and grades 1 through 8 would be major beneficiaries of the publication of textbooks by small presses with students, teachers and college-level help as editors. The National Endowment for the Humanities recently (1987) issued its report, *American Memory,* a report ordered by Congress. This study reports, amongst other things, that textbooks which emphasize skills instead of content leave children ignorant of history and literature. The author of *American Memory,* Lynne V. Cheney, said in it: "Most elementary reading books contain little literature," and, she said: "Knowledge of the ideas that have molded us and the ideals that have mattered to us function as a kind of civic glue. In our schools today, we run the danger of unwittingly proscribing our heritage." *American Memory* also quotes Cicero as saying: "To know nothing of what happened before we were born is to remain forever a child." Are we going to systematically destroy our historical memory by ignoring it in our schools? Are we going to ignore the competition of ideas, including those thought to be alien to our own system of a government with all its checks and balances as well as the First Amendment? Are we going to allow education specialists to dictate that skills, not history or literature, be the core curriculum for our schools? Nothing would be more certain to cause more drop outs to occur, since many children are not even taught to read well enough to learn the past in the textbooks of today.

Most teachers would agree that the growth of a child's self-esteem is the single most important factor in the entire learning process. It begins at home and sometimes continues in the classroom. A child, even a 4-year old will happily respond to praise of something he or she has drawn as a picture when nothing more complicated than hanging it on the wall occurs where peers may enjoy it, too. Now, however, 33 years after Brown v. Board of Education, the case which desegregated the public schools by holding that "separate but equal" schools denied equal protection of the laws, self-esteem amongst black children is no better than it was in 1954. According to Dr. Kenneth Clark, emeritus professor of psychology at the City University of New York—he and his wife did the study considered by the Supreme Court in Brown v. Board of Education—the situation today is no better than 40 years ago, the date of the original study. "We've tried," he said, "to hide the damage racism does to black children, but the damage is there, and will continue as long as racism continues." Teachers must have to ask themselves whether textbooks which tend to cripple self-esteem amongst all children, including black children, should any longer be adopted by state boards of education. Small presses may want to consider publishing books which tend to re-inforce self-esteem in the classroom and elsewhere.

Many people know or sense that fostering self-esteem does not stop with graduation from kindergarten, elementary school, high school or college. Indeed, it continues into life, including the selection of a spouse and later. The late Stanley Coopersmith was the author of *The Antecedents of Self-Esteem*, and a child psychologist at the University of California at Davis. One sign of a child with little or no self-esteem, he noted was an inability to make up his or her own mind. This is often the the result of parental ridicule of the child's emerging ideas or opinions. Many parents of college-age students find it impossible to allow these students to *choose* between two or more controversial ideas. Choice fosters self-esteem and allows the development of a sense of self. Attempts to suppress choice very often lead to regimentation, eg., ideological groupings with little or no flexibility, as in George Orwell's *1984*. Exposure to controversial ideas allows choice and either rejection, acceptance or something in between.

In some cases, students may be getting short-changed in a global village (suppression of choice by educators). For example,the existence of the Soviet Union and Marxism-Lenism as practiced there is a fact of life. It won't go away. It seems better to have Marxism at least discussed in the clasroom, probably by an avowed Marxist. Students who don't get credit for half the native intelligence a lot of them have, would be the first to ridicule and reject Marxism. "It hasn't worked where it's practiced," they would say. "Why is anyone foolish enough to argue it would work in the United States?"

A case decided four years ago declined to make this possible — Ollman v. Evans, 750 F.2d 970 (C.A.D.C. 1984). Curiously enough, the Department of Justice cited it as one of several cases in support of Judge Bork's confirmation to the Supreme Court. It should be read carefully in view of some of his statements *not* cited by the Department of Justice.

This case (Ollman v. Evans) seems significant today, since Judge Robert Bork, recently nominated for a seat on the Supreme Court by President Reagan and rejected over-whelmingly by the Senate, agreed with the plurality opinion in a libel case. Judge Antonin Scalia, already a Justice of the Supreme Court after being appointed by President Reagan and affirmed by the Senate, dissented. The key issue in this case was whether a newspaper column's statement that Ollman, an avowed Marxist who had "no status in the profession (of political science) was a constitutionally protected statement of opinion, or an unprotected statement of fact which was false and libelous. Judge Bork found the statement to be one of opinion, while Judge Scalia found it to be one of fact, the falsity of which was a question for a jury.

Small presses, and there are an estimated 12,000 to 15,000 of them, may also want to read the opinion in Ollman v. Evans, but for different reasons, more books (satire). The film, *Moscow on the Hudson,* is one good model. Ridicule of absolutist views is, or can be devastating. Do those who argue for a *jurisprudence of original intent* really believe that divine intervention will help discover what the Framers of the Constitution intended in 1787? Or will the Attorney General, Edwin Meese, 3rd disclose this intent in some sort of spiritual revelation in a First Amendment case involving free speech? Or even a right of privacy case by arguing for a rehearing in Griswold v. Conneticut? Even Fourth Amendment cases (no unreasonable search and seizure except on a warrant issued on probable cause describing what may be searched) are not immune from attack on the basis of original intent—what did the Framers of the Bill of Right really mean in 1791? Some Courts have felt impelled to read definitions into words and theories that the Framers of the Constitution and the Bill of Rights could not even dreamed of in the contemporary environment of 1988. California v. Greenwood, decided on May 17, 1988 by the U.S. Supreme Court, now allows the police to search sealed trash bags without a warrant. A warrant is required by the Warrant Clause of the Fourth Amendment, and must be supported by "probable cause." None was shown in this case, so one more encroachment on the privacy of all citizens, even the innocent, has been sanctioned by the Supreme Court.

Thus, it is curious to find Judge Robert Bork concurring with the majority in a First Amendment case, Ollman v. Evans.

The facts in the Ollman case indirectly involved a college-level classroom and the collision between academic freedom and constitutionally protected expressions of opinion under the First Amendment within the context of an action for libel. The eleven judges on the Court of Appeal—it was a hearing *en banc,* instead of the usual 3-judge panel—might have been decided differently, had Judge Bork not been the conservative ideologue that so many people seem to think. He is quite different—an absolutist in radical disagreement with the mainstream of free speech.

People may merely think that the presence of Professor Ollman in the classroom, an avowed Marxist, was no more than distasteful. They shouldn't, since his views may well affect other areas of free speech. They already have in a case, Finzer v. Barry, which the Supreme Court will decide in the Session which began on October 5, 1987. In a case decided in 1987—Board of Directors of Rotary International v. Rotary Club of Duarte, 481 U.S.___, the Supreme Court, per Justice Powell, found proper a California statute requiring the admission of women to membership, also found a First Amendment right of *expressive associa-*

*tion,* under which individuals have the freedom to associate for the purpose of engaging in protected speech. What the court does with this expansion of fundamental rights, even though not expressly guaranteed, will be interesting in view of earlier cases recognizing them as indispensable to the enjoyment of rights explicitly defined.

The decision of the Court of Appeals in Ollman v. Evans filled about 63 pages with the Court's opinion and many separate concurring and dissenting opinions.

The facts must be summarized briefly for a better understanding of the Court's holding. Bertell Ollman was a teacher of political science at New York University who had been named or appointed as Chairman of the Department of Government and Political Science at the University of Maryland. Rowland Evans and Robert Novak were nationally syndicated columnists. On May 4, 1978 they published a column which appeared in *The Washington Post* and many other newspapers through the United States. The column was entitled "The Marxist Professor's Intentions." Ollman's principal work was *Alienation: Marx's Conception of Man in a Capitalist Society,* which Evans and Novak described as "a ponderous tome in adoration of the master ('Marxism is like a magnificantly rich tapestry'). Published in 1971, it does not abandon hope for the revolution forecast by Karl Marx in 1848." The column continued with the statement specifically identified as libelous: *Such pamphleteering is hooted at by one political scientist in a major eastern university, whose scholarship and reputation as a liberal are well known. 'Ollman has no status within the profession, but is a pure and simple activist,' he said.* Would he say that publicly? No chance of it. Our academic culture does not permit the raising of such questions." (Italics are in the Court's opinion).

Bertell Ollman filed his complaint in 1979 in the U.S. District Court for the District of Columbia alleging that the column was libelous and had caused the University of Maryland to withhold approval of his appointment as Chairman of the Department of Government and Political Science. In its opinion, the Court of Appeals affirmed a judgment in favor of Evans and Novak in the District Court. Throughout the 63 page opinion, the notion that

Ollman would use his new academic forum to *indoctrinate* his students with Marxist dogma was subtly ignored even though the newspaper column was all part of the record. Because it said in part that Ollman had "(avowed) his desire to use the classroom . . . for preparing what he calls the 'revolution' " To Judge Bork, the "revolution" seems to have meant the violent ovverthrow of the government. In another setting, Judge Bork had written that speech which advocated "forcible overthrow of the government" was not constitutionally protected by the First Amendment—free speech. It seems absurd to think that Professor Ollman's speech in the classroom would do any more than expose him to ridicule from most, if not all of his students. In 1919, Justice Holmes said in Abrams v. United States: "But when men have realized that time has upset many fighting faiths, they may come to believe even more than they believe the very foundations of their own conduct that the ultimate good desired is better reached by free trade in ideas, — that the best test of truth is the power of the thought to get itself accepted in the competition of the market; . . . " Today, almost 69 years later, the free exchange of ideas in the market place is still the best test of truth. Justice Powell said as much in 1974—"However pernicious an idea may, we depend for its correction . . . on the competition of *other ideas.* The classroom is clearly a forum for the competition of ideas.

The fear of many teachers then and now of a very real threat to academic freedom had a historical origin—the hysterical mouthings of the late, unlamented Senator from Wisconsin, Joseph McCarthy. After wrecking the lives of many people, he finally disappeared from the political scene after first being censured by the Senate. In another part of the country, Professor Herbert Marcuse was the focal point of protests at the University of California at San Diego. His writings were filled with turgid, forgettable prose—convoluted Marxist dogma—and he seems to have disappeared from the academic scene without leaving a trace. Those of the radical right in the United States—extreme conservatives is a more diplomatic phrase—fear the results of indoctrination from the liberal left and other more radical ideas.

Accommodations between these competing ideas are not always left to the courts. Therefore, it seems appropriate to read and analyse the views of Judge Bork and Judge Scalia in the concurring in part and dissenting in part opinions in Ollman v. Evans.

Judge Bork's opinion, three other judges concurring, begins at page 993 of 750 F.2d. Here are his views in part: "I write separately because I do not think he (Judge Starr for the plurality) has adequately demonstrated that all of the allegedly libelous statements at issue here can be immunized as expressions of opinion. The dissents, on the other hand, while acknowledging the importance of other factors, seem actually premised on the idea that the law makes a clear distinction between opinions, which are not actionable as libel, and facts, which are. In my view, the law as enunciated by the Supreme Court, imposes no such sharp dichotomy . . . .Any such rigid doctrinal framework is inadequate to resolve the sometimes contradictory claims of the libel laws and the freedom of the press . . . .This case illustrates that point. It arouses concern that a freshening stream of libel actions, which often seem as much designed to punish writers and publications as to recover damages for real injuries, may threaten the public and constitutional interest in free, and frequently rough, discussion Those who step into areas of public dispute, who choose the pleasures and distractions of controversy, must be willing to bear criticism, disparagement, and even wounding assessments. Perhaps it would be better if disputation were conducted in measured phrases and calibrated assessments, and with strict avoidance of the ad hominem; . . . But that is not the world we live, even have lived, or are ever likely to know, and the law of the first amendment must not try to make public dispute safe and comfortable for all the participants. That would only stifle the debate. In our world, the kind of commentary that the columnists Rowland Evans and Robert Novak have engaged in here is the coin in which controversialists are commonly paid."

On page 994, Judge Bork's opinion moves into a grey area, and one in which publishers are often uncomfortable. He said, again in part: "The temptation to adhere to sharply-defined categories is understandable. Judges generalize, they articulate concepts, they enunciate such things as four-factor frameworks, three-pronged tests, and two-tiered analyses in an effort, laudable by and large, to bring order to a universe of unruly happenings and to give guidance for the future to themselves and to others. But it is certain that life will bring up cases whose facts simply cannot be handled by purely verbal formulas, or at least not handled with any sophistication and feeling for the underlying values at stake." In effect, Judge Bork seems to reject what he described as mechanical jurisprudence, the application of formulas to somewhat comparable facts.

Senior Circuit Judge MacKinnon, who joined in Judge Bork's concurring opinion, wrote a separate concurring opinion which begins at page 1010. He noted that the University of Maryland was a public university in which a 15-member Board of Regents was the governing body. With one exception, the Governor appointed them all with the advise and consent of the Maryland Senate. The University was tax-supported and received very substantial sums for its operations in the form of appropriations by the legislature. When all the facts about Ollman became known, an intense public controversy arose, most of the content being political — tax-paying citizens should not support a professor who taught or might teach Marxism to their sons and daughters. After the Evans-Novak column appeared, the president of the University ultimately refused to approve Ollman's appointment. Ollman had been selected over 100 other candidates for the position at the University of Maryland. In his concurring opinion, Judge MacKinnon limited his comments to the part of the column which stated that "Ollman has no status within the profession, but is a pure and simple activist." On page 1012, he stated in his opinion: "Here also is a university, an arm of a constitutional government, which is dedicated, among other things, to educating its citizens in the principles of politics. Ollman's nomination thus must inevitably have raised questions about the mission of a public university, the scope of academic freedom, and the responsibilities, if any, of public universities and the political science profession in a society like ours dedicated not only to free debate, but to preserving the institutions that make free debate possible."

The discussion of "status" in Judge MacKinnon's opinion caused him to concur with his colleagues, because he said: "its meaning is variable, unverifiable, controversial, a matter of opinion . . . The word does not have a 'precise core of meaning.'" Accordingly, he came down on the side which held the column was constitutionally protected opinion, referring with approval to Judge Bork's concept of "a public, political arena." In the dissenting opinion from Judge Wald and one which Judge (now Justice Scalia) joined, it was thought that saying Ollman had "no status within the profession, but is a pure and simple activist" was "an assertion of fact for which its authors can be made to answer, consistent with the requirements of the first amendment, in a suit for libel."

All Judge Bork had to do to allow Ollman his day in court was to rule that the "status in his profession" comment by Evans and Novak in their column was an constitutionally unprotected statement of fact. By doing so, Ollman would have been entitled to a trial by jury on the issue of its falsity. The 7th Amendment to the Constitution, ratified in 1791, gave him this right if he could show an injury in fact to his reputation. The U.S. District Court granted Evans and Novak summary judgment (no jury trial) on the grounds that these defendants' opinions "did not imply underlying false and defamatory statements of fact." Three judges of the U.S. Court of Appeals, including Judge Scalia, disagreed, holding that the statement made in the column — he (Ollman) had no status within his profession — was defamatory. Accordingly, they said, Ollman was entitled to a trial by a jury on the issue of its truth or falsity. Even though Ollman was selected over about 100 other applicants, his appointment as Chairman of the Department of Political Science at the University of Maryland was withdrawn after the Evans-Novak column appeared in the *Washington Post* and other newspapers throughout the United States. This question was not addressed by either the Court of Appeals or Judge Bork, except by the dissent in which Judge Scalia (now Justice Scalia) joined.

The plurality opinion, together with the separate concurring and dissenting opinions, represent a conscientious attempt by all of the judges to work out an intellectual accommodation of competing interests, the very accommodation which was withheld from plaintiffs in Mozert v. Hawkins County Board of Education. As Judge Boggs said in his concurring opinion in that case decided by the U.S. Court of Appeals for the Sixth Circuit on August 24, 1987: "In my reading of the testimony, the (trial) judge's finding is not only clearly erroneous, but it can only be reversed by a failure to recognize a distinction between the ideal education the parents want, and that level of accommodation and education which they believe is constitutionally required and which they 'want' here." And in another separate, concurring opinion, Judge Kennedy said: The state and the Hawkins County School Board also have a compelling interest in avoiding disruption in the classroom (a divisive by-product of the opt-out remedy)."

Courts very often seem to decide difficult cases on the basis that certain conduct may be "divisive" and interfere with either the educational function of the schools or, in an artistic setting interfere with the "artistic integrity" of a performance in a theater. There are other ways of minimizing both.

Recently, in a civil case brought by Vanessa Redgrave, a well known, talented and controversial actress (she supports the claims of the Palestinian Liberation Organization), the limits of the First Amendment were tested. See Redgrave v. Boston Symphony Orchestra, Inc., 602 F. Supp. 1189 (D.C. Mass. 1985). Redgrave sued the Boston Symphony Orchestra for breach of contract and violation of her civil rights under the Massachusetts Civil Rights Act. The Boston Symphony had cancelled her appearance as narrator in a performance of Stravinsky's *Oedipus Rex*. She also sought damages for her loss of a role in *Heartbreak House,* playing at the Circle in the Square Theatre in New York City with Rex Harrison as the star.

The District Court awarded Redgrave damages for breach of contract for cancellation of her appearance. The record at trial showed that Vanessa Redgrave had not been offered a role in

*Heartbreak House* because of this action of the Boston Symphony. Rex Harrison, who was star of this play, also had cast control. The reason given was, as one witness said, "we would not hire her because of all the events that had happened, the cancellation by the Boston Symphony and the effects that we felt it would have on us (audience reaction or interruption of the performance) by having her."

In a 2-1 decision on October 14, 1987, the U.S. Court of Appeals for the First Circuit reversed the District Court. See Redgrave et al v. Boston Symphony, Inc., 831 F.2nd 339–360 (1st Cir. 1987). Since the opinion was withdrawn, a hearing *en banc* having been granted, the Slip Opinion dated October 14, 1987 is the only source currently available for the opinion's text. In writing for the majority, Judge Bownes said the Symphony's defense of its artistic integrity was really a request for "the right to perform without interruption from the audience." Later, however, the Court of Appeals reversed itself in 1988.

History and experience teach that the risk of catcalls, boos, disruptions and even being the target of vegetable projectiles is inherent in any public performance by artists who seek to entertain and/or educate the public. Indeed, it could be argued that the audience has a First Amendment right to object vociferously to an artistic performance."

Then, Judge Bownes discussed the recognition of a First Amendment defense of artistic integrity. He wrote: "This would mean that a performing artist or group of artists could deny another artist her statutorily protected right to perform because of the *fear* that the audience might interrupt the performance." (Emphasis added). The trial record does not appear to have any evidence tending to show what others in the audience might have done to silence such interruptions.

Additionally, the U.S. Court of Appeals also found the *communicative link* between the Symphony's action and the loss of Redgrave's professional role in *Heartbreak House,* a link closely analogous to recognized elements of the law of defamation. By necessary implication, the Court of Appeals found that this *link* involved some unprivileged statement by the Boston Symphony, the contract termination itself because of Vanessa Redgrave's politically unpopular support of the PLO. It held that she was entitled to $12,000 in damages for loss of her role in *Heartbreak House.*

The Slip Opinion, however, was not the last word. On August 31, 1988, the U.S. Court of Appeals for the First Circuit, in an opinion *en banc,* reversed itself in what can be described as a judicial aberration. Amongst other things, the court held that Vannessa Redgrave was not entitled to recover damages sought under the Massachusetts Civil Rights Act (MCRA). This is a somewhat novel act that creates a private cause of action for injunctive relief and damages against any person who interferes by threats, intimidation or coercion with the exercise by any other person of rights secured by the Constitution or laws of the United States and the Commonwealth of Massachusetts. Redgrave had a right "secured" by a contract to perform as narrator of *Oedipus Rex,* with the Boston Symphony Orchestra. The Sypmphony cancelled this contract only because of her unpopular political views and for no other reason. Notwithstanding some anonymous telephone calls threatening disruption of this performance, the Symphony still cast a pall of orthodoxy over political speech by Vannessa Redgrave. The Symphony invoked the defense of "artistic integrity," a defense never before used in a case with First Amendment implications, and the U.S. Court of Appeals agreed with this wholly specious argument. The court did not even balance the competing interests of free speech outside the Symphony Hall with its claimed right to have a performance free of interruption or catcalls within the Hall. "Political speech" is a particularly valuable and protected form of speech and has been ever since the decision of the U.S. Supreme Court in Keyishian v. Board of Regents of New York (385 U.S. 589) in 1967, a case which involved the academic freedom of certain faculty members of the State University of New York. Vannessa Redgrave deserves no less freedom in the Symphony Hall than Keyishian got in the classroom. The Boston Symphony Orchestra has now joined the long, dishonorable list of censors which began in Boston as the *Watch and Ward Society* over 80 years ago.

The holding in this case is arguably relevant to attempts, many of them successful, to ban, remove or restrict certain books used in public schools throughout the United States—a freedom to learn from the constititionally protected speech of others. A report, *Attacks on the Freedom to Learn,* was compiled and recently issued by a Washington, D. C.-based anti-censorship group, *People for the American Way.* The report listed 153 attempts to remove or otherwise restrict certain books from the public schools. They include some literary classics, such as the following:

*The Chocolate War* (1974) by Robert Cormier
*The Catcher in the Rye* (1951) by J. D. Salinger
*Of Mice and Men* (1937) by John Steinbeck
*The Adventures of Huckleberry Finn* (1884) by Mark Twain
*Anne Frank: The Diary of a Young Girl* (1954) by Albert and Frances Goodrich
*To Kill a Mockingbird* (1960) by Harper Lee

This is only a partial list, but according to a spokesman for *People for the American Way,* the number of attempts to remove or restrict such books was up by 168% over 1982. This kind of censorship seems clearly analogous to secrecy in government—a paranoid fear that somehow people will read something of harm to themselves, not to national security.

Secrecy in government has become so pervasive and all-embracing that what we learn or can learn from books, including textbooks, is slowly being eroded. After all, in *Newspeak,* Ignorance is Strength. Even the *display* of books with sexually explicit material is under attack from the radical right. We are "shrink-wrapping" knowledge with opaque covers, so it can't even be seen, much less read or, as in the Redgrave case, even heard. And, as the dissenting opinion in Bethel School District v. Fraser noted, it's being done by our own United States Supreme Court by some Justices of that Court who are at least a generation older than those exercising their right of free speech and a long distance away from the scene of the speech.

A precisely defined "national security" clearly has a place in our government. Moreover, every person has a right not to have his privacy invaded by judicial interference, either in the privacy of his or her own home or to speak freely so long as the speaker does not subject his audience to statements that are false and defamatory within the standards established by New York Times v. Sullivan. However, it is the responsibility of the courts to protect these rights, even to the point of developing different jurisprudential standards for all of them instead of what appears a political litmus test and applying it without any regard to the diversity of our society. Many people are denied access to the courts for lack of standing—they must show an injury in fact, some compensable interest the law protects. Courts might want to see what governmental interests the Department of Justice think can show an injury in fact before going further than so advising the court—confession of error in defending those interests without any injury in fact.

In Ollman v. Evans, a careful reading of Judge Bork's concurring opinion leads inevitably to the conclusion that he wanted to and did head off what he clearly felt would be disruption in the college classroom were an avowed Marxist allowed to asume the position to which he had been appointed by the University of Maryland. In Mozert v. Hawkins County School Board, the Court of Appeals managed to minimize any interference with the school's educational function by recognizing the divisive nature of the so–called "opt out," allowing students to be excused from attending classes where certain textbooks were required reading. These textbooks were alleged to have burdened the rights of some students to their free exercise of religion under the First Amendment. See Mozert v. Hawkins County School Board, 827 F.2nd 1058 (6th Cir. 1987).

Indeed, almost the entire rationale of this case rests on a 1948 case, Illinois ex rel. McCullum v. Board of Education. There the late Justice Jackson said: "Every parent has as good a right as this plaintiff to demand that the courts compel the schools to sift out of their teaching everything inconsistent with their doctrines. If we are to eliminate everything that is objectionable to any of these warring sects or inconsistent with any of their doctrines, we will leave public education in shreds. Nothing but educational confusion and a discrediting of the public school system can result from subjecting it to constant law suits." La plus ça change, la plus le même chose.

Had so-called educators appointed to sit in judgment on textbook selection only trusted their own children and those of others to learn how to read—to read and think—the courts would only be deciding cases involving education and academic freedom of minors instead of teachers and professors, all of this to the great relief of teachers and parents of the minors involved. Parents send their children to public schools to learn how to read so they can function effectively in the global village after graduate. Now parents blame the schools and the textbooks used to fuel the fires of educational reform. They might consider taking a look at their own actions, since almost all actions involving the education of warring sects is brought by parents on behalf of their children. It's time to give the children a chance to change the learning process, at least for reading skills.

# Chapter 15
# Epilogue

During the last year of the Reagan administration, the head of the Office of Legal Policy, a division of the Department of Justice, had a lot to say about what he called "a narrowly defined range of pseudo civil liberties" involving both the First and Fourth Amendments. Here's what he said:

> "For far too long, individuals have been successfully propagating the notion that the principal concern of the justice system should not be the determination of the truth, but rather the promotion of a narrowly defined range of pseudo civil liberties which may be claimed by criminal defendants. Typically, the claim is made that the Constitution requires no less. This is sheer nonsense.
>
> "Our present difficulties stem from having allowed these ersatz civil libertarians to stand our Constitution on its head, and their tragic legacy can only be overcome if we put the Constitution back on its feet. To do so, it is only necessary to interpret the Constitution as it was originally written and as it was understood for virtually the entirety of our nation's history."

This statement is both inaccurate and poor history. For over 198 years, the Supreme Court has construed First and Fourth Amendment cases as "meaning freedom of speech and protection against all governmental invasions of the sanctity of a man's home and the privacies of life."

The First and Fourth Amendments to the constitution were both ratified in 1791. The text, insofar as it protects free speech and protects persons from a violation of the constitutional guarantee against unreasonable search and seizures follows:

> Congress shall make no law respecting an establishment of religion, or prohibiting the the free exercise thereof; or abridging the freedom of speech, or of the press; or the right of the people

peaceably to assemble, and to petition the Government for redress of grievances.

The right of the people to be secure in their persons, houses, papers, and effects, against unreasonable searches and seizures, shall not be violated, and no Warrants shall issue, but upon probable cause, supported by Oath or affirmation, and particularly describing the place to be searched, and the persons or things to be seized.

In Schenck v. United States, the Supreme Court in 1919, examined the basic principles underlying free speech by holding that expression may be regulated where it creates "a clear and present danger that [it] will bring about the substantive evils that Congress has a right to prevent." In 1925, Gitlow v. New York modified this standard by restricting expression if "acts [overthrow of the government by force and violence] were advocated in general terms; and it was not essential that their immediate execution should have been advocated." The speech in Gitlow could be restricted by the state, because it led to a "substantive evil." In Cohen v. California, the state sought to regulate offensive speech, but the Supreme Court held that a state cannot excise epithets ["Fuck the Draft" worn on defendant's jacket in the Los Angeles County Courthouse] as offensive by functioning as a guardian of public morality. In New York v. Ferber, decided in 1982, the Supreme Court unanimously upheld a state statute prohibiting "persons from knowingly promoting a sexual performance by a child under the age of 16." "States," the Supreme Court said, "were entitled to greater leeway in the pornographic depictions of children . . . because it bears so heavily and pervasively on the welfare of children, the balance of compelling [state] interests is clearly struck, and it is permissible to consider these materials as without First Amendment protection." In 1985, however, the Supreme Court held that a state could not ban "lustful" material, noting in Brocket v. Spokane Arcades, Inc. that material that did no more than "arouse good, old-fashioned, healthy interest in sex" was constitutionally protected. In 1957, the Supreme Court, in Kingsley Books, Inc. v. Brown, upheld restrictions on the sale of obscene materials upon a court order allowing injunctive remedies against "the sale and distribution of written and printed matter found after due trial to be obscene," and to obtain an order for "the seizure . . . of the condemned publications." Chief Justice Warren, joined by Justices Brennan, Douglas and Black, dissented, saying that the statute "savors too much of book burning" and that the provision for injunctive relief during litigation was excessive in that it gave the state "the paralyzing power of a censor."

It was not until 1974 that the Supreme Court tried to define obscenity in Miller v. California. It held that material, such as books which, taken as a whole, appealed to a predominantly prurient interest in sex or which portrayed sex in a patently offensive way. The Miller court also held that the material, taken as a whole must lack serious literary, artistic, political or scientific value. Miller v. California which has successfully confused courts, juries and law enforcement officers ever since 1974, was a departure from a case decided in England in 1860, Queen v. Hicklin. The Hicklin test allowed "material to be judged [as obscene] by the effect of an isolated excerpt [one page] upon particularly susceptible persons." Now, however, courts and juries have to take the book "as a whole" and find it obscene by applying statewide or community standards.

The problem with all these disparate standards of obscenity is an almost total failure of legislatures to recognize that a fine line must be drawn between protected and unprotected speech in cases alleging obscenity. America's obscenity laws are rooted in this country's religious antecedents, of governmental responsibility for communal and individual 'decency' and 'morality.' Obscenity is not suppressed primarily for the protection of others. Much of it is suppressed for the purity of the community and for the salvation through religion of the 'consumer,' the person who reads for whatever reason. However distasteful some material may be to some of us, it is nevertheless a form of communication and entertainment to a substantial segment of society; otherwise it would have no value in the marketplace of ideas. Obscenity is not a crime. It is no more than a sin. Neither the Supreme Court nor Congress seems willing to treat it as such. In Fort Wayne Books, Inc.v. Indiana *et al*, decided by the Supreme Court on February 21, 1989, a draconian remedy in Indiana's Racketeering Influenced and Corrupt Organizations statute (RICO) was sanctioned. If two or more books found at trial to be obscene had been sold by a bookstore, all of its real and personal property could be seized. This means that these two books could result in the seizure of literary classics. This is a blunt legislative instrument, not a scalpel, and Congress has joined this pathetic parade toward further erosion of rights guaranteed under the First Amendment.

Congress, under the guise of preventing the commercial exploitation of minors for pornographic purposes, enacted the Child Protection and Enforcement Act of 1988 in the closing session of the 100th Congress. It was signed by President Reagan in 1989. Hardly anyone will ever defend the commercial exploitation of minors for pornographic purposes, but the act is misnamed. Beginning with Chaper 2 which amends Title 18 U.S.C. 1465, *inter alia*, the act might better be named as the Book Burning Act of 1988. It not only allows a court to order the forfeiture of an offending book, this act also allows a court to order the forfeiture of *all* property used in the business of publishing, distributing or selling two or more copies of a book found to be obscene. Not only that, but Congress has made it simple and profitable for informants from the political or religious right to spy on their neighbors. The Attorney General may "award compensation to persons providing information resulting in a forfeiture." As a result of the decision in Riley v. Florida in 1989, spying has become relatively simple. All a person needs is the money to charter a helicopter and "search" for obscene material at an altitude of not less than 400 feet using sophisticated photographic technology to photograph one or more pages of a book. This is not an "unreasonable search and seizure" within the language of the Fourth Amendment. In dissenting from a majority of six, Justice Brennan asked his colleagues if they were unconcerned about the implications of this decision which allowed conduct described as "a dread vision of the future" in George Orwell's *1984*, a contemporary version of the police state.

Congress need take only one more step to convert the United States into a police state. Cocaine is a "controlled substance," as it should be, and possession for sale is a criminal offense. The next step requires only that Congress make the possession for sale of printer's ink a "controlled substance." While we are losing the war against drugs and, in some cases, bringing cities close to bankruptcy because of the costs of dealing with the results of "crack," a cocaine derivative, Congress seems to have nothing better to do than act in an arbitrary and capricious manner by authorizing the destruction of books found obscene by application of ambiguous definitional standards. What is needed is a clear and unambiguous definition of obscenity and one which will put publishers on fair notice as to what is permissible under the First Amendment and does not confuse the courts, juries and law enforcement officers. In the meantime, satire may be useful as a way of directing the attention of the Supreme Court to the route Congress seems determined to follow.

The following satire, all of it fictional, combines modern technolgy with judicial confusion to show what results are very likely to occur. The monologue which follows takes place in the office of the Attorny General's Obscenity Enforcement Unit, a division of the Department of Justice.

"Look, you fellows, we have waited around until January 20, 1989, and we now have an environment all of us have been waiting for. We've gotten convictions in that obscene books case. You know, United States v. Educational Books, Inc. and God only knows we can't run all over the country reading books to see if their sexually explicit material is enough to get a conviction. To get one, we'd have to show a pattern of corrupt conduct under RICO, and that takes more manpower than the Department of Justice has right now. But the Supreme Court has just given us a new weapon, the helicopter, and I know the president wants to use the military to stamp out obscenity. Even if the Secretary of Defense says he has more important uses for helicopters, just think of all those traffic reports on the radio, all of them reported from helicopters during commute hours. We can just reward their pilots as informants from the proceeds of forfeiture. There may be some of them who will decline to spy for us, but there are literally thousands of helicopters available for charter by the right people, and we know who they are.

All present nodded in agreement, and the article which follows will attempt to describe, in fictional terms, what happened next.

———————

Hear Ye, Hear Ye, the U.S. District Court for the Northern District of Euthansia is now in session, the Honorable Mark Antony presiding. All rise.

As the reed-thin, black-robed judge slowly seated himself and adjusted his horn-rimmed glasses, he told the Clerk: "Call the first case on the criminal calendar."

Reading his notes, the Clerk intoned, "United States versus Nolo Contendere Press, its publisher, Peter Erante and others. For arraignment under Rule 10."

Counsel, are you ready to proceed with your case?"

"May it please the Court, we are ready," replied the Assistant United States Attorney. "However, I have stipulated with counsel for defendant that he may proceed first with his Motion to Suppress Evidence under Rule 12, Federal Rules of Criminal Procedure. Counsel has persuaded me that he raises a serious, but novel constitutional question arising under the Fourth Amendment—unreasonable search and seizure."

"Very well, counsel, you may proceed with argument on your Motion. It's a little unusual, but the law clearly holds that a defendant aggrieved by an unlawful search and seizure may move the District Court to suppress for use as evidence anything so obtained on the ground that the arrest warrant was defective on any of several grounds."

The Judge paused a moment and then said: "Since a trial by jury has been waived, it would not be prejudicial for me to note that the arrest warrant, even though issued after the search complained of was made, showed probable cause that defendants possessed and were reading a book alleged to be obscene and in violation of Title 18 U.S.C. 1465 as amended in 1989. The arrest warrant also shows defendant was found to be in possesion of a controlled substance, namely, printer's ink, a violation of a new law Congress, in its infinite wisdom has enacted.

Yes, sir. My client was arrested on a warrant alleging a violation of 18 U.S.C. 1562, a pattern of corrupt conduct, even though he has never been convicted of anything worse than a parking violation. Accordingly, I will concentrate on the issues of probable cause and good faith conduct of government law enforcement personnel in illegally obtaining evidence. It is our contention that no such showing was or could be made under all the circumstances of this case. The U.S. Attorney's Office has a copy of the motion and affidavits attached. Accordingly, I will summarize their contents for the Court."

"Please proceed, counsel," said Judge Antony.

"My clients are the Nolo Contendere Press, its publisher, Mr. Peter Erante, the national distributor for the publisher, National Books, Inc., the owner of MoreBooks, Inc., a retail bookstore, Peter Rep, a commission representative who was calling on the bookstore to obtain orders for the defendant's books and his two children, one a minor who had accompanied him to see how their father did his job. He is charged with a violation of the new Child Protection and Obscenity Enforcement Act of 1988 along with conspiracy to violate 18 U.S.C. 1465.

Because the day was clear and warm, all the individual defendants were seated in a fully enclosed garden area behind the bookstore, and the commission rep was showing the owner a book. It was open to page 48. The children — one was 24 and the other was 17 — were looking at this page. One was even pointing to a line on page 48 and smiling benignly. Helicopters were not considered routine by the defendant bookstore owner, but the sight of one with the call sign of a local radio station clearly visible from the ground was simply ignored, even after it made another pass over the garden where they were all enjoying the sun.

The commission rep had written an order for the book the defendants were examining, but made a mistake, threw it in a nearby waste basket and started to re-write the order. Defendant bookstore owner then agreed on the quantity ordered — 10 copies of the book. Exactly two days later, an F.B.I agent, at least he identified himself as one, appeared and asked defendant to accompany him to the Courthouse. Defendant was not worried, because the F.B.I. agent had told defendant that he was "acting in reasonably good faith."

At the Courthouse, however, things took a turn for the worse. A representative of the Department of Justice's Obscenity Enforcement Unit had removed the discarded purchase order from the trash bag left out in front of the bookstore for collection as required by local ordinance and had noted the quantity ordered. Then, defendant was shown three pictures of page 48 of the book shown on the purchase order. The print or text of this page was almost as good and legible as the text in the book itself. The picture, I discovered, had been taken from a helicopter flying at 400 feet. Counsel from the United States Attorney's office has stipulated that no warrant for this search had been obtained from a Magistrate and based on probable or any other cause.

Then, may it please the Court, the nightmare began. They had stripped-searched my client, Mr. Erante, and examined him thoroughly. They found no printer's ink on him or in his clothes, except a copy of the purchase order. Even before this happened, defendant had asked for a lawyer. His request was denied, and he did not have one during the entire period of his prolonged detention — 27 hours. Two agents even told Mr. Erante that a lawyer would only obstruct justice by telling him how to avoid being searched at all. They had not even sought judicial authorization for the strip-search and did not have sufficient facts to support the issuance of an order from a neutral Magistrate for what happened next."

Then, if you can imagine the indignity of it all, they brought in one of those Doberman Pinschers that are trained to 'sniff' for printer's ink. My client was forced to lie down while this dangerous dog sniffed all over my client, drooling and licking him."

Then, when the dog got up to my client's left ear—there he was, your Honor, with a savage dog, slavering, with a tongue like sandpaper, right over my client's face. However, when he 'sniffed' behind my client's ear, the dog went into convulsions and had to be taken away before he bit someone."

Judge Antony had leaned forward, removing his glasses as he did so, his eyes expressing some interest.

"Then, what happened?" The Judge looked at the lawyer from the United States Attorney's Office. He was trying to keep a straight face, knowing what Judge Antony might say. The Judge had once commented publicly that his namesake was an example of what Imperial Rome did in 31 B.C, saying that he would never allow himself to be found in the same compromising situation, an impermissible dalliance with someone like Cleopatra which was a source of gossip in Rome and public immorality and one which led to Mark Antony's fall from favor in the Roman Senate. The United States Attorney waited for what might happen next.

"Then, your Honor," continued counsel for the defendants, "those present made a terrifying mistake. They said they would take my clients to the laboratory which had developed the pictures and make them submit to interrogation by the technician who was said to be an expert in matters involving obscenity, even though his only formal education consisted of high school and vocational training. The pictures had been taken from the helicopter using satellite photography technology.

Your Honor, he had no choice, because the agents said they'd detain him forcibly otherwise. Mr. Erante is a citizen of the United States, as are all the defendants here. This case is clearly distinguishable from those which give Customs agents broad latitude to search 'all persons coming into the United States' under 19 U.S.C. 1582. We are not talking about drugs here, only one page of a book and printer's ink. What happened here was an impermissible search and a flagrant denial of due process of law.

So he went through the same interrogation he'd first experienced, only much worse. The government-hired technician was pretty rough, and my client suffered severe emotional distress and suffering. Naturally, the technician savagely interrogated defendant, asking all kinds of personal questions about his sex life and what it felt like to be selling junk that appealed only to a prurient interest and had no redeeming social or political value.

So your Honor, I submit that there has been a violation of my client's rights under the Fourth Amendment-an unreasonable search and seizure. Not only that, he suffered emotional distress intentionally inflicted by agents of the United States. He was subjected to humiliation plus pain and suffering. The law seems clear. The Supreme Court held in Johnson v. United States that a right of privacy can be invaded only when a decision to do so is made by a judicial officer, at least for Fourth Amendment purposes. This is not a case where one page of a book was or even could be visible from outside the curtilage of the property. A helicopter was literally spying on my clients in an enclosed garden. Therefore, I again move this Honorable Court to suppress the evidence obtained."

"Have you completed your argument, counsel?"

"Yes, sir."

Turning to the United States Attorney's representative, Judge Antony asked him, "Do you have anything you'd like to call to the attention of this Court?"

"No, sir. I do not. Counsel has made a persuasive case that government agents acted illegally. He has submitted affidavits in support of his motion. So I think, with all due respect for this Court, I will have nothing to add."

There was a moment of absolute silence in the courtroom. Then the judge began. "The Court will deny the motion to suppress this evidence. The case cited in support of the motion to suppress is absolutely unprincipled. A warrant for an arrest may be based on hearsay evidence, even a paid informant, and, without more, it need not show where the property to be found is actually located or that help from a dog or an under-educated technician may be required to find it. The fact that the Doberman Pincher went into convulsions when he sniffed defendant ear is completely irrelevant. Mr. Erante cannot claim any reasonable expectation of privacy outside his home. In United States versus Thomas at 757 F.2nd 1359, the Court noted that, with a trained dog, police may obtain information about what is inside a dwelling that they could not derive from their own sensory perceptions. A trained dog's nose is a superior sensory instrument. Here, the convulsions may be treated as empirical evidence that printer's ink, a controlled substance was present, even though behind defendant's ear only in trace or *de minimis* amounts. The convulsions were a positive 'alert' from a dog and justified the use of a government technician."

The claim that an anonymous tip from a dissatisfied book-buyer, even though seduced by the possibility of making money, led to the search of defendant's trash and the helicopter's over-flight is irrelevant. Defendants collectively and individually have no standing to assert it, even though it led to the search complained of here. Even if defendant bookstore and its buyer or owner had complained that the search of his trash had been made without a warrant in order to find a purchase order for this obviously obscene book, he could not object on Fourth Amendment grounds. In O'Connor v. Ortega, Justice Scalia told us that 'we have recognized exceptions when special needs, beyond the need for law enforcement, make the warrant and probable cause requirement impractical.' The plurality opinion, written by Justice O'Connor, did, in fact, recognize that Dr. O'Connor had a reasonable expectation of privacy in his office. However, a tip from a dissatisfied customer, if it leads to the discovery of incriminating evidence, is sufficient to dispense with the need for a warrant. We cannot place obstacles in the path to justice by requiring one. As Justice O'Connor noted in her opinion, 'A determination of the standard of reasonableness applicable to a particular class of searches requires balancing the nature and gravity of the intrusion . . . against the importance of the governmental interest alleged to justify the intrusion.' I agree, and a warrant is simply not appropriate when the difficulty of obtaining one is likely to frustrate the purpose behind the search. Recently, Justice White approved the search of sealed trash bags without a warrant. A purchase order for an obscene book, as this was, is no different from garbage left for collection, and it was found where the Supreme Court has held law enforcement officers may search without a warrant, in a sealed trashbag.

The Judge paused for a moment, as though collecting his thoughts.

The requirement that the book must be "taken as a whole," as in Miller v. California, is judicial activism. One page is sufficient.

"May it please the Court, I must interpose an objection," and counsel for the defendants rose to his feet. "Miller v. California appears to control here and the requirement there is that the book must be 'taken as a whole' may not be ignored.

"Counsel, sit down immediately, or I will hold you in contempt of court. I control what goes on here, and I expect to continue without any interruptions from you."

As I was about to say, judicial activism is impermissible here, and arguments touching on the prolonged period of defendant's detention are frivolous, a subtle form of activism. There are no hard-and-fast time limits in a case like this. Rigid criteria lead to mechanical jurisprudence, and original intent jurisprudence is what I must apply here.

As you know, I am a strict constructionist and believe in the jurisprudence of original intent. We must not allow ourselves to announce unenumerated rights without adequate authority in the text of the Constitution itself. This is particularly sound policy where the constitutional text and its immediate implications are traceable by some historic link to the ideas, the intent, if you like, of its Framers. I am a jurist who believes his role is to interpret the law and not to make it, even though the contours of original intent are not always clear cut. I am guided by the text of the Constitution, and the intent of its Framers. The language of the Fourth Amendment is unambiguous. It clearly states that the 'place' to be searched must be particularly described."

It is nonsense to expect a purchase order to be 'particularly described.' Government agents can scarcely understand their own regulations, much less one page of a book or a purchase order. The Framers of the Constitution could certainly read, even though they failed to define words like 'dog,' 'sniff' and 'privacy.'

"Unlike amendments ratified after 1791, the Fourth Amendment does not provide that Congress may enact such legislation as it deems necessary and proper to carry out the intent of this language. It does not, for example, define the word 'unreasonable' as it applies to searches and seizures. Congress could have, but has not defined 'unreasonable' for Fourth Amendment purposes. Accordingly, the Supreme Court has the obligation to define 'unreasonable,' just as it did recently in United States v. Montoya De Hernandez at 473 U.S. 531. There, Justice Rehnquist felt that the 'expectation of privacy was less at the border than in the interior.' Los Angeles, where the events in that case occurred, is only 109 miles from the border with Mexico. As one moves toward it, any person's reasonable expectation of privacy diminishes. In San Diego, there is only a 'trace' amount of privacy left. The critical significance of distance in miles or feet is clear from other cases involving a reasonable expectation of privacy, such as California v. Ciraolo and People v. Sabo. Were it not for FAA regulations and the wind, dust and noise of a helicopter, as it descended to 100 feet, the privacy of defendants would have diminished even more."

"In Montoya De Hernandez, however, the Court of Appeals held that her initial detention was permissible only if the inspectors had a 'clear indication' of ailimentary canal smuggling of cocaine. In reversing the Court of Appeals, the Supreme Court held that the detention beyond the scope of a routine customs search was justified if the customs agents, considering all the facts, 'reasonably suspected' that Montoya De Hernandez was smuggling cocaine in her ailimentary canal. Thus, we have three standards of 'reasonableness' since the decision in United States v. Leon at 468 U.S. 897: reasonable suspicion, clear indication and probable cause. A search warrant obtained in objectively reasonable and good faith reliance on a subsequently invalidated warrant does not justify the substantial costs of exclusion. Here, there was no warrant at all, because the law enforcement officers were busily engaged in the 'often competitive enterprise' of locating bookstores that might be prosecuted for selling obscene books. Had they taken the time to get a search warrant from a neutral Magistrate, they might have his finding of probable cause invalidated as being based on 'knowing and reckless falsity' of the officers' affidavit. The Magistrate might even have been removed for 'incompetency or mental disability' for relying on the ambiguous nature of a dog's 'sniff.' Multiple standards all too often produce mechanical jurisprudence and compel law enforcement officers to think before acting. For the 'unfit and ruthless,' this is too much of a burden to expect them to carry. The wrong under the Fourth Amendment cannot be *fully accomplished* until the evidence of a crime is actually discovered, that is to say, until the defendant's privacy has been *fully invaded*. The benefits of multiple standards are outweighed by the costs of applying them. The burden of the exclusionary rule is unacceptable here, even though only one page of a book was produced and a copy of a purchase order for that book was found on defendant publisher's person and removing it may have caused severe emotional distress intentionally inflicted.

In this case, any single standard, even if induced by the infliction of 'distress,' is sufficient to support the additional steps taken by government agents. Congress has not defined 'distress' as a component of unreasonable search."

In Montoya De Hernandez, Justice Rehnquist found that 'prolonged and humiliating' detention was justified without an order from a judicial officer. I agree, even though this defendant had requested a lawyer and none had been present during his 27 hours of prolonged and humiliating detention.

The use of a dog was no doubt humiliating here, and the use of a government-hired under-educated technician was probably humiliating and intrusive as to defendant. But the standards we fashion to discover the guilty apply equally to the detention of the innocent and may be exercised by the most unfit and ruthless officers as well as by the fit and responsible. Here, officers caused the infliction of both humiliation and pain. They did this to discover what later turned out to be present, even though a minute amount—*de minimis*—was actually found. It was still printer's ink, strictly construed. Even if they found no ink at all, the level of suspicion as to the content of one purchase order for a book independently said to be obscene was high enough to justify a painful and humiliating search.

It is the proper function of the Supreme Court to define 'distress,' just as it has the obligation to define 'obscenity' and other words which are used literally in Congressional enactments. The reason is simple. Title 18 U.S.C. 1465, purported to define 'obscenity.' It was not broadly enough defined, even by community standards in 1955. This section had a legislative history going back to 1872, and Senate Report No. 113 of March 16, 1955 merely said it was trying to prevent the mails from being used to corrupt public morals. Naturally, when the legislative history is so ambiguous, we are occasionally compelled to look at the statute itself. There we find words like 'obscene,' 'lewd,' and 'filthy.' We must define them as the Constitution's Framers might have done had they faced the same dilemna–corruption of public morals using the postal system of 1787. This means, of course, that we must sometimes overrule Congress. Only the Supreme Court may overrule Congress. It, for example, has not chosen to define 'distress' inflicted as part of a search and seizure authorized by the Fourth Amendment, and nothing in the Annals of Congress from 1791 provide any help in divining what the Founding Fathers meant by 'unreasonable.' Certainly, there is no reference to 'distress' there. Nor can pain and suffering be what I would call make-weight add-ons — to buttress an argument clearly without merit.

"In 1984, Justice White, writing for the majority in United States v. Leon, noted at 468 U.S., page 919, an exclusionary rule may deter some police misconduct. He said: 'It should not be applied to deter objectively reasonable law enforcement activity.' I agree, particularly since the FBI agents told Mr. Erante that they were acting in reasonably good faith.

"The point made by counsel that his client suffered from intentional infliction of severe emotional distress is also without merit. Congress did not enact legislation defining this, so I hold that this cannot be a future actionable tort. It clearly does nothing to limit the reach of unreasonable search and seizure.

"We all suffer some emotional distress at the hands of publishers, and that's why bookstores return books for credit when they can't be sold, even if marked down. But our records show no case in which a bookstore owner was ever enjoined from practicing what he was trained to do — deal with publishers and commission reps. Moreover, the fact that two minors, or so they were thought to be at the time of the overflight, were present, is convincing evidence of an intent to exhibit obscene material to minors in a place where they could 'peruse' it.

The notion that Mr. Erante was somehow humiliated by being searched using a dog is wholly without merit. He had no reasonable expectation of privacy outside of his home. Cases holding that use of a trained dog impermissibly intrude on that expectation are completely without any redeeming judicial support. Fortunately, our Courts are beginning to see that a so-called right of privacy would never have been considered worth protecting by the Framers of the Constitution in 1787 or 1791.

"In California v. Ciraolo, decided in 1986, the Supreme Court has allowed a fixed wing plane to photograph property from an altitude of 1000 feet, where suspected activities were going on. This was not an unreasonable search. A state court case, People v. Sabo, 185 Cal. App. 3rd, held in 1986 that a helicopter flying at an altitude of 400 feet invaded the reasonable expectation of privacy of defendants. A terrifyingly frivolous opinion by a state court, and the Supreme Court improvidently denied a petition for certiorai in 1987. However, the Supreme Court closed this unfortunate gap in a case decided on January 23, 1989, Riley v. Florida. The zone of privacy has now been reduced to 400 feet.

Griswold v. Conneticut held that an absolute right of privacy began in the bedroom, but only for the benefit of married couples. People v. Sabo held that a reasonable expectation of privacy existed at 400 feet. By denying the People a hearing in the Sabo case, the Supreme Court missed a golden opportunity to decide what happens to privacy between the bedroom, 400 feet and 1000 feet. It overlooked an opportunity to spell out a new social agenda for airspace. In the dissent by Justice White, one in which the Chief Justice joined when the petition for certiorari in

People v. Sabo was denied, the dissenting opinion noted that the helicopter was lawfully positioned. Federal regulations allow operation of helicopters at altitudes lower than those allowed by fixed wing aircraft. See 49 U.S.C. 1301(29), which defines 'airspace' as that needed 'to insure safety in take-off and landing of aircraft,' including helicopters. Thus, a helicopter, to insure either, could land or take off right next to a bedroom without invasion of the privacy of its occupants for Fourth Amendment purposes. The use of a trained dog and a government-retained technician to discover what the dog could not 'sniff' does not represent an impermissible intrusion on defendant's expectation of privacy, even though he could not know what either might find. Society does not accept his expectation as objectively reasonable.

It is these fine distinctions that make the law such an intellectual challenge. As I see it, the Constitution is least precise where it is the most important. Original intent is the only legitimate basis for constitutional decision. This means that I must construe the language of the Fourth Amendment and what its Framers intended at the time, namely, 1791. Since the full record of the Constitutional Convention was never entirely reduced to writing—only about 7% of it—ascertaining it is not without a few minor problems. However, the remaining 93% has been revealed to me by the Attorney General of the United States. Accordingly, I must defer to the revelatory powers of the Executive Branch of the government, even though it means disregarding the principle of *stare decisis*, to uphold precedents or to stand by decided cases.

As a result, and without any evidence of original intent or definitions, I see no material difference between a dog at sea level and a fixed wing plane at 1000 feet or a helicopter at 400 feet. Two fly, and the other sniffs."

The motion to suppress evidence is denied. All defendants will now stand. How do you plead, Mr. Erante and others?"

"Guilty."

# Partial Table of Cases

New York v. Ferber, 458 U.S. 747, 73 L. Ed. 2d 1113 (1982). The New York Court of Appeals reversed conviction of Ferber for selling films in a bookstore in violation of statute prohibiting persons from knowingly promoting sexual performance by children under 16 on grounds statute violated First Amendment (424 N.Y.S. 2d 967). The U.S. Supreme Court reversed this case.

O'Connor v. Ortega, 480 U.S.___, 94 L. Ed. 2d 714 (1987)

Old Dominion Branch No. 496, National Association of Letter Carriers v. Austin, 418 U.S. 264, 41 L. Ed.2d 745 (1974)

Miller v. California, 413 U.S. 15, 37 L. Ed. 2d 419 (1974)

Perry Education Assn. v. Perry Local Educators' Assn., 460 U.S. 37, 74 L. Ed.2d 794 (1983) Dissent at page 55 notes application of viewpoint discrimination in violation of First Amendment.

Roberts v. U.S. Jaycees, 468 U.S. 609 (1984)

Smith v. United States, 431 U.S.291, 52 L. Ed. 2nd 324 (1977)

Rosenbloom v. Metromedia, Inc., 403 U.S. 29, 29 L. Ed. 2d 296 (1973)

New York Times v. Sullivan, 376 U.S. 254, 11 L. Ed. 2d 686 (1971)

Philadelphia Newspapers, Inc. v. Hepps et al, 475 U.S. 767, 89 L. Ed. 2d 783 (1986)

Pope v. Illinois, 481 U.S.___, 95 L. Ed. 2d 439 (1987). In this case, Justice Brennan, who wrote for the majority in Roth v. United States, dissented, noting that " . . . my view [is] that *any* regulation of such material with respect to consenting adults, suffers from the defect that 'The concept of obscenity' cannot be defined . . . to provide fair notice to persons who create and distribute sexually oriented materials, to prevent substantial erosion of protected speech as a byproduct of the attempt to suppress unprotected speech, and to avoid very costly institutional harms." Paris Adult Theater I v. Slaton, 413 US 49, 103, 37 L Ed 2d 446, 93 S Ct 2628"

Roth v. United States, 354 U.S. 476, 1 L. Ed. 2d 1498 (1957)

Time, Inc. v. Hill, 385 U.S. 374, 17 L. Ed. 2d 456 (1967)

Time, Inc. v. Pape, 401 U.S. 279, 28 L. Ed. 2d 45 (1971)

Virginia v. American Booksellers Association, 484 U.S.___, 98 L. Ed. 2d 782 (1988)

American Booksellers Association, Inc. v. Commonwealth of Virginia, 792 F. 2d 1261 (4th Cir. 1986)

American Booksellers Association, Inc. v. William Hudnut, Mayor of Indianapolis, 771 F. 2d 323 (7th Cir. 1985)

Apple Computer, Inc. v. Franklin Computer Corp., 714 F. 2d 1240 (3d Cir. 1983

William M. Brinton v. Department of State, 636 F. 2d 600 (D.C. Cir. 1980)

Buckley v. Littel, 539 F. 2d 882 (2d Cir. 1976), cert. den. 429 U.S. 1062

Cianci v. New Times Publishing Co., 639 F. 2d 54 (2nd Cir. 1980)

Educational Testing Services v. Katzman, 793 F. 2d 533 (3rd Cir. 1986)

Falwell v. Flynt, 797 F. 2d 1270 (4th Cir. 1986)

Falwell v. Flynt, 805 F. 2d 484 (4th Cir. 1986)

Forro Precision, Inc. v. International Business Machines, 673 F. 2d 1045 (9th Cir. 1982)

Hustler Magazine, Inc. v. Falwell, 796 F. 2d 1148 (9th Cir. 1986)

Information Control, Corp. v. Genesis One Computer Corp., 611 F. 2d 781 (9th Cir. 1980)

Ollman v. Evans and Novak, 750 F. 2d 970 (D.C.Cir. 1984),separate concurring opinion by Judge Robert H. Bork beginning at page 993

Pring v. Penthouse, Inc., 695 F. 2d 438 (10th Cir. 1982), cert. den. 462 U.S. 1132

Raftery v. Scott, 756 F. 2d 335 (4th Cir. 1985)

Redgrave et al v. Boston Symphony Orchestra, Inc., 831 F.2d 339 (1st Cir. 1987) Slip Op. of October 16, 1987, reversing judgment for defendant in Redgrave et al v. Boston Symphony Orchestra, Inc., 602 F. Supp. 1189 (D.C. Mass. 1985) Opinion withdrawn from circulation.

Salinger v. Random House, Inc., 811 F. 2d 90 (2nd Cir. 1987)

Smith v. Board of School Commissioners, __ F. 2d __ (11th Cir. 1987) Slip Op. August 26, 1987

Upper Midwest Booksellers Association v. City of Minneapolis, 780 F. 2d 1398 (8th Cir. 1985)

Planned Parenthood Federation of America v. Heckler, 712 F. 2d 650 (D.C. Cir. 1983)

United States v. Morison,___F. 2d___(4th Cir. 1988)

United States v. One Book Called Ulysses, 5 F. Supp. 182 (S.D.N.Y 1933)

United States v. Petrov, 747 F. 2d 458 (2d Cir. 1984), cert den 85 L. Ed. 2d 318

American Booksellers Association v. Stroebel, 617 F. Supp. 699 (D.C. Va. 1985)

American Booksellers Association, Inc. v. Webb, 643 F. Supp. 1546 N.D. Ga. 1986)

Matthew Bender & Co., Inc. v. Kluwer Law Book Publishers, Inc., 672 F. Supp. 107 (S.D. New York 1987)

Macmillan, Inc. v. Craft, 667 F. Supp. 120 (S.D. N. Y. 1987)

Masson v. The New Yorker Magazine, Inc., Alfred A. Knopf, Inc. and Janet Malcolm, ___F. Supp.___ (N.D. Cal. 1987) Slip Op. of August, 1987)

Ollman v. Evans and Novak, 479 F. Supp. 292 (D.C.D.C.1983)

Smith v. Board of School Commissioners, 655 F. Supp. 939 (D.C. Ala. 1987)

American Booksellers Association, Inc. v. Superior Court, 129 Cal. App. 3rd 197 (1982)

Baker v. Los Angeles Herald Examiner, 42 Cal. 3rd 254 (1984)

Bindrim v. Mitchell, 92 cal. App. 3rd 61 (1979), cert. den. 444 U.S. 984

Burnett v. National Enquirer, Inc., 144 Cal. App. 3rd 991

Institute of Athletic Motivation v. University of Illinois, 114 Cal. App. 3rd 1, fn. 4 (1980)

People v. Sequoia Books, Inc., 518 N.E.2d 775 (Ill. App. 1988)

Royer v. Steinberg, 90 Cal. App. 3rd 490 (1978)

Yorty v. Chandler, 13 Cal. App. 3rd 467 (1970)

Tattered Cover Bookstore, Inc. et al v. Dale Tooley, District Attorney, et al, 696 P. 2nd 780 (1985)

## Statutes

5 U.S.C. 550 et seq., Administrative Procedure Act

17 U.S.C. 101 et seq., Copyright Act of 1976, amended to include definition of "computer program" in 1980. See Section 107 for definition of "fair use."

18 U.S.C. 1961, et seq., Racketeer Influenced and Corrupt Organizations Act

18 U.S.C. 1461 et seq. as amended in 1989. Obscenity

Deerings California Codes Constitution, Article III, Section 6, added Nov. 4, 1986

Deerings California Education Code, Sections 60061, 60202.5 and 62500.